14.75

P9-CKX-983

WITHDRAWN

JUN 2 8 2024

DAVID O. McKAY LIBRARY
BYU-IDAHO

WHITTIER ❧ BARD OF FREEDOM

JOHN GREENLEAF WHITTIER

From a photographic copy of a daguerreotype. On the back of
the photograph appears in Whittier's handwriting the following
inscription: "To Edmund Clarence Stedman this photo taken at
the age of 30 is from his friend John G. Whittier."

WHITTIER

BARD OF FREEDOM

WHITMAN BENNETT

"All honor and praise to the right-hearted bard
Who was true to The Voice when such service was hard,
Who himself was so free he dared sing for the slave
When to look but a protest in silence was brave."

—*Lowell*, A FABLE FOR CRITICS

KENNIKAT PRESS
Port Washington, N. Y./London

WHITTIER

Copyright, 1941, by Lillian Barbour Bennett
Reissued in 1972 by Kennikat Press by arrangement
with the University of North Carolina Press
Library of Congress Catalog Card No: 76-159082
ISBN 0-8046-1624-8

Manufactured by Taylor Publishing Company   Dallas, Texas

TO

THOMAS FRANKLIN CURRIER

Honorary Curator of New England Literature and
Consultant in American Literary Bibliography in
the Harvard University Library, whose Bibliography of Whittier and whose personal coöperation
have been of indispensable assistance

AND TO

CARROLL A. WILSON

Preëminent among American Rare Book Collectors, for equally vital information, criticism,
and encouragement

PREFACE

MY ENDEAVOR in attempting this interpretative biography of John Greenleaf Whittier is to draw a convincing portrait of him as he really was—the most effective literary man in direct personal influence on our political and social system that this country has ever produced; a paid propagandist of much sagacity; a "rabble-rowsing" anti-slavery rhymster in the service of God Almighty against the demon of human physical bondage, saying his say with such intensity that no verses of equally fiery righteous indignation are to be found in English later than the seventeenth century; an astute editor, a graceful essayist, a thundering prose controversialist, and, in middle life and later, a truly masterful indigenous poet.

Today, almost a century and a third since his birth and a half a century since his death, Whittier is little known to the younger generation of readers. It is important that his work be revived not merely for studious analysis but for voluntary reading of all moderately well educated young Americans. He was certainly a progressive and a liberal of his times, and no greater teacher of the American Way ever lived.

I shall do my best to show how this poor Yankee small-town Quaker farm boy, though never an office-holder in any serious degree, became a force in national politics; how he literally selected Charles Sumner to be Massachusetts Senator in charge of anti-slavery legislation and deliberately engineered his election. Then I shall strive to explain, so far as such a mystery can be explained, how the germ of real poetry grew in Whittier's soul; how, knowing his limitations of education and viewpoint, he was inspired, when already nearing middle life, to emulate his more literary contemporaries; how, by marvels of self-discipline and industry, he learned to use his faculties to such purpose that he was able to make himself a superb balladist and to compose the American rural masterpiece, *Snow-Bound*.

I have made no attempt whatever to find new scraps of unpublished writings or doubtful anecdotes. The amount of positively authentic material already printed in one form or another is tremendous. My problem has been to assimilate it all, to reread Whittier's own writings against the background of correlated current events, and to draw as faithful a picture as modest abilities will admit of the man and his mission in life.

Quaker Yankee Whittier had naturally a personality as aggressive and uncompromising as Catholic Spanish Loyola, but this was restrained by the tenets of the peculiar faith into which he was born and which he refused to renounce however much its restrictions chafed. Never robust, frequently ill, almost always "ailing," he was a prodigious worker. In political life he was a great poor man of spotless integrity. As an author he was modest almost to a fault. In personal life he was a bachelor celibate—a notable example of sublimation.

Virtuous and conventional men, living upright private lives, are generally supposed to be less interesting than vicious and eccentric exhibitionists. But circumstances alter cases. Good men have lived in times past and, let us hope, live today, who are neither goody-goody nor namby-pamby. Anybody who ever assailed Whittier on the theory that he was too good to fight must have had a very rude awakening—when he regained consciousness.

The general misconception of John Greenleaf Whittier is directly traceable to the long twilight of his life, passed comfortably and prosperously in revered semi-retirement. He lived to see his large part in the triumph of emancipation generally recognized, to know that his best poems were definitely American classics. Though the more active phases of his life ended in his late fifties, he lived and wrote with ability until he had passed the meridian of his eighty-fifth year. His intellect never faltered.

During this long Indian Summer of Whittier's later exist-

ence, a whole generation of Americans was born and reached
maturity. These boys and girls did not know him as the alert,
clean-shaven, hawk-eyed, restless and tireless Champion of
Freedom, forever publishing rhymed clarion-calls to recruit
volunteers for the abolition cause and writing, at intervals,
brief ballads that naturally clung to memory-strings. To them
he was an austere old man with a white beard, whose picture
hung in all the school rooms; a person much given to religious reflections, author of numberless school recitations; a
sort of Yankee Quaker Living Buddha, regarded by their
parents with a deference approaching holy awe. This first
post-Civil-War generation was too impressed not to be re-
spectful. But to the second generation, Whittier, then dead,
became only a name attached to tiresome verses, all too
familiar. And to the third generation he is fast becoming a
mere symbol in the Epic of America.

Born and raised in the very heart of Cambridge, Massachusetts, I myself grew to young manhood with a cloying
overdose of Emerson, Longfellow, Lowell, Hawthorne,
Holmes, and Whittier. Therefore, in urging new appreciation of Whittier, I fully understand the obstinate inhibitions
to be overcome.

My determination to essay this biography was reinforced
by a conviction that I have certain specific accidental qualifications for the task.

First—As my boyhood winters were passed in Cambridge, so my boyhood summers, for some ten or twelve
years, were spent in Hampton, New Hampshire, the sea-shore
edge of the Whittier country, where the poet found so many
of his legends and his characters; where flows the Hampton
River with its famous Rivermouth Rocks; where lie the sand
dunes on which Whittier pitched his "Tent on the Beach";
where spreads that great salt marsh which so fascinated him
that, when he was dying, he was content to gaze upon it from
the house of a friend in Hampton Falls and never suggest a
return to the old home in Amesbury. That beach, that river,
those rocks, that marsh, and that town with its quaint legends

of colonial days—I know them all even better than Whittier knew them, and it is a strong bond of understanding to have loved the same things.

One of my early and vivid boyhood recollections is of my mother and aunt returning from Whittier's funeral and telling me how it was held in the garden because the house was too small to accommodate the throng of mourners.

Second—My enthusiasm for Whittier is such that almost endless rereading of both his prose and verse has failed to dull the edge of the pleasure and satisfaction he invariably affords me. If it is true that the final test of a great painting is one's ability to live with it, then I have proved the greatness of Whittier, for familiarity breeds only profound appreciation. His outer life is spread on the record of nineteenth-century America, obviously and variously. His inner life, honestly reflected in his writings, is a perspective without horizon this side of Eternal Goodness.

Third—Many years spent in large-scale publicity operations should give me an advantage in expounding Whittier's anti-slavery campaigns in prose and verse.

Fourth—For the past fifteen years, as a professional book dealer, I have had a special interest in Whittier and have bought and sold Whittier books, broadsides, pamphlets, and letters to the value of many thousands of dollars.

I must make some mention of the many quotations of Whittier verse—a very few complete short poems, numerous parts of poems, and a digest of *Snow-Bound*—with which these pages abound. Since the average reader cannot be expected to peruse this biography with Whittier's Collected Poems at his elbow, I see no other means of letting the poet speak for himself. I appreciate, of course, that any abbreviated version of *Snow-Bound* is sacrilege, but in making it I did my prayerful best. My hope is that these excerpts will illustrate the critical analysis of the biography and will excite interest rather than satisfy it. My work will have justified itself if the reader, as he finishes this book, resolves to check and amplify the impressions I have conveyed by studying for himself the whole body of Whittier's work. There will perhaps be an added interest in the fact that the earliest texts have been used in quoting from the poems by Whittier. The poet made many minor changes from time to time. The final forms, for comparison, may be found in the 1888 edition of Whittier's Collected Poems. While the variations are usually slight, some of them are of considerable interest.

I must also say a word relative to the chapters concerning the decade immediately preceding the Civil War and the undeniable tendency of the book at that period to overflow the banks of individual biography and to become a condensed history of the anti-slavery movement in the United States. In extenuation, I can only protest that, as Whittier affected history, so history had its effect on Whittier—as his deeds influenced events, so, more generally, all events in the anti-slavery epic, whether or not directly instigated by him, reacted upon him. I abandoned my effort to pare away part of this background of history when I found it resulted in ruining the third-dimensional qualities of the Whittier portrait.

A friend of Whittier's—equally celebrated but otherwise very different indeed—wrote an early poem containing this quatrain:

> Lives of great men all remind us
> We can make our lives sublime
> And, departing, leave behind us
> Footprints on the sands of time.

John G. Whittier left giant footprints. But the sands of time have been dust indeed, for the winds of time have almost filled up the impressions once so deep and well-defined.

My task—to brush them out.

CONTENTS

Preface   vii

1. The Whittier Ground and Background   3

2. The Quaker Inheritance   10

3. The Barefoot Boyhood   18

4. Greenleaf Becomes the Town Poet   27

5. White-Haired Boy of the Academy   40

6. To Boston and Home Again   46

7. To Hartford and Back Again   53

8. Transition   62

9. Dedicated to a Cause   70

10. *Justice and Expediency*   79

11. Poetical Writings of 1833-1834   85

12. The First National Anti-Slavery Convention   92

13. The New England Anti-Slavery Riots   100

14. Getting Back into Harness   107

15. The Year 1837   115

16. The Burning of Pennsylvania Hall, May 17, 1838   123

17. Conclusion of the Philadelphia Engagement   130

18. The Perennial Invalid   139

19. Emotional Onslaught on Slavery   146

20. Frustrations and New Foundations   156

21. The Anti-Slavery Movement Formally Enters Politics   165

22. Back in the Anti-Slavery Conflict   173

23. The Rebirth of a Poet   181

24. Legends and Reminiscences   188

25. Whittier Reforms His Prose   196

26. The Hammer Returns to the Anvil   203

27. The End of Literary Prose Efforts   211

28. The Pulsating Fifties   221

29. Whittier Drafts Sumner for the Senate   228

30. Thunderheads of War   235

31. Whittier Emancipates His Own Inspiration   244

32. *Maud Muller* and *Skipper Ireson*   253

33. The Year 1860   263

34. Whittier in War Time   269

35. *Snow-Bound*   278

36. *The Tent on the Beach*   292

37. Twilight Inspiration   298

38. Devotional Writings   305

39. The Celibate Patriarch   314

40. Eternal Goodness   321

Appendix: A Recently Discovered "Round Robin"   329

A Note on Sources and Method   335

Index   343

ILLUSTRATIONS

John Greenleaf Whittier. From a photographic
copy of a daguerreotype taken at about the
age of thirty   *Frontispiece*

                                             FACE PAGE

The Whittier Homestead at Haverhill. From a recent
photograph   8

The Quaker Meeting House in Amesbury. From a
recent photograph   9

The Whittier Home in Amesbury. From a recent photograph   9

Facsimile of the famous Whittier letter in which Mogg
Megone is characterized as an Indian in Walter Scott
plaids   66

Facsimile of an early broadside, "Our Countrymen in
Chains"   86

Pennsylvania Hall in Flames. From an old engraving   128

Portrait of Charles Sumner   129

Title-page of the First Edition of *Snow-Bound*   280

The Fireplace of *Snow-Bound*, in the Homestead. From
a recent photograph   281

Portrait of Whittier in Later Years   320

Whittier's Bedroom in the Amesbury Home. From a
recent photograph   321

WHITTIER ❧ BARD OF FREEDOM

1

THE WHITTIER GROUND
AND BACKGROUND

WE HAVE ALL HEARD of the small boy who asked his nineteenth-century grandfather to come out from behind his whiskers. Whiskers—visible and invisible—largely explain why so many Americans of today regard the New England authors of a hundred years ago as stuffed shirts. Enlarged photographs of these worthy men, still hanging, half a century old, in many primary and grammar school rooms, have done the originals most unjust injury, being contemporary wooden-image likenesses. Whittier, Longfellow, Bryant, and Lowell are generally shown as elderly men peering over or around their whiskers. It is true that Hawthorne wears only a wilted version of a grenadier mustache—but the great stone face is not less revealing. Emerson, with his intelligent but immobile horse countenance, and Dr. Holmes, with his perennially puckered smile, like a slightly withered apple, though clean-shaven have whiskers just the same—invisible all-overs.

These faces, betraying nothing of the active minds, humanitarian souls, and multiple geniuses behind them, have literally frozen the sprouting admiration of some two generations of Americans. The fault was entirely the period's conception of how a man should look, plus the necessarily fixed pose to coöperate with slow-recording early cameras. What child wouldn't be wary of literary product from such specters of the eighteen-seventies and eighties? Also it is a fact that poems and speeches drilled into us in early youth, unless approached in later life from an entirely fresh viewpoint, somehow in retrospect seem fit only for children. Every man at about thirty-five should set himself the task of rereading his pet school-room aversions.

New England in the nineteenth century produced no Wordsworth, Coleridge, Byron, Shelley, Keats, Robert Browning, Elizabeth Browning, or Francis Thompson, but it did produce something which, though less expert, is of great importance—something genuine, unaffected, exceedingly quotable and inspiring—something in which characteristically forthright phrase make big thoughts seem simple instead of making little thoughts appear mighty. This very simplicity of speech, like the simplicity of Lincoln's addresses, is so translucent as to seem colorless until the words are scrutinized and the phrases examined. Our youthful literature expressed itself in the purest English idiom of modern times, clothing basic truths, entirely worthy of mature reflection, in language understandable by the young in so far as immaturity can appreciate the thing it has not experienced in fact or sympathy. Such simplicity is not trivial or trite. One cannot study Whittier without reference to poems which seem commonplace from familiarity, for, second only to Longfellow, the conscious phrase-maker, Whittier, the unconscious phrase-maker, is by a very wide margin the most quoted American poet. The number of Whittierisms that have passed unlabeled into the common speech is astonishing.

The reader must help remove the whiskers. And he can do this by remembering that Longfellow was not only a gifted poet but the most charming and charitable of men, who met personal tragedy with rare courage—and was the best judge of wine in Cambridge; that Lowell was a master in criticism, a fine human being, and a highly successful minister to England; that Emerson was not only a true thinker but great in secret local charity and in his internationalism, and that it was to his house John Brown's widow came directly after the execution; that Dr. Holmes, besides being poet and novelist and humorist, saved the lives of thousands of American mothers by his crusade proving the contagiousness of child-bed fever; that Whittier, through his self-denial and anti-slavery activities, exerted on American history an influence so great that in all the field of English poetical writing it is difficult to find a comparable instance.

John Greenleaf Whittier, the poet, was the second of four children in the fifth generation of a race of vigorous and respectable but otherwise undistinguished Massachusetts farmers. First of Whittier's direct paternal ancestors to arrive in America was Thomas, born in England the year the Pilgrims landed at Plymouth. In 1638 he came to New England and settled at Salisbury, Massachusetts, on land now within the township of Amesbury, establishing himself at the very outset not on the exact location of the "homestead" but within the limits of what is now frequently described as the Whittier country. From Salisbury, Thomas moved to Newbury and thence, nine years after landing in this country, to the East Parish of Haverhill, which became his permanent home. Meanwhile, he had married Ruth Green, said to have been a distant relative, who had made the voyage to America on the same vessel that brought Thomas over.

In the very first paragraph of his *Life and Letters of John Greenleaf Whittier,* Samuel T. Pickard (official biographer and husband of the poet's niece) states that "Thomas Whittier ... is supposed to have been of Huguenot descent." If this is true in any sense, the French origin must have been extremely remote or on the distaff side, for the now clearly established fact is that the ancestors of Thomas were British yeomen, and the name—which Thomas spelled with one "t" as Whitier—is English to the core. A highly qualified informant, who had family reasons of his own for the most exhaustive inquiry, summarizes the record thus:

"The known facts about the ancestry of Thomas Whittier (1620-1696) are that he was the son of Richard Whittier, whose marriage to a woman by the name of Rolfe is recorded in the parish registers of White parish, Wilts. The name Whittier is not uncommon in the neighborhood of Salisbury (England) and Richard Whittier may be connected with a branch of the family living at Langford. If so, his ancestry can be traced back three generations more. I cannot find any mention or suggestion of Huguenot origin."

The name Whittier itself does not bear out the idea of French origin. It is generally believed to be occupational, signifying a whitener of leathers—a combination of the obvious "white" with "taw," meaning to tan. A "whittier" is thus a "white-taw-er." The possibility of the name's being, in this instance, a merely phonetic transfer from the French (it is manifestly no translation or exchange based on root similarity of either sense or sound) is negligible, for the combination "wh" is practically unknown in French. If Thomas Whittier's father was allied to the Whittiers of the Salisbury district in England, the removal of the family to Salisbury, Massachusetts, would make a particularly complete and characteristic picture. The manner in which early settlers were frequently drawn to localities bearing the dear and familiar names of home is well known and recognized.

The original Haverhill home of the Whittier tribe was a crude dwelling about half a mile from the comparatively spacious homestead which Thomas built when he was nearly seventy years old, in the year 1688, just half a century after his arrival from England. Thomas Whittier, by the way, is described as an enormous seventeenth-century Englishman weighing over three hundred pounds, of prodigious physical strength and of unusually forceful mind.

The Whittier homestead—still standing in good condition and owned by self-perpetuating trustees—is set back from the main Amesbury-Haverhill highway. Originally there was an old-type doorless barn on the same side of the road and also a small grist mill, turned by a stream which was much more active formerly than today. The stepping-stone to the porch doorway of the house is said to be one of the original millstones. The present "modern" barn across the road, described in *Snow-Bound,* was built in 1821 and enlarged later. The Whittier place never had the winter-defying continuous house-woodshed-barn structure evolved by Yankee common sense to meet the Northern New England climate and characteristic of nineteenth-century construction thereabouts.

The homestead, with its thirty-foot kitchen, remains substantially in its original seventeenth-century form except for the addition of a second-story room where once was a slanting roof. Though this is no Yankee mansion such as semipiratical sea captains built in Portsmouth and Newbury, it is constructed firmly around an enormous chimney and is definitely superior to the average isolated farm dwelling of the time and place. This house and its 148 acres of land remained in possession of the direct male Whittier line until 1836. Here the poet was born and here he grew to manhood.

Successive generations of Whittiers, from the procreative founder Thomas to the unmarried and childless poet John Greenleaf, were as follows:

Thomas (to repeat certain information) was born in England in 1620, came to America in 1638, moved to Haverhill in 1647—seven years after the founding of the town—and, having married Ruth Green, begot ten children. He built the homestead in 1688, and he died in 1696.

Joseph, youngest son of Thomas, was born in 1669; married Mary Peasley in 1694; bought the homestead property from the other heirs; and died December 25, 1739, leaving nine children.

Joseph II, youngest child of Joseph I, was born in 1716, married Sarah Greenleaf in 1739, and begot eleven children, of whom only six survived to maturity and only three married. He died in 1796, precisely a century after the death of Founder Thomas.

John (father of the poet) was the youngest son of Joseph II to marry. He was born in 1760 and remained on the Haverhill farm in partnership with a younger unmarried brother, Moses. John and Moses paid the other heirs $1,700 for complete possession. John married Abigail Hussey in 1804, when he was forty-four and she was only twenty-one. John and Abigail had four children: Mary, John Greenleaf (the poet), Matthew Franklin, and Elizabeth Hussey. John Whittier died in 1830, six years after the death, through accident, of his younger brother, Moses.

John Greenleaf, the poet, the second child of his parents, was born on December 17, 1807, and never married. Mary, the older sister, was born in 1806, married Joseph Caldwell of Haverhill, had two children—Louis Henry and Mary Elizabeth—and died in 1860. Matthew Franklin, the younger brother born in 1812, spent his middle years in Portland, Maine, and then removed to Boston, where he held a customs house appointment until his death in 1883. While in Portland, he published a series of caustically humorous antislavery letters under the name of Ethan Spike of Hornby. Matthew Franklin was survived by three children—Charles Franklin, Elizabeth Hussey, and Alice Greenwood.

The poet's younger sister Elizabeth, born in 1815, never married. Throughout life she was his closest companion, the active head of his household, and his most trusted critic. The association might almost be compared to that of Charles and Mary Lamb, with the tragedy of Mary's insanity fortunately eliminated. Elizabeth—"Lizzie," as she was called—was a brilliant and vivid conversationalist, supplying the family circle with vitality and charm. She was endowed with qualities of loyalty to her brother, appreciation for all fine things in literature, and personal magnetism far exceeding the slight poetical talent shown by her occasional verses, which Whittier could never judge impartially because he loved her too profoundly.

The poet's mother, to whom he was devotedly attached, lived until 1857, surviving her husband by twenty-seven years. Her younger spinster sister, Mercy Evans Hussey—the poet's "Aunt Mercy"—a most lovable character and throughout mature life a charter member of the Whittier household, predeceased her by eleven years.

After the death of his uncle in 1824 and his father in 1830, Whittier, who had already begun editorial work, decided that for a man of his tastes and his delicate physical constitu-

Photo John Blacklock

THE WHITTIER HOMESTEAD AT HAVERHILL

ilt by Thomas Whittier in 1688, the homestead is constructed
nly around an enormous chimney. It remains substantially in
original seventeenth-century form except for the addition of
a second-story room where once was a slanting roof.

Photo John Blacklock

THE QUAKER MEETING HOUSE IN AMESBURY

Photo John Blacklock

THE WHITTIER HOME IN AMESBURY

It was in the "garden room" of the Amesbury home that Whittier
did the bulk of his most important literary work,
including the writing of *Snow-Bound*.

tion, carrying on the large and comparatively unproductive farm was obviously impossible. For this reason in 1836 he sold it to Aaron Chase for $3,000 and reinvested $1,200 in a little one-story cottage almost opposite the Quaker meeting house in the center of the town of Amesbury. This meeting house was the same one which the Whittiers attended when living in Haverhill, and its proximity was a great convenience, especially in the winter.

Some years later a second story was built on one side of the Amesbury cottage; but it always remained a plain, unpretentious house—just as it may be seen today. Whittier's little bedroom, with narrow bed and Franklin stove, speaks a volume of Spartan philosophy. After the death of his sister Elizabeth in 1864, the aging poet found himself literally alone and spent much of his time away from Amesbury, though he continued to regard it as home until his death in 1892—fifty-six years after its purchase and 196 years after the death of Founder Thomas.

It was in the downstairs "garden room" of this Amesbury cottage that Whittier did the bulk of his most important literary work, including the composition of *Snow-Bound*.

From this small-town center, on the shores of the Merrimack, the galvanic force of an overwhelming and slow-maturing genius and personality gradually unfolded itself. From a little old desk in that humblest of rooms, an extraordinary man—laboring under the handicap of perfectly genuine physical limitations of energy—sent out a cry for peace but not at the price of slavery, for brotherhood but not at the price of compromise with evil, and exercised, through personal associations, political insight, public meetings, propagandist prose, and popular verse, an astounding influence on the minds and emotions of millions.

2

THE QUAKER INHERITANCE

ALL ACCOUNTS AGREE that Whittier's mother, Abigail Hussey Whittier, many of whose qualities were reproduced in her son, was a woman of native refinement and responsive temperament, with full face and fair complexion emphasized by her notably dark eyes. She was not, as stated by Pickard, one of the Husseys of Hampton and therefore a descendant of the famous unfrocked preacher, the Reverend Stephen Bachiler, but the descendant of one Richard Hussey of Dover, New Hampshire, a weaver. Moreover, these two Hussey families, though settled no great distance apart, seem not to have been related.

Since Whittier himself believed that he was a descendant of Bachiler—Pickard even made an effort to whitewash the talented old reprobate—and since that genealogy established his distant cousinship to Daniel Webster—really a Bachiler descendant—extended research has been made in this matter. Roland H. Woodwell of Amesbury, one of the foremost Whittier students, supplied the correct information in the *Essex Institute Historical Collections* for January, 1934; and, as a matter of fact, the genealogical lines of both Hussey families had been previously established by material which John Osborne Austin and Victor C. Sanborn had published. Wherefore, the dark and gleaming eyes under overshadowing brows, so often cited as evidence of the cousinship between Whittier and Webster, came from no common source though in each case they revealed a peculiar fervor of temperament.

It is not a little amusing that Whittier, always profoundly

interested in New England tales and histories, seems to have been wrong not only as to the vaguely traditional early Huguenot origin of his race but also in the very specific matter of his mother's immediate family. However, it must be remembered that, except for the matter of slavery in all its aspects and details, Whittier was far more poet than intensive analytical scholar. The appeal of the romantic and the legendary and the fabulous was very strong to his nature and these genealogical errors, which added a touch of glamour to the rather drab farmer and weaver ancestry, are no stranger than his equally honest mistakes as to the "facts" on which he founded two of his greatest ballads. Whittier was without the least suggestion of that false pride which leads men to "build up" their family histories.

As a matter of psychology, the more prosaic Whittier's inheritance becomes under dissection, the more remarkable is his achievement as an individual. Yet who can say conclusively what qualities produce greatness? The extraordinary mind and soul may result from no one inherited strain but from just the right variety and quantity of many elements in fusion. So far as is known, the Whittiers seem to have been English-Yankee provincial stock except for the Latin drop brought into the race by the poet's grandfather, Joseph II, when he married Sarah Greenleaf, of positively French extraction, bearing a name translated from the original Feuille-Verte. That Greenleaf should have been given to the poet as his middle name and that he should have been known as Greenleaf (not John) to intimates all his life is a bit of a coincidence, for there was certainly an un-Saxon spark of intensity in his nature.

Whatever the sources may have been, all the contrasting elements of impulse, fervor, self-control, and persistence were evident in Whittier's contradictory personality. As steam gathers force confined within a cylinder, so his large emotional endowment, compressed within Quaker theories of life and sublimated by habitual celibacy, achieved an extraordinary ardor of the spirit. His whole life force found its escape in the battle for right and justice.

It must always be remembered—and the reader will learn that this applies most definitely to the Whittier family—that the early nineteenth-century farmer of the modestly prosperous and self-respecting type was no "peasant" in the European sense. He and his family were people who had come to this country seeking intellectual and religious freedom as well as a livelihood and who often cherished ideals which their city cousins had forsaken for more practical standards. The magnificent purposes and stern self-denials of Revolutionary days had not been entirely forgotten.

To understand either the work or the life of Whittier requires some general knowledge of the "people called Quakers," members of the Society of Friends, established in Northern England by John Fox in 1649 and brought to New England only seven years later, while the antinomian troubles with Anne Hutchinson were still fresh in mind. Though the two first missionaries to this country, Mary Fisher and Ann Austin, were put under restraint as soon as they reached Boston and shipped back to the mother country at the first possible moment, more missionaries followed; and the "heresy," though it never had a broad appeal to the Yankee mind, took firm root in various localities.

The early persecution of the New England Quakers culminated with the executions of three men and one woman who insisted on returning from banishment with the avowed purpose of martyrdom. Startling though this record is, one must in justice remember that the Quakers gave serious provocation and that they were insistent intruders. Also, such punishments as whipping at the cart-tail, cutting off ears, and piercing tongues were merest child's play compared with the barbarous method of execution for High Treason then still being actively employed by Charles II against the men who voted for the beheading of his father. To be "hanged, drawn, and quartered" meant to be only half hanged, and cut down living; to be eviscerated; and to be hacked into four parts. Nearly a century later—in 1743— thirteen Negroes, accused of forming an utterly nonexistent arson conspiracy, were burned at the stake by order of the court in New York City.

Because of the highly individualistic character of his movement and the lack of church discipline, Fox's idea in the early stages attracted many fanatics who "testified" not only by quaking and trembling—whence the familiar name of the sect—but by interrupting church services, invading law courts, wearing filthy sackcloth, smearing themselves with lampblack, and even going naked in public places. After all, Endicott, then Bay Colony Governor and a stern one, had to do something when a wholly virtuous young woman by the name of Deborah Wilson "testified" by running naked through the streets of Salem; and another, Lydia Wardwell, appeared entirely nude at church in Newbury. What became shortly thereafter the church of contemplation, where worshipers awaited in silence the promptings of the spirit, began with a plenitude of emotional frenzy, especially on the part of its missionaries.

However, persecution brought sympathy in its train—and sympathy brought the Whittiers into the Quaker fold. Thomas Whittier, the founder, though no Quaker himself, was one of the signers of a petition seeking the pardon of a certain Robert Pike, who had been censored by the General Court for daring to protest against an order forbidding Quakers Thomas Macy and Joseph Peasley to conduct Quaker meetings on Sundays in their own dwellings. The General Court was obdurate, as usual. Instead of forgiving Pike's temerity at protesting on behalf of the Quakers, the magistrates took revenge on all the petitioners who had asked for Pike's pardon, excusing only those who formally retracted their share in the application. Thomas Whittier, grandfather of the poet, was among the hardy signers of the Pike petition who refused to retract and consequently lost their rights as freemen.

Though tyranny as arbitrary as this might well have inspired revolt in the most temperate of minds, Thomas Whittier continued to be a member of the congregation in the established local church, became a leading figure in the village through some elemental knowledge of construction engineering, and achieved full citizenship fourteen years later, in 1666. The important result was the after effect. Mary Peasley, who became the wife of the first Joseph Whittier, son of Thomas, was a devout Quakeress and granddaughter of that very Joseph Peasley for whose rights to conduct Quaker services old Thomas had braved the authorities. Joseph Whittier, either before or at the time of his marriage, became a professed Quaker, establishing Quakerism in the family. But that was in 1694, when Quakers had become recognized as entirely respectable people.

Sarah Greenleaf, the poet's paternal grandmother, and Abigail Hussey, his mother, were Quaker women when they married the Quaker Whittiers.

In later life, the orthodoxy of John Greenleaf Whittier's Quakerism was often challenged. Though he had doubtless become more of a humanitarian than a theologian of any stamp, he clung to the conservative Quaker practices and opposed both evangelical and formalist innovations. Pickard quotes his dryly humorous advice not to forbid the groans at Quaker meetings because there might be nothing left. But Whittier, in saying this, was merely seeing the humorous side of a worship-form very close to his heart.

The poet, whose appearance was always scrupulously neat, used throughout life the long Quaker coats (said to have been made for him by the same Philadelphia tailor for nearly half a century) but in later years never wore the broad-brimmed Quaker hats—and perhaps this mixture was the outward and visible sign of his adherence to the sect with avoidance of conspicuous and unessential queerness. Though Whittier could cast them aside completely at will, Quaker forms of speech came most familiarly to his lips and appear in all his intimate letters. Regarding himself always as a member of the Society of Friends in good standing, but no zealot, he retained one fundamental Quaker virtue bred in his bones all his days. He never put pen to paper unless the spirit moved him, and then, if seriously moved, he was the most sententious of poets. In him temperament and restraint were the polarities engendering dynamic power.

Though he did not consecrate himself to the anti-slavery cause until his twenty-sixth year, Whittier was literally born into the movement, and therefore he took up what he had come to regard as his appointed task with no trace of self-righteousness or professionalism. In demanding freedom for the slave he was merely urging upon others what he had always known to be right, trying to convince them of the need for immediate action as he had convinced himself.

Whittier was actually the fifth in a line of noteworthy anti-slavery Quakers—the one destined to have the glory of seeing the dream realized. Chalkley, seventeenth and early eighteenth-century American Quaker leader and itinerant organizer, was first of these five great advocates of freedom for the Negroes and his mantle fell on the shoulders of two extraordinary men who carried the movement forward almost to the dawn of the nineteenth century—John Woolman and Anthony Benezet, a Frenchman who gave his life to this country. Between them they preached the doctrine of freedom in virtually every Quaker meeting in America, until they made it almost impossible for slaveholders to remain Quakers or for Quakers to remain slaveholders. Woolman's *Journal*, edited by Whittier, is the record of a great life.

Early in the nineteenth century Benjamin Lundy took up where Woolman and Benezet had ended, the interval having been filled by another liberty movement—the American Revolution and the permanent organization of these United States. It was Lundy who inducted Garrison into the anti-slavery movement and who was his partner in his first anti-slavery publication—previously Lundy's own organ. Though the Yankee Garrison proved too much of a fire-eater to work with the Quaker Lundy and they separated, they were both working for the same objectives. In 1839, Lundy died, and John Greenleaf Whittier, then in Philadelphia—already trained in the work by five years of experience—took over Lundy's last publication and continued it more vigorously under a new name.

The Pennsylvania Quakers as a group were the first religious sect absolutely to forbid slaveholding to its members. Vermont, by her constitution, when she joined the Union as the fourteenth state, was the first government in this country specifically to forbid slavery.

The family tree of anti-slavery agitation in the direct line is indeed close-pruned: Quaker Whittier succeeded Quaker Lundy, who had taken over the eighteenth-century work of Quakers Woolman and Benezet and who had "discovered" Garrison, who literally discovered Whittier. The spreading of the movement toward the West is more difficult to trace except on the theory that some of the early seed fell on fertile soil. The only actual martyr to anti-slavery publicity —Elijah P. Lovejoy, who was killed by the mob that attacked his printing press in the supposedly free territory of Alton, Illinois, in 1837—seems to have had an almost independent inspiration of his own. But the sensation caused by his death fed directly back into the main channel of the movement, for it was at his memorial services in Faneuil Hall, Boston, that Wendell Phillips made one of the most famous extemporaneous speeches in American history, reaching his climax by unconsciously paraphrasing Whittier, and instantly became the chief orator of the anti-slavery cause. Nor should it be forgotten that it was Whittier who, through his careful study of personalities and his painstaking political manipulations, was the prime mover in getting Charles Sumner elected to the Senate, thus giving the anti-slavery group already in Congress the most drastic and uncompromising leadership humanly possible.

The earliest published attack on slavery in this country is supposed to be *The Selling of Joseph,* a little three-page pamphlet issued in the year 1700 by Samuel Sewall, penitent witchcraft judge and author of New England's most famous diary. Though no preacher he was a professing moral philosopher, interested in proving, for instance, that there would be women in Heaven. But, by and large, American religious thought—apart from the Quakers, who had virtually eliminated slavery from their membership both North and South by 1800—was curiously indifferent. The Southern ministers had no difficulty in finding examples of slavery galore in the Old Testament and insisted that slavery was a divinely created institution. The vast majority of Northern ministers, well aware that their more prosperous parishioners saw no need of interfering with "property rights" or a Southern system which supplied cotton for Northern mills, either accepted slavery as a normal state for the Negroes or at least did their best to bar the unpleasant subject from their pulpits. It was not until after the Mexican War of 1846, which the North believed to have been waged primarily to increase slave territory, that the anti-slavery movement began to obtain general religious indorsement. Whittier had bitterly opposed this war, and his anti-slavery verses had made an immense emotional appeal to the humanitarian instincts of all Northern people—an appeal to which women in particular could not turn a deaf ear. And the women were largely responsible for bringing the church into line with progressive thought on the slavery question.

Quaker Whittier certainly did not constitute in himself the entire nucleus of the anti-slavery propaganda nor individually achieve freedom for the Negro. But the influence of his guiding hand appears in every multifarious phase of this colossal national upheaval.

3

THE BAREFOOT BOYHOOD

BECAUSE CERTAIN Whittier poems, like *The Barefoot Boy* and *In School-Days,* clearly indicate a humble walk of life, and because the younger generation of today naturally does not understand the special conditions of New England farm life somewhat more than a century ago, an erroneous impression prevails that the poet endured an especially impoverished youth and lacked even the most rudimentary opportunities for education.

The boy Greenleaf certainly was not raised in the lap of luxury. He undoubtedly had less cash to spend than the tenement child of today, but he was always respectably clad according to the standards of time and place, he was never hungry, and his schooling, though limited, was not neglected. That he even had encouragement to write is shown by the fact that mother and sister preserved juvenile efforts. It is true that his father, compelled to see all the more practical aspects of life, took no stock (as the Yankees say) in Greenleaf's literary talents, but his mother, his Aunt Mercy, and his two sisters were all most sympathetic. Many writers have struggled for first expression in a far more hostile atmosphere. Even his father's brother and partner in ownership of the farm, Uncle Moses, was impressed.

A farm good enough so that more than a century ago the poet's father and uncle paid $1,700 to buy out the other heirs; a farm which the poet thought worth freeing from mortgage debt with his own initial earnings; a farm which supported four children and four adults with all respectable creature

18

comforts; a farm which the poet himself sold for $3,000 just a bit more than a hundred years since, was a pretty good Yankee homestead. This writer's Vermont Green Mountain great-grandfather would joyfully have swapped house and acres, regarding an equal exchange as incredible good fortune and proof positive of insanity in the Whittier family.

As to the significance of *The Barefoot Boy*—God knows Whittier never thought of him as underprivileged and makes no suggestion to that effect in his verses. Any boy in that neck of the woods compelled to wear summer shoes and stockings would have considered that he was being inhumanly tortured and would have been almost as ridiculous to his village comrades as if he had sported a Fauntleroy hair-cut. Bare feet for a country boy in 1817 were no more indication of poverty than bare legs for a city girl in 1941.

To work laboriously in the fields, to suffer cold in the winter, to eat plain but plentiful food, were universal conditions among even prosperous farm families. The lives of the comparatively few very poor country people were something quite different, tragic beyond or below the concepts of modern living standards—something to make twentieth-century families on relief downright fortunate by comparison. Pie for breakfast with pork and beans and hot doughnuts, eaten after a couple of hours of hard work, would not be the prescribed diet of any modern sanitarium, but it can taste mighty good, and possibly it killed no more people than sawdust breakfast food and weight-reducing counted calories. Yankee farmers should be judged by their barns rather than their houses. Everybody from North of Boston knows the story of the farmer's wife who moved into the barn while her husband was at the County Fair and stayed there until he repaired the house and put on a new front porch. The Whittier barn-barometer still stands as mute, positive evidence of thrift and substance.

Pickard says that Whittier had to milk seven cows—which may have been a task but proves there were seven cows to milk. The livestock included one horse, a yoke of fine oxen,

poultry and pigs and probably Thanksgiving turkeys gob-
bling in the backyard. Fresh fish were readily found in brook
and river and in the not too distant ocean. Greenleaf's
mother and his Aunt Mercy both seem like just the sort of
Quaker women who could perform miracles in a "chimley"
oven. Greenleaf was thin by nature, not from poverty or
secret sorrow. Starved-looking Quakers are not quite as rare
as two-headed calves—but almost.

As to Greenleaf's difficulties in obtaining an education,
his father's opposition did not concern the obviously useful
"three R's"—Reading, 'Riting, and 'Rithmetic—but had to do
with what the old Quaker characteristically regarded as
superfluous learning. Whittier, like all the other village children, acquired the fundamentals at the short and irregular
terms of the local district school, taught by a series of young
masters. Moreover, his mother and Aunt Mercy were able
to give more help at home than most boys received. Old John
himself was no fool and could probably do trick sums that
would tangle many a modern college-trained teacher, for
such problems were almost as much a standard diversion of
the time as spelling bees or our modern cross-word puzzles.

The point is this—that Whittier matured under better
than average country conditions and his "socialistic" pro-
clivities, which seem ridiculously conservative today and
merely indicate his basic love for fair play, were no more
resultant from personal suffering or embittered youth than
his anti-slavery activities. He belonged emphatically to the
"common people" in an era when America was far more class
conscious than today and when transition from class to class
was infinitely more difficult, and he never earned more than
a frugal living until he was sixty. But there was not a germ
of actual Marxism in his entire mental composition. Glorify-
ing honest labor and indorsing movements to obtain reasonable privileges represented to his mind not revolt but normal
progress.

The fact that the Whittier library apparently contained
only some thirty titles and that the famous gift of Burns's

Poems was indeed an awakening revelation for the boy who in his early teens had already begun to make verses, does not spell hearthside ignorance. There was a world of reading in those thirty books, and at least two of them were rather surprisingly broad for a Quaker household. The family doubtless borrowed other books and obtained certain periodicals of the time as well as the weekly news sheets of the vicinity, including the one in which Greenleaf's own first printed contributions appeared.

The story of Whittier's limited high-school education, to speak in modern terms, and of his later self-education will appear as the narrative proceeds. The object of this advance comment is merely to assure the right approach to the panorama of his life: for, although Whittier's boyhood in Haverhill was no such perpetual lark as Thomas Bailey Aldrich's boyhood in Portsmouth seems to have been—more than just twenty miles of geographical distance separated the old sea-faring merchant town at the mouth of the Piscataqua and the farming families on the banks of the Merrimack— the barefoot boy whistled through his early years cheerfully enough.

Written in the retrospect of half a century, Whittier's picture of winter time in his boyhood days as depicted in *Snow-Bound* is probably a bit idealized, but the reality cannot have been too uncomfortable physically or too stultifying mentally. The poet's brother and two sisters remained deeply attached to him and to each other throughout life; he had the kindest of mothers; a simple but saintly aunt; an easygoing and friendly uncle; a silent, determined, prosaic, and practical father, more concerned with tilling his farm and reducing the mortgage than with higher education or literary aspirations. All four children lived to ripe maturity—unusual in those days and proof of very adequate creature comforts. In fact, the entire family group of eight souls remained unbroken throughout the poet's youth.

That Greenleaf's laborious share of field work and such chores as attending to cows, horses, oxen, and sheep (the

"women folks" generally took charge of the poultry) over-
taxed his strength is undoubtedly true, for he was far less
robust than his five-years-younger brother, Matthew. That
his father was any slave driver beyond the limits of characteristic Yankee diligence is nonsense. When he once understood that Greenleaf had injured himself, he was deliberately
considerate and probably blamed himself too late. Only sentimental biographers have magnified into unfair burdens the
boy's share of the tasks on the fairly prosperous farm which
supplied his family with life's necessities in a good deal of
abundance but which was still under the shadow of the
mortgage put on it by his father and uncle when they bought
out the other heirs.

Pickard questioned Whittier closely about his boyhood
from the age of six—as far back as the poet would admit any
specific memory. Though he points out repeatedly in the
course of his biography that Whittier had a fondness for
gentle spoofing, he seems never to have suspected that the
solemn old Quaker was amusing himself a bit on unessentials
at the expense of his admiring Boswell.

For instance, there is the story of how the heroic ox, Old
Butler, saved Greenleaf's life. This ox, the partner of Old
Buck, being a very hefty animal, one day started lickety-split
(as Uncle Remus would say) down a steep hillside on which
Greenleaf had posted himself shaking a bag of salt—chocolate creams to Mr. Ox. Unable to stop himself, Old Butler
took a flying leap over the boy, who, it is conceded, was
stooping down. Says Pickard, "The noble creature leaped
straight out into the air, over the head of the boy, and came
to the ground far below with a tremendous concussion and
without serious injury to himself." Anybody familiar with the
Yankee ox, which can be hastened only the merest trifle if
you drive nails into him, would doubtless have admired to
see that jump. It is the best recorded since the same ox's
sister jumped over the moon.

The present writer had a very stern Yankee grandfather

with a penchant for remembering barefoot days. His favorite form of locomotion appears to have been riding a ferocious bull bare-back. The real virtue of the ox story is that it shows Whittier's very Yankee sense of suppressed drollery better than any of the incidents cited by Pickard for that purpose.

The same ox, by the way (and he was no cousin of Paul Bunyan's blue ox) stuck his head through an open window to listen to a Quaker meeting in the Whittier house while a sweet-voiced woman was holding forth—but withdrew and disappeared "rarin'" and bellowing when a gusty brother took up the torch.

When Whittier was nine, President Monroe and the circus (*vide* Pickard) came to Haverhill on the same day; and, being Quaker, Greenleaf got no chance to see either. Next day he went to Haverhill to seek out at least the footprints of the "greatest man in the country" and was delighted to locate elephant tracks which he felt sure were the president's. Certainly, Pickard could "take it"—and chatting with him about old times must have been a real pleasure for the aged poet.

The district school which Whittier attended in East Haverhill, instead of being worse than most seems to have been better than average. At least two men of some distinction taught the poet there in his boyhood—George Haskell, fresh from Dartmouth, who attained a notable position in after life both as physician and educator, and Joshua Coffin, also Dartmouth bred, historian and antiquarian of Newbury. In fact, Coffin was the very first teacher in that district school to have Greenleaf as a pupil—when he went with his sister Mary and could only join the alphabet class. After a lapse of several years, Coffin was again teacher and Whittier pupil; and Coffin was the man destined to influence him most just as he was entering his teens.

Pickard categorically denies the story that Whittier refused to learn the Westminster Catechism at school. His Quaker father said he need not learn it because of its errors, and the boy was excused from this duty.

Though the one-room district school was obviously the

worst possible form of education for a slow or stupid child, it may have been surprisingly effective for eager and precocious minds, continually overhearing the recitations of more advanced pupils. Nobody then mistook education for play. Whittier's rapid advance during his two self-earned terms at the Academy (high school) which he did not enter until nineteen, and his immediately successful editorial employment thereafter, show that home and district school and natural intelligence had combined to provide by no means inadequate elementary training.

The Whittier home library of some thirty items has already been mentioned—the Bible, Quaker journals, works by Penn and other Quaker worthies predominating. One of Whittier's earliest rhymes was a sort of catalogue of these literary treasures, which, though Quakerish, were not all too sanctified. Rather surprisingly, the list includes Franklin's *Autobiography* and the *Memoirs* of both Stephen Burroughs and Henry Tufts, who were the first two self-confessed and self-exploited Yankee rascals to capitalize their misdeeds by turning author.

John Whittier, the poet's father, had been an itinerant merchant before his marriage—something a grade above the typical Yankee peddler—and had traveled from Haverhill up into Canada, becoming a bit less provincial than most of his neighbors. Physically strong and alert, prompt, and practical in daily affairs, he served several terms as a town selectman. From him the poet inherited the unexpected patience and industrious common sense he invariably showed toward the practical application of his emotion-born theories.

That the Whittier social background was entirely respectable and above the average of the locality is proved by recorded visits of the traveling Quaker leaders who, from time to time, attended the Amesbury meeting near by, which was "church" for the Whittier group. Also, the school teachers, local editors, and other passing strangers of intellectual caliber—note the description of the Second Adventist Harriet Livermore in *Snow-Bound*—found in the heart of this family more than the usual understanding and hospitality. Yet nothing here must be misinterpreted to belittle the self-made quality of Whittier's life achievement. The purpose is to reduce legends to facts which are wonderful enough in themselves. Our Barefoot Boy started on his career not ill equipped for routine life but with a commonplace foundation on which only he could have erected the living statue of a world-famous poet-patriot.

Whittier's earliest journey from home appears to have been to attend a Quaker meeting in Salem some thirty miles away but still in Essex County. Gradually he seems to have become familiar with the entire district intervening between the two places and to have been fascinated by the witchcraft and folklore legends which abound there as nowhere else in America. This interest led to the writing of his very first book, *The Legends of New England,* followed by *The Supernaturalism of New England* not many years later. Whittier knew in particular all the folklore of the neighboring old town of Hampton and used many local traditions in tale and poem. These Hampton legends of things beyond human ken are familiar to the writer as stories heard from the lips of natives in his own boyhood—including some that Whittier never utilized.

That Whittier never traveled abroad or even in far distant parts of his own United States was due partly to health, partly to very limited means, and partly to his extreme regard for family ties. He followed world events with absorbed interest and in his later years, when he had leisure and means, he did not have to go to the world because the whole world had acquired the habit of coming to him. Nothing is more absurd, therefore, than the picture of him as a plowboy poet. The permanent directness of his literary style, both in prose and in verse, was not for lack of vocabulary or of phrase-coining power, nor was it assumed. It was a part of his personality. In early days Whittier learned that this was his most potent, instinctive method of speech, and he had the rare wisdom never to outgrow it. He remained homespun as he remained Quaker, from conviction and from a canny, common-sense appreciation of both his strength and his limitations.

No small part of Whittier's special importance was the eminent practical determination and sanity imbued in him during his boyhood on a Yankee farm.

4

GREENLEAF BECOMES THE
TOWN POET

WHITTIER WAS MOST EMPHATICALLY not a child genius. He seems to have been born with some aptitude and instinct for rhyming—but little more. He acquired distinction of phrase and conscious art in simplicity only after years of effort and after having written more than a hundred published poems. His personal estimate of his own early efforts was so very modest that only a handful of them were ever included in the various collections of his works and it is possible that a considerable body of unsigned work still remains unidentified. In later years, he wrote that ten thousand boys could compose better poetry. As a matter of fact, Whittier's early prose averages far better than his verse.

Despite the immense amount of rhyme which Whittier produced from his eighteenth year onward, he never considered the serious development of his poetical talents as a major interest in life until some years after he had abandoned his individual political ambitions to promote the anti-slavery cause, when he was about thirty. Before that time, he had written thousands of stanzas because he felt in the mood, because he could use them in papers he was editing, and because he found they brought him a certain distinction. Of Whittier's early poetry it may probably be said with justice that no equally unliterary avalanche of verse ever brought equally wide recognition for its author, a fact that can be explained only by a note of intense sincerity, so contagious that the average mind responded without criticizing.

Bryant, writing *Thanatopsis* and *To a Waterfowl* when scarcely more than adolescent and never greatly surpassing them in later years, is the exact antithesis of Whittier, who came into his full glory with the writing of *Snow-Bound* at fifty-eight.

Whittier's earliest known efforts are mere childhood jingles. His earliest poem between covers did not appear until he was twenty-one, though he had published numerous verses in papers and periodicals before that time. A single sample of his very juvenile efforts, taken from Pickard's *Life and Letters*, is more than sufficient:

> And must I always swing the flail,
> And help to fill the milking pail?
> I wish to go away to school;
> I do not wish to be a fool.

These verses must have been considered precocious by the family because his older sister committed them to memory and repeated them years after. The only analytical interest is that even in these four lines the little boy had something serious to say and said it with a punch.

The to-be-expected stories of how the boy Whittier filled his slate with verses both at school and at home abound—and are doubtless true. Such verses were probably about on a par with the still-extant boyish manuscript—a series of two-line stanzas—cataloguing the books in the family library.

Pickard, in his work, preserves a portion of a very early unpublished poem of somewhat more advanced character—an imitation of *The Old Oaken Bucket*. Apparently several other unpublished boyish manuscript poems, written between his sixteenth year and before he entered the Academy in the middle of his nineteenth year, are still extant. The four earliest poems which Whittier could be induced to include in the appendix to the compendious 1888 edition of his *Collected Poems* were compositions of his eighteenth year. By contrast, note that Bryant's *Embargo*, a poem based on an international political situation, was published when he was fourteen.

Whittier produced his best work at an age that Poe never reached; an age at which Whitman was merely repeating himself; Longfellow was engaged in the writing of amiable poetic exercises interesting to critics only; Bryant was no longer a poet at all; Lowell was still an active influence in other fields but had long since written all his essential verse; and poor, wonderful Emerson was no longer of sound mind. Only that strange irrepressible personality, Dr. Holmes, could still turn the trick at the same age. No man ever wrote more consistently good verse of its special caliber from dawn to dusk of an octogenarian life than Holmes, but even his greatest verse work was all done at a time of life when Whittier was still in comparatively early stages of development.

Fortunately there is an entirely provable story of Whittier's first great inspiration. The specific volume of Burns's *Poems,* which first aroused poetic emulation in the soul of the country boy, remained in the poet's possession throughout life and is still preserved in the Haverhill home. The incident of its acquisition occurred in 1821, the boy's fourteenth year. Joshua Coffin, the historian of later days already introduced as Whittier's teacher at the East Parish District School, had become an intimate of the household. One night, on a typical visit to the Quaker family, he read aloud many selections from a copy of Burns which he had chanced to bring with him and explained the dialect. Greenleaf's attention was so concentrated, the obvious impression on him so profound, that Coffin left the book with him and never took it back.

As Irving stated that he learned to write from Goldsmith; as Cooper undoubtedly learned from Scott; as Bryant stemmed from Wordsworth; so Whittier undoubtedly acquired much from the naturally sympathetic Scotch countryside poet. That he showed the Burns influence in countless compositions of the less aggressive type is beyond dispute, and that this inspiration remained with him all his days is proved by *Snow-Bound* itself.

As a matter of fact, Burns exerted a much more direct influence on early American verse than is generally recognized. In those days, the New England states in particular were inhabited mainly by small farmers, independent tillers of a rocky soil, who understood the appeal of nature and country life as expounded by the Ayreshire graduate plowboy or, as a Yankee would say, farm hand. Two American reprints of the Kilmarnock Burns—faithfully reproducing even the errors—appeared in Philadelphia and New York within two weeks of each other in 1788. So Whittier, in attuning himself to Burns, was not deliberately seeking a model for compositions but merely responding more keenly than less gifted individuals. The best evidence of this affinity is Whittier's own poem, *Burns*, and especially this stanza:

> Let those who never erred forget
> His worth, in vain bewailings;
> Sweet Soul of Song!—I own my debt
> Uncancelled by his failings!

Two years later Whittier made his first trip to Boston, then self-confessed hub of the universe and of all American culture. Mrs. Nathaniel Greene, wife of the Boston postmaster, was among the Whittier relatives who had visited Haverhill, and the boy's trip was a return visit. Nathaniel Greene was not only postmaster but editor and publisher of the *Boston Statesman*, an influential and notably well conducted journal.

The official biography account of this visit is that Whittier cut it short because he met a brilliant actress and feared she might lure him into attending a theatrical performance, thus breaking an essential Quaker prohibition. The writer cannot rid himself of the impression that this is another example of how the old poet enjoyed laying it on a bit thick when he reminisced about his youth for his eager biographer. The statement that Whittier bought his first Shakespeare in Boston is probably more factual.

It was not until 1826, when the boy was eighteen, that fate took a hand in definitely shaping Whittier's career, bringing him by apparently mere chance into contact with another young Man of Destiny, with whom he was to remain in intimate contact until the days after the Civil War. This other youngster, who became the most famous of all the extreme anti-slavery agitators, was William Lloyd Garrison.

Garrison, two or three years older than Whittier, was born at near-by Newburyport, seaport at the mouth of the Merrimack, son of a father who either died or disappeared shortly after that event. When his first childhood had passed, his mother had apprenticed him to a shoemaker in Newburyport, and when they both went to Baltimore for a time in 1815 he continued at the trade. From Baltimore, mother and son had moved to Haverhill (apparently without meeting the Whittiers) and there young Garrison had tried cabinetmaking. From Haverhill he had gone back to his original home of Newburyport and had become apprenticed, in 1818, as a printer, to Ephraim Allen, proprietor and editor of the *Newburyport Herald.*

In the eight years between 1818 and 1826 Garrison had made rapid and precocious progress. Apparently a natural born printer, he learned the mechanics of the trade without effort almost over night and, like Franklin, first broke into print by submitting anonymous compositions to the paper which employed him. He soon established himself as a regular contributor to his own paper and began writing political articles for other publications. Before long he had become foreman printer and temporary editor of the *Herald* in the owner's absence. Then, coming of age, he had started his own paper, the *Free Press,* really the old *Herald,* which he took over and to which he gave this new name.

The instrument chosen by fate to establish connection between eighteen-year-old Whittier and twenty-one-year-old Garrison, was Whittier's very practical elder sister, Mary, who privately sent one of Greenleaf's poems to the *Free Press,* to which father John Whittier had subscribed because of its editor's liberal and humanitarian views. This poem, which was submitted without any clew as to its authorship and which appeared in the issue for June 8, 1826, had been written about a year earlier and may be found in the appendix to the 1888 Whittier *Collected Poems* under the title of *The Exile's Departure*. It is an Irish exile's Byronic farewell to Erin, in four romantic stanzas of eight lines each.

As usual, Pickard supplies humanizing details. He says that the young poet received the paper from the postman, who passed that way on horseback, while he and his father were mending a stone wall; that he saw his own work in print, was amazed and almost dazed. This is possible, for though farmers generally had to go to the postoffice for their mail—a century before rural delivery—the Whittiers lived on the main road and the postman may have been in the habit of leaving whatever he had for them as he rode by to the next town.

Another poem, *The Deity*—a rather creditable blank verse effort—was soon dispatched to the *Free Press*, and appeared in the June 22 issue, with a commendatory editorial note describing the author (then actually eighteen) as a lad of sixteen. The two poems aroused Garrison's interest so much that he traced the source through the postman and drove to Haverhill for the express purpose of seeing his contributor. There the spruce, self-confident young editor and the shy, immature poet began a life-long friendship during much of which they were the two most celebrated literary co-workers for freedom even when in disagreement as to means and methods.

Garrison, who always went straight to any objective, introduced himself to old John Whittier and urged that Greenleaf should have more advanced schooling. The taciturn Quaker was anything but pleased with this casual meddling in his domestic affairs and apparently said so. However, the parental objections must have been less harsh and unreasonable than generally represented in accounts of this famous incident. In a letter written to Garrison himself thirty-three years later, Whittier defended his father, saying, "My father did not oppose me; he was proud of my pieces, but as he was in straitened circumstances, he could do nothing to aid me." The simple truth is that the farm had not grown more prosperous. It produced plenty to eat but little that could be sold for cash and the remaining $600 of the old mortgage was the family nightmare.

Although Garrison, the piping-hot young enthusiast, failed to convince the elder Whittier that it would be common sense to give young Greenleaf a smattering of the higher education, a far less important man, by patient argument, obtained his consent on the condition that it should entail no further cash burden on slim family resources. In the latter part of 1826, Garrison had moved from Newbury to Boston and Whittier had begun offering his verses to the *Haverhill Gazette*, recently acquired by Abijah W. Thayer, formerly an editor in Portland, Maine; and it was Thayer who persuaded old John Whittier to yield the point. In all probability the Quaker father foresaw that this defection of his eldest son might ultimately lead to his abandoning the farm on which several generations had expended such herculean labors.

As a matter of fact, Thayer had an ally in fate. The higher education was suddenly to become more convenient. Instead of having to go to Newbury, Whittier would be able to get the necessary instruction in Haverhill, where a new Academy was to open in 1827—so near that he could tramp home for the week-ends. Even so, the money problem had to be analyzed literally to the last cent. It seems to be a matter of undeniable record that the poet calculated the exact cost of his first term at the Academy minutely, said that he would have just twenty-five cents left, and proved to be exactly correct.

Greenleaf earned the small required sum for board and tuition during the winter of 1826-1827 by making cheap slippers or sandals at eight cents a pair. No choice of work could have been more natural. It will be remembered that Garrison was originally an apprentice shoemaker, and he may have suggested the idea. Moreover, Haverhill and Amesbury are two of the oldest shoemaking centers in America, and part of the system of the old-time factories was to send out certain types of work or parts of the work to be done by the poorer people of the neighborhood in their homes. The writer well remembers seeing women making shoes in the doorways and windows of near-by Salisbury. And it will be remembered that whereas Hood wrote *The Song of the Shirt*, Hannah, the underprivileged heroine of the first factory girl poet, Lucy Larcom, was "binding shoes" instead of sewing seams. Probably Whittier's shoe-shop, mentioned in various biographies, was just a corner in barn or woodshed. Be that as it may, he earned enough money to be one of the pupils for the first term of the Haverhill Academy, beginning on May 1, 1827. He arranged to board in Editor Thayer's family.

The formal opening or dedication of the Academy occurred on April 30 and the *Gazette* recorded that the exercises included the singing of an ode "composed for the occasion by John G. Whittier of this town," whose name, however, did not appear on the program, of which there are two known copies.

According to an old gazetteer, Haverhill and Amesbury were both very prosperous local manufacturing towns at this period, in which connection it must be remembered that the Whittier homestead was in the East Parish, not in the village of Haverhill, but on its outskirts. In Yankee speech, Amesbury, in particular, was no slouch of a town, and rural in only a comparative degree. Though the first locomotive did not appear in America until 1829 and some twenty years elapsed before there were elementary networks of railroads, both Haverhill and Amesbury, by virtue of the Merrimack River, had water power and water transportation. In fact, towns of this class enjoyed early in the last century special advantages that were neutralized by the coming of railroads and steam.

The Haverhill Academy apparently did an all-around job,

for it enrolled pupils as young as ten and as old as twenty-five. Whittier at nineteen was one of the "big boys." The sacrifices he had made to attend assured his diligence, and his progress was remarkable. Piecing in what he had already learned at district school or at home, he put together the framework of a not inadequate American education, though he seems to have essayed no foreign tongue except French. As the town poet he was already a marked individual and was accepted readily into the most cultured families. He showed immediate interest in politics and international affairs.

This first term lasted six months, and at its end the wallet needed replenishing. During the winter of 1827-1828, Whittier taught school in the Birch Meadow district of West Amesbury (now Merrimac) and earned enough to assure a second term at the Academy, presumably beginning in May, 1828, which passed under much the same conditions as the first. Apart from his school-teacher savings, Greenleaf apparently earned a little money doing book-keeping for a local merchant. For a young man of Whittier's temperament and character, the school-teaching interlude between his two terms at the Academy must certainly have been a period of determined self-education. Virtually unchanged influences of environment and education were therefore in play from May, 1827, to November, 1828—within six weeks of his approaching twenty-first birthday.

What little is known of Whittier's adolescent affections during this period—he was bashful and almost as retarded in emotional as in poetic maturity—is discussed in the next chapter. The subject cannot be treated as casually as the facts warrant because it is necessary to refute certain absurdities of the psychoanalytic type printed in a recent biography by one Albert Mordell. There is surely nothing new or odd or revolutionary in the fact that young poets, especially if good-looking (as Whittier was), excite the interest of girls and have been known to return the interest. However, the picture of Whittier as a particularly callow, mooncalf lover, who became ill through sexual repression and ended up as a "male flirt" is too objectionably false to pass unanswered. Various commentators state that, in the numerous poems of his Academy period, Whittier shows a Byronic flair. Bless us all! What serious young poet—even young Quaker poet—doesn't get the Byron fever at some time? True, there have been exceptions like Bryant and Holmes, but the "ayes" have it by an overwhelming majority. And it must be remembered that in 1827-1828 George Gordon, Lord Byron—having died in 1824 for Greece and his own sins—was the most glamorously romantic influence in the drab Northern world. Any sensitive young poet who doesn't try to write like Byron at some period of development really ought to be shot at sunrise as a traitor to his craft—or excluded from the union.

Whittier's early productivity was so stupendous that, for years, bibliographers and biographers have been struggling not only to trace original printings, but to separate real Whittier efforts from spurious attributions. Thomas Franklin Currier, whose father was a friend of the poet and who has long been an assistant librarian of Harvard College, printed very recently (1937) a bibliography of Whittier surpassing any similar effort on the subject of any American author. It is the fruition of years of delving and, though not absolutely without possible errors—especially in some deduced probabilities—is amazing and exhaustive. The conclusions at which he arrives must be accepted as very much the best to date and definitive in 99 per cent of the disputed questions.

Between June 6, 1826, and December 9, 1826, Currier lists nineteen Whittier poems—seventeen signed with the initial "W" and two unsigned—all published in Garrison's *Newburyport Free Press*. The first piece to appear in Thayer's *Haverhill Gazette* was *The Execution of Louis XVI*, which was printed on January 6, 1827. From that date up to December 8 of the same year no less than fifty-seven Whittier poems are recorded, all but four of which are to be found in the files of the *Haverhill Gazette* or *Essex Gazette*, the second name being merely a change of title for the same journal,

effective as of February 10, 1827. The poet used the following signatures: the initial "W" twenty times; his full surname
only for the *Ode* at the opening of the Amesbury Academy,
as printed in the *Gazette;* the name "Adrian" twenty-four
times; the signature "Donald" (for Scottish dialect poems)
seven times; and the signature "Peter" for a single humorous
parody (very possibly not his work at all).

For the year 1828, Currier locates no less than seventy
Whittier published poems. Six of these are unsigned but
definitely authenticated. The other sixty-four bear these
various signatures: "W," "Whittier," "J.G.W.," "Adrian,"
"Donald," "Timothy," "Nehemiah," "Ichabod," and "Micajah."
These verses appeared in several publications—*Essex Gazette,
Boston Statesman, National Philanthropist, New England
Weekly Review, Journal of the Times,* and *American Manufacturer.* This list foots up to the truly amazing total of one
hundred forty-two published poems during a three-year
period while the author was between eighteen and twenty-
one—including just one poem which appeared after his
twenty-first birthday on December 17, 1828. Yet this was
only a sample of what was to follow.

As to the connections between Whittier and the various
journals printing these early poems: Whittier boarded in
Haverhill with the editor of the *Gazette* and was his protégé;
the *Boston Statesman*—authoritative and widely read—belonged to Whittier's cousin, Nathaniel Greene, at whose
house he stayed (as has already been mentioned) during his
first boyhood trip to Boston; the *National Philanthropist* and
the *Journal of the Times* (Bennington, Vermont) were both
edited transiently by Garrison; the *National Philanthropist*
was under the same ownership as the *American Manufacturer,*
of which Whittier himself was soon to become editor. The
only journal, among all those publishing the early Whittier
poems, with which he had no personal introductory contact
was the *New England Weekly Review,* most important of
the group. The fact that he was able to break into this periodical "cold" shows that his writings were being recognized

as of popular interest. At the time, this paper was being edited by the brilliant and satirical George D. Prentice.

It has been fad and fashion with Whittier biographers to discover and inflict upon their readers unpublished childhood or youthful poems by J.G.W.—possibly, probably, and positively not. This activity should really be forbidden by law. Such early verses as Whittier himself thought worthy of preservation by even the most liberal standards he reluctantly included in the appendix to the 1888 edition of his *Collected Poems*, and there the curious may slake their thirst.

In 1828 Whittier had for the first time the pleasure of seeing one of his poems in a "regular book." That book, published after long preparation by Editor Thayer, was entitled *Incidental Poems by Robert Dinsmoor, the Rustic Bard*. The verses by Whittier, entitled *J.G.W. to the Rustic Bard*, appear on pages 248-250. They are in the same Burns-inspired Scotch dialect Whittier had already used repeatedly in his *Gazette* poems over the "Donald" signature—a dialect more artificial for Whittier than for Dinsmoor, whose forebears, though they had lived and died in America for three generations, had resided in a strictly Scottish community. These verses were printed in the *Gazette* at about the same time that the volume was published and probably before it got into circulation. They are conventional and complimentary; and the simple truth is that old Dinsmoor was then at least as much of a poet as young Whittier. Though Whittier must have known Dinsmoor through Thayer, there is no iota of genuine evidence that he either edited the volume or wrote the sketch of the author. He merely helped out, in a friendly way, by writing a favorable criticism which was first published in the *Boston Statesman* and then reprinted in the *Gazette*.

It has long been tradition to claim that *The Song of the Vermonters*—the first poem in which Whittier found himself and surrendered to his instinct for vital balladry—was written in 1828 though not published until 1833. Mr. Currier refutes this belief with data, arguments, and probabilities, explaining the vagueness of Whittier's only known reference to the problem. A better reason for believing that it was written in 1833 rather than in 1828 is inherent in the work itself. The poem is definitely beyond the author's capacity in 1828 but about what might logically have occurred five years later.

The special nature of Whittier's inspiration was for some years unrecognized even by the poet himself. Once he grasped it, he exercised it continually and developed it consistently. No man knew better than he that the slightest touch of sophistication was fatal and that basic truths, simply stated as such or unfolded in brief action episodes, were keystones for his thought and expression. As has already been indicated—and as cannot be too frequently emphasized—the vast popularity which Whittier acquired in youth with his torrent of second-rate poetry is explainable only by its poignant sincerity.

If ever a man learned to drive nails by swinging a hammer, Whittier learned to write poetry by writing it.

5

WHITE-HAIRED BOY OF
THE ACADEMY

OBVIOUSLY THE YOUNG POET who wrote the ode to be sung at the opening of the Academy must have been the star pupil or, as the young folks say today, the white-haired boy. Not only was young Whittier a poet with his piece in the paper almost every week, but he was tall, good-looking, serious, ambitious, and engagingly shy. He was poor, but a member of the editor's household and distinctly a marked young man. In addition to his verses, the *Gazette* also printed his prose articles—his study of *Robert Burns* (November 8, 1828); his review of Dinsmoor's *Incidental Poems* (March 1, 1828); *Reginald Heber* (June 21, 1828); *Juvenile Productions* (October 18, 1828); *The Prose Works of Milton* (May 24, 1828); *Poets and Poetry*, four numbers (June 14, 21, 28, and July 19, 1828); *Review of "Charlotte's Daughter," by Mrs. Rowson* (May 17, 1828); *The Smuggler* (May 31, 1828); *War* (August 9, 1828). If the young women of the town, especially the female students of the Academy, had been unconscious of this phenomenon in their midst they would have had to be congenitally deaf, dumb, blind, and sexless.

Judge Minot, a leading citizen of Haverhill, with a son and a daughter of his own at the Academy, opened his house and its comparatively extensive library to young Whittier. In later years, the daughter recalled Whittier's conversations with her father on political matters and his surprisingly detailed information. Judge Pitman and Dr. Elias Weld—the most broadly cultured man of Amesbury—also opened their houses and libraries to the Quaker youth.

Whittier was indeed getting intensive education—by direct study under supervision of Oliver Carlton, the very capable master of the Academy; by his own never satisfied thirst for good literature, now readily available; by contact with mature minds; by the local reactions to his various printed productions. He must really have been little short of an assistant editor for Thayer. He wrote the *Carrier's Address for 1828*, and he cannot possibly have ignored the chance to learn the rudiments of composition, make-up, and printing which every old-time editor had to bear continually in mind. In short, while acquiring general education and the rudiments of such social amenities as his rather embarrassed and self-conscious personality could absorb, Whittier was learning at close range from Thayer—a very competent instructor—the editorial trade, which he practiced himself thereafter for many years. And it is to be taken for granted that politics in general—and of Essex County in particular— must have been the salt and pepper of table talk in the home of Editor Thayer.

In January, 1828, between his two terms at the Academy, Thayer tried to give his local prodigy another boost by issuing the prospectus of a book to be entitled *The Poems of Adrian,* the mysterious Adrian being J.G.W. This prospectus has none of the semi-patronizing atmosphere of the indorsements printed by Garrison in his *Free Press* or by Greene in the *Boston Statesman,* when introducing the novice author. Says Thayer: "It is believed by his friends that these poems indicate genius of a high order, which deserves all possible culture. The design of thus offering his juvenile writings to the public is to raise money to assist him in obtaining a classical education." In a word, Thayer wanted to send his protégé to college, but the needed subscriptions for the book —200 pages for only 75 cents—failed to materialize.

According to the official biography Whittier accumulated, during his second term at the Academy, the bulk of the material for the *History of Haverhill* which was completed by B. L. Mirick and published by Thayer in 1832. All in all,

J.G.W. was certainly a very busy young man, living abstemiously and bent on learning practical things. If he had the disposition to play the clownish, moon-calf amorous rôle of this period assigned to him in Mordell's *Quaker Militant* (of which there is not the least proof or indication) he must have discovered the secret of manufacturing the time to do it in.

According to Mordell, an unsuccessful love affair during this Academy period was the first step in Whittier's misguided use of the sex urge which resulted in his health's suffering from repression and in his becoming an incurable "male coquet." Whether his ill health was from early eye-strain, as one authoritative physician insists; from repression, as Mordell is absolutely certain; from early bodily overstrain at farm tasks, as tradition asserts; or from heart trouble as Dr. H. I. Bowditch, his very competent Boston physician, contended is uncertain to this day—with no evidence or general credence for the Mordell hypothesis. The facts of Whittier's love-life—if one may use the term at all for anything so blandly innocuous—were assembled by Mordell so completely, in his ardent endeavor to prove his pet theory, that further investigation would be time wasted. Moreover, the facts seem themselves to be well documented, and the problem is purely one of interpretation.

Answering the very unimportant self-posed question of whom Whittier commemorated in his love poems *Memories* and *My Playmate*, Mordell states that in these and other verses Whittier enshrined a distant relative, Mary Emerson Smith, granddaughter of Mary Whittier, who was a second cousin of his father and the wife of Nehemiah Emerson, a veteran of the Revolution. Mary Emerson Smith and Greenleaf met as children, says Mordell, and Whittier recited his poems to her. It appears that she had Grecian features, brown hair, hazel eyes (like Adela in the poet's *Moll Pitcher*) and an " 'aughty" disposition based upon her father's prosperous circumstances.

That this affair was consumingly intense Mordell "proves"

by quoting from two Whittier prose sketches, which really have nothing to do with the case—*Confessions of a Suicide*, which satisfies him that Greenleaf reached a suicidal state of mind, and *The Opium Eater* (in which the earlier *Confessions of a Suicide* was incorporated), adding "dope" to the woes of the earlier fragile trifle.

"What though the other village girls idolized him and sought his attentions!" says Mordell. "That good fortune could not allay the fiery tempest which swept over him."

Briefly, isn't it possible that Greenleaf had a high-school crush on Mary and that though Mary just couldn't bring herself absolutely to cut the town poet loose, she wouldn't get down to cases or to his standard of living? Mordell may even be right in contending that she rejected the poet after he left town to work in Boston, though Whittier did his best to show her the worldliness of such vanities as dancing and even though he wrote verses and might perhaps have given up his beloved Quaker meeting to marry her.

Mordell states that Whittier, after leaving Haverhill for Boston, persisted in dangling, and quotes an authentic silly letter to prove it. Poems on this episode are identified as *Stanzas, The Dream of the Misanthrope*, and *To S.E.M.*— none of them worthy of quotation and all of them so vapid that the inspiration may as well have been imaginary as specific.

"The gusts of furious blasts of inhibited sex passion now swept over his poetic work," says Mordell, pointing dramatically to a very conventional rhymed version of a Roman legend, *The Vestal*, and a charmingly ingenuous farewell poem, *To Mary*. This *To Mary*, not in the *Collected Poems*, was printed first in the *Boston Courier* and then deliberately reprinted by Whittier in the *New England Weekly Review*, of Hartford (which he was then editing) as a joking rejoinder to the charge that he was using too much love poetry in his columns—scarcely the use that the always cautious and courteous Whittier would have made of any personal bleeding wound.

In 1831, when Whittier retired from the editorship of the *New England Review*, he suffered a severe nervous breakdown which Mordell insists on connecting with the fact that, at about this same time, stick-along Mary left the East and went to Cincinnati, from which Western point of vantage she still occasionally wrote to the sorrowful rejected knight. The climax of all this nonsense is reached when Mordell identifies Mary as the *Demon Lady*—really far worse punishment than her blandishments deserved!

In conclusion regarding Mary, be it noted that she married a Kentucky judge by the name of Thomas and had ten children—wherefore she seems to have known the right man when she found him. In her subsequent widowhood, she would now and then meet Whittier on his trips to the New Hampshire Mountains and chat over old times. There is no reason to deny this episode of somewhat more than averagely sentimental calf-love—nor is there the faintest evidence that it shattered Whittier's soul or nervous system. His natural instinct was for celibacy, not passion.

To return to Academy days—Greenleaf also met one Evelina Bray, whose affections, Mordell says, he trifled with because he could not conquer his love for Mary and was no bigamist at heart. Though one may be sure the attachment was not unconventional, Mordell says Whittier felt that he had behaved very badly and consequently wrote poems about wicked men who broke ladies' hearts—such as *The Church Yard, Forsaken*, and *The Farewell*, none of more than the slightest significance. Worse, much worse—he even wrote a prose story entitled *The Forsaken Girl* and sometimes penned editorials against philanderers.

In later years Whittier sent Evelina books, and she wrote letters to him, and in her widowhood (after an unfortunate marriage, ended by the death of her husband through mob violence) she went a-visiting him, just like Mary. She had a habit of talking for publication and liked to be advertised as Whittier's early sweetheart. It was so romantic and so very harmless! The episode of the Philadelphia lady will be narrated in due course—and she also used to visit Whittier in her widowhood. Did any man ever have such an incurable harem-after-widowhood of platonic sweethearts—human boomerangs all?

In all seriousness and with all absurd exaggerations eliminated, Whittier doubtless had a youthful love for Mary Smith, and he admitted this to various friends with typical quaint hesitation. He probably did refer to her in *Memories*, which is good romantic verse of the gently reminiscent type, and possibly in *My Playmate*, which is better.

To a mind not of the Mordellian persuasion, it is evident that Whittier dramatized these slight experiences (serving him in place of the more explicit experiences acquired by most young men) in prose and verse. His enormous practical industry was certainly not that of a youth emerging from a late adolescence into storms of ungratified passion.

If America has ever produced a genuine instance of male sublimation, John Greenleaf Whittier is the shining example. His ruling passions were Justice and Freedom.

6

TO BOSTON AND
HOME AGAIN

IN THE LATE AUTUMN of 1828, Whittier found himself confronted with the problem of earning an immediate livelihood or seeking a college education, which could be done only on borrowed money.

Garrison, who had just left his Boston job as editor of the *National Philanthropist* (which had published its first Whittier poem on June 6 of that current year) was engaged in establishing his more outspoken Bennington, Vermont, publication, the *Journal of the Times* (which published its first Whittier poem on October 24) and recommended Whittier for his own old position. The *National Philanthropist* was the first prohibition paper and was one of a group of three papers—two weeklies and a monthly—operated by the Reverend William Collier, a Baptist clergyman, and his son, William R. Collier. According to Pickard, Whittier wrote an article on temperance which Thayer published in the *Gazette* on November 15, and this may have been done with an eye to business because the negotiations between Whittier and Collier, for the *Philanthropist* editorship, were just then coming to a head. Thayer, who was himself a temperance enthusiast, undoubtedly knew temperance-minded Collier; and Collier would naturally have been impressed with the recommendations of his own former editor, Garrison, and of Thayer, with whom the prospective employee had worked and lived on terms of exceptional intimacy. Possibly Whittier's influential Boston relative, Editor Nathaniel

Greene of the *Statesman,* also put in a good word at the right time. On the basis of three such sponsors it seems natural enough that Collier should finally have offered Whittier his first editorship at $500 a year.

At just about this same time, November 27, 1828, Whittier's first contribution to the *American Manufacturer,* the second Collier weekly, appeared in print. This was an unsigned article on the Haverhill Academy. A letter written by Whittier to Thayer the very next day states clearly that he cannot go through college on charity, that he cannot abide the thought of teaching, and that the offer from the *Philanthropist* is both respectable and sympathetic because he believes in the cause it represents.

Within a month Whittier was in Boston working for the Colliers and living in their household, which seems to have been a combination of home and boarding house, at 30 Federal Street. But instead of becoming editor of the *Philanthropist* he found himself, on January 1, 1829, formally installed in charge of the *American Manufacturer.* Just how or why this switch occurred is absolutely unknown, but the change was advantageous because it put the young editor into much closer touch with current events. Reformers of every type haunted the Collier home and shop. It was there, in 1828, that Garrison first met Benjamin Lundy—fourth in the dynasty of Quaker prophets to carry the torch of emancipation and the man who first enlisted Garrison's active interest in the slavery cause. It was written in the stars that Garrison and Lundy were to work together and then separate and that the mantle of Lundy was to fall on the shoulders of Whittier.

The *American Manufacturer* was distinctly a pro-Clay political organ, advocating protective tariffs (for which Clay was the outstanding sponsor), urging the creation of American industries, and naturally opposing any and all ideas emanating from Andrew Jackson. Clay, coming from the border state of Kentucky, was then the only leading figure in politics striving to combine the best commercial interests of both North and South. In fact, he foresaw that the North must become a manufacturing center, at a time when most Northern capitalists opposed the idea on the theory that it would kill the shipping and merchandising business with England and Europe. In theory, at least, Clay was opposed to slavery to the extent of honestly wishing that some peaceful means for abolishing it could be found.

The chance that put Whittier into this political editorship had a vast influence on his entire career. He was intensely ambitious at this dawn of his "grown-up" life—ambitious for success, not for self-sacrifice—and had always been fascinated by politics; and here was his ready-made opportunity to break into the game. But even in his rôle of political editor of a manufacturing trade journal, Whittier could not restrain his poetic impulse. His first three poems for the *Manufacturer* were *The Conscript's Farewell* and *The Old Oak Tree*, both published on November 27, 1828, and *Take Back the Bowl*, published on Christmas. During the calendar year of 1829, despite all his other activities, he published forty-five definitely identified poems—fifteen in the *American Manufacturer;* eleven in the *Essex Gazette;* four in the *New England Weekly Review*, of Hartford; six in the *Boston Courier*—a new medium for him; three in the *Yankee and Boston Literary Gazette*—also a new medium; four in the *Philadelphia Album*—new again; one in the *Ladies' Magazine*, of Boston—likewise a first contribution; and one in the *Columbian Star*—the fifth fresh connection of a single season. Increasing scope and increasing popularity need no further evidence.

Two of the 1828 poems, *The Earthquake*, first printed in the *Boston Statesman*, and *The Sicilian Vespers*, first published in the *Journal of the Times*, and one of the 1829 poems, *The Spirit of the North*, first printed in the *Ladies' Magazine*, were widely reprinted and added greatly to his persistently growing reputation. These three poems are all included in the 1888 appendix to the *Collected Poems* and show the development of that graphic, visual simplicity which became

Whittier's special gift. The final stanzas from *The Spirit of the North* will serve to illustrate:

> Dark and desolate and lone,
> Curtained with the tempest-cloud,
> Drawn around thy ancient throne
> Like oblivion's moveless shroud—
> Dim and distantly the sun,
> Glances on thy palace walls,
> But a shadow cold and dun
> Broods along its pillared halls.
>
> Lord of sunless depths and cold!
> Chainer of the northern sea—
> At whose feet the storm is rolled,
> Who hath power to humble thee?
> Spirit of the stormy north!
> Bow thee to thy Maker's nod—
> Bend to him who sent thee forth—
> Servant of the living God.

Of course the captious critic might point out many immaturities and might note the fact that Whittier could not finish even this without the religious tag, which many people feel to be a frequent blemish but which others recognize as merely a part of the whole in Whittier's compositions.

The amount of prose from the editor's pen—editorials and articles of all sorts and "fillers"—that went into the *Manufacturer* must have been tremendous and can be traced only in part with any certainty. About thirty-five years ago, as assistant editor of a New York trade weekly, the present writer turned out about one-fourth of a very sizeable journal every seven days. Merely to imagine what Collier probably expected in 1829 for $500 a year is enough to bring on an attack of pen palsy.

Whittier was disposed to take everything he did seriously, and for the time being he became sincerely attached to the fortunes of Clay. This enthusiasm proved advantageous because of other connections it brought about. It was also in the *Manufacturer* office that Greenleaf Whittier first met Charles Sumner, then a Harvard student. Sumner came to the printshop with some of his father's copy for an anti-Masonic paper which his father was promoting and which was printed by the Collier Press. Of course neither young man could have had the remotest idea of the years of joint soldiering that lay ahead for them.

In August, just as he was really digging in, Whittier was called back from Boston to the Haverhill farm by his father's failing health. He had saved half of his $9 weekly salary and that fund went to reducing the old farm mortgage. For a bit more than half a year he had lived in the Hub of the Universe; had met men important in literary and political activities; had increased his poetical reputation; had become a thoroughly professional editor; and had made good self-educational use of access to libraries many times greater than those available in Amesbury or Haverhill.

At very nearly the same time that Whittier left the *Manufacturer*, Garrison abandoned his *Journal of the Times* in Bennington and became Lundy's partner in publishing the *Genius of Universal Emancipation* at Baltimore.

The most widely quoted of all Whittier sentimental letters was written while he was editing the *American Manufacturer*, to his friend Edward Harriman. Part of it is printed here just to show how very un-Mordellian, unsuicidal, un-torn-by-passion his attitude was, even if admittedly a bit poetico-mawkish.

Says Greenleaf: "Here I have been all day trying to write something for my paper, but what with habitual laziness, and a lounge or two in the Athenaeum Gallery, I am altogether unfitted for composition. . . . There are a great many pretty girls at the Athenaeum, and I like to sit there and remark upon the different figures that go flitting by me, like aerial creatures just stooping down to our dull earth, to take a view of the beautiful creations of the painter's genius. I love to watch their airy motions, notice the dark brilliancy of their fine eyes, and observe the delicate flush stealing over their cheeks, but, trust me, my heart is untouched—cold and motionless as a Jutland Lake lighted up by the moonshine. I always did love a pretty girl. Heaven grant there is no harm in it!" What sentimentality could more unconsciously reveal the utter soul of innocence?

Back in Haverhill, Greenleaf devoted himself for four months to farm and father. But he had neither the disposition nor the cash to remain idle through the winter. By January 1, 1830, he was back in harness, editing the *Gazette* for his old friend Thayer, doing most of the work at home. While editing this local paper, he entered into correspondence, at some length, with George D. Prentice, the young and brilliant editor of the *New England Weekly Review,* of Hartford, who has already been mentioned and in whose publication several Whittier poems had already appeared. Like the *Manufacturer,* the *Review* was ardently pro-Clay politically, and Prentice, only about five years older than Whittier (though far more sophisticated) was a man of veritable wit and no little talent.

In June, John Whittier died, leaving Greenleaf to provide for himself and three women—his mother, his aunt, and his younger sister, Elizabeth or "Lizzie." His older sister, Mary, had married and his brother had left home to make his own way in the world.

Problems connected with his father's death were only half settled when Whittier received an offer he could not reasonably refuse. This completely unexpected proposition was that he should substitute for Prentice of the *New England Weekly Review* in Hartford while Prentice went South to prepare the official campaign life of Clay, who was already slated to run against Jackson for the presidency in 1832. His services would be required by midsummer.

During these domestic upheavals and changes of occupation Whittier seems to have relaxed his habit of poetical composition very little if at all. From January 19 to August 21 of 1829—practically the first six months of his twenty-second year—he published twenty poems in the *Gazette*, two in the *New England Weekly Review*, one in the *Ladies' Magazine*, one in the *Cincinnati American*, and one in the *London Literary Gazette*.

Mr. C. A. Wilson, world's foremost collector of nineteenth-century New England first editions, has pointed out that the poem first printed in London—*To the Author of the Improvisatrice*—appeared before a single line by Longfellow, Holmes, Poe, Hawthorne, or Emerson had been published in the British Isles. It was presented to the public with a commendatory editorial note on the talent of its author, "a young American poet editor of great promise in the United States." The poem in the *Cincinnati American*, published on May 30, 1830, was a ballad entitled merely *Henry Clay*. Though Whittier absolutely refused to have it printed in his collected works, because of obvious crudities, it became the recognized Clay campaign song and was the first Whittier ballad to sweep the country.

7

TO HARTFORD AND
BACK AGAIN

WHITTIER TOOK OVER from Prentice on the *New England Review* in midsummer of 1830 and surely had full charge by August. This was serious responsibility for a youth of twenty-two who had been attending his first term of high school only four years earlier. His work included not only the usual routine of high-class editing but the political publicity and maneuvering preceding a presidential election in which the patron saint of the paper—Henry Clay—was to oppose the fire-eating Andrew Jackson. The situation was complicated by the opposition of Daniel Webster, already the giant-orator-statesman of New England, to Clay and his policies. Webster feared that Clay's program for the industrialization of American life behind a barrier of protective tariffs would disproportionately injure New England's very important commerce.

The contrast between the sarcastically witty, wine-loving, dashing Prentice and the earnest young Quaker must have been something of a jolt to the owners and other employees of the *Review*. But Greenleaf had come to do a job and he did it with North-of-Boston thoroughness. However ingenuous he may have looked, his naturally shrewd political instincts and his pro-Clay training on the *Manufacturer* gave him the necessary grasp of essentials.

Except for two or three weeks spent in New York during January of 1831, Whittier seems to have remained in Hartford continuously until March of that year—a period of about nine months—when he went back to Haverhill on business connected with his late father's $6,000-estate. In June and July he seems to have left Haverhill on a trip down east, apparently his first pilgrimage in search of health, and not to have returned to Hartford until August, about a year after his first arrival there. He went back to his editorial desk, but after a month or six weeks of work he had a severe nervous breakdown. This collapse must have been serious if not dangerous because he went back home this time accompanied by a physician, a Dr. Crane, as being considered unfit to travel safely alone.

After a rather prolonged period of recuperation, he left Haverhill again, planning to pass through Hartford on his way to the National Republican Convention in Baltimore on December 12, but by the time he reached Boston he was too ill to go farther. As of January, 1832, Whittier reluctantly surrendered his editorship of the *Review*. Prentice had not returned to his old post, and except for illness permanent control of the *Review* had been within Whittier's grasp.

In a letter to his friend Jonathan Law, written at Haverhill on January 5, 1832, and quoted in the official biography, Whittier flatly denies that he is "hypo" and insists that his sickness is "as real as the nose on my face." In this long epistle, Greenleaf first bewails the blue devils of despair that assail him and then protests that he is not really morose; speaks of visits to Boston, Salem, Marblehead, and Andover; and even adds the very un-Hamletesque remark, "The girls here are nice specimens of what girls should be."

This breakdown—nervous or physical or both combined—is the attack which Mordell seeks to establish as "love melancholy" (to quote good old Burton) caused by the emigration westward of persistent Mary Emerson Smith—on her predestined way to husband and ten children. True to his thesis of making a sex problem, willy-nilly, Mordell supplies Whittier with yet another Hartford inamorata, Mary Anonymous —but still a Mary, the name itself being a symptom of the obsession. Also there was one Cornelia Russ (shameful infidelity to Marys Ltd.), daughter of Judge Russ of Hartford —seventeen years old, beautiful, and, according to New England prejudices of the time and place, of high degree. Mordell quotes a letter from Greenleaf to Cornelia—and a pretty sappy letter it is—asking for an appointment he didn't get and didn't deserve to get on such an application. In all sober seriousness, Mordell says: "Cornelia was proud and snobbish like Mary. Meanwhile, his high passions, clogged again, brought suffering upon him. He brooded and brooded till physical agony and mental torture wrecked him."

This is just so much unmitigated tosh. If Whittier could return from the grave he certainly would tell Mordell a thing or two with Quaker simplicity. The spare-time day-dream sillinesses of a rather sickly youth who has worked himself to death should be no mystery and scarcely subject for comment. Any personable widow of thirty-five or forty has had more than one such case on her doorstep and generally knows enough to treat it with human compassion.*

Consider the immense labor that this slightly undeveloped youth had crammed into four and a half years—from May, 1827, to September, 1831. He had studied with hungry concentration for two six-month terms at high school—teaching school himself between those terms—while continually writing for publication besides doing bookkeeping on the side. He had edited the *American Manufacturer,* the *Essex Gazette,* and the *New England Review,* writing, learning, and earning at the same time. He had run the homestead farm and edited the *Gazette* while his father was dying, and he had taken up his task on the *Review* within sixty days of his father's death. He had lived and saved money on a pittance. Throughout the period he had published almost a

---

* A remarkable "Round Robin," written in 1832 by Whittier and two Haverhill girl friends to a young woman who had visited in Haverhill, has just been discovered and has come into the author's hands too late to incorporate in this book except as an Appendix. It will be found on page 329. It is illuminating to one of the least known periods of Whittier's life, revealing him as pictured by himself and as pictured by two intimate young women friends.

poem a week and must have written prose enough to fill a sizable volume. With his fragile physique, the wonder is that he stood the grind so long. As a premise for problems of wild and ungovernable passion this record is clearly preposterous.

The genuine social summary of Whittier's much interrupted life at Hartford is brief. First he boarded at the old Lunt Tavern and then at the house of Hartford's former postmaster, Jonathan Law. He made the acquaintance of Mrs. Sigourney, the first of the many famous women authors who were to be his friends, of Dr. Todd, the Honorable Mr. Trumbull, and the Honorable Martin Wells. Trumbull and Wells were his special political mentors. He also became acquainted with Isaac E. Crary, later both a general and a congressman; Charles M. Emerson, a young lawyer who acted as his attorney; and F. A. P. Barnard, later president of Columbia, whose name is preserved in Barnard College. These men were all contributors to the *Review*. He was invited to join the exclusive club of local literary bloods but was a determined water drinker and never reappeared after his first experience with the group.

While Whittier was officially editor of the *New England Review*—from August of 1830 until January of 1832, a period of about eighteen months—he published fifty-one poems in periodicals, all but three in the *Review*. One of these, *To William Lloyd Garrison*, published in the *Essex Gazette* for November 26, 1831, was his first out-and-out anti-slavery poem and appears as such in his collected works. Another, *New England*, printed in the *Review* on October 18, 1830, was finally incorporated into his long poem, *Moll Pitcher*, published two years later. This is the earliest Whittier composition to be widely known and quoted in parts today; and, in a sense, *New England* is his credo of Yankee loyalty.

Besides this steady stream of verse, Whittier flooded the columns of the *Review* with editorials, sketches, short stories, book reviews, and what-not. Even during his absences the steady flow of material continued uninterrupted. Indeed, these absences were his induction into that specialty of editing by mail which he practiced so largely in later life.

The two or three weeks' trip to New York in January of 1831 constituted Whittier's introduction to Manhattan and was for the specific purpose of gathering facts to complete Prentice's *Life of Clay*, which had arrived in manuscript lacking two or three chapters needed to round out the work properly. Accompanied by his friend Crary, Greenleaf journeyed from Hartford to New Haven by stage and thence to New York by boat, encountering a severe storm. On arrival he was invited to a convivial evening by Forrest, then the dominant figure of the American stage, Halleck, and Leggett, sure proof that he was indeed becoming somebody; but he managed to escape. His time seems to have been spent mainly in library research, but he did meet Mordecai Noah, of the *New York Courier and Enquirer* at the office of that very influential paper, and Jerome Brooks, of the same publication, at his residence. The only importance of the visit was to broaden the country Quaker's background still further and to supply him with the stimulus of new impressions.

From May, 1827, to January, 1832—from the middle of his nineteenth to the beginning of his twenty-fourth year—Whittier had developed from high school freshman to veteran writer. It was only natural that his work should now begin to appear in permanent form. In fact, two first examples of his work in book form appeared in February, 1831, shortly after his return from the New York trip and while he was actively editing the *Review*. The first of these was the *Life of Clay*, with the last two or three chapters, as well as various corrections and interpolated passages, from the hand of Whittier. The second was Whittier's own first complete published volume, *The Legends of New England*, published by Hanmer and Phelps of Hartford, a slim volume of prose and verse, 142 pages of text in addition to the introduction and customary preliminaries.

Five of the nine poems contained in *The Legends* had previously appeared in the *Gazette,* and of the whole nine

Whittier ultimately "collected" only two, *Metacom* and *The White Mountains*. The seven prose sketches all appeared in the published volume for the first time. In later life Whittier had almost a mania for destroying vestiges of what he considered bad early work and is said to have paid five dollars for any copy of this book he could find, just for the privilege of tearing it up.

Though *The Legends* preserves a number of Yankee traditions of the supernatural and early-settler type always beloved of Whittier, it is commonplace enough in concept and treatment. It is amusing to note that he is not absolutely accurate as to his facts, even when he names the two Indians who first appeared at Plymouth in the spring of 1621, being just half right and half wrong, for all through life he had the habit of never being quite exact, twisting the facts of legends or events he commemorated. In his preface, he says that he shall have accomplished his purpose if the book inspires further investigation and recording of New England antiquities, which have been sadly neglected. And here again he is not quite right, for Drake and Upham had already begun their researches and publications. Whittier was not originating a movement but participating in the early phases of one already started. *The Legends* is today mainly interesting as Whittier's first complete book. Because of that fact, because of its great rarity, and because there are three minutely different bibliographical variants, constituting first, second, and third state, the item will always be valuable and a nugget for collectors.

Though it did not make its appearance until early in 1832, one other book must be mentioned in this distinctly prefatory period of Whittier publications. This is Mirick's *History of Haverhill*, published in Haverhill by Thayer. As already mentioned, Whittier collected much of the data for this book during his Academy days and it seems to have been prepared along the general lines he had indicated. It is a "Whittier item" which Whittier never claimed for himself in any degree whatever.

Despite the fact that he had given up his editorial position in Hartford and was living at home with no very pressing work to do, the year 1832 was comparatively sterile in literary production, except for the publication of his first long poem in book form, *Moll Pitcher*, which was issued in April by Carter & Hendee of Boston. This is a typical twenty-three-page octavo-size pamphlet with blue paper covers—front wrapper printed, back wrapper blank. The poem was copyrighted and printed by Joseph Buckingham of Newburyport, to whose *New England Magazine* Whittier contributed his first poem almost simultaneously, in the May number. It was dedicated to Dr. Todd, Whittier's old friend of Hartford days.

Today *Moll Pitcher* is the most valuable of all Whittier first edition items. Though he excluded the poem as a whole from his authorized works, he used parts of it over again, just as he used part of his *Gazette* poem, *New England*, in *Moll Pitcher*. The first two stanzas of *Memories* came from *Moll Pitcher* and so does *Extract from a New England Legend* in the 1843 collection known as *Lays of My Home*. As suggested by the title of this excerpt, *Moll Pitcher* might well have been included as a longer poem in *The Legends of New England*. The heroine is not the female cannoneer of Revolutionary fame but a Yankee witch who upsets the wits of the heroine by convincing her that her lover is to meet disaster at sea—a prophecy which is fortunately not fulfilled, so that everything can end happily, with the daughter of the heroine, who has fully recovered her senses, comforting the witch on her deathbed.

The whole of *Moll Pitcher* was reprinted with the author's tacit consent just once, eight years later, in a much smaller sized paper-covered volume entitled *Moll Pitcher and The Minstrel Girl*. The importance of this volume and its rarity are generally underestimated. It is not only the sole form in which *Moll* is available to the average collector but it is the one and only issue of *The Minstrel Girl*.

Also, in 1832—probably in July or early August—appeared

the *Literary Remains of John G. C. Brainard*, with a sketch of his life by Whittier, published by Goodsell of Hartford— an item rare in original board covers but comparatively common in original cloth. Though Poe literally tore his reputation to pieces at a later date, Brainard was a Connecticut bard of some genuine lyrical inspiration, especially in his feeling for nature; one of those short-lived consumptive geniuses so characteristic of early American letters. Whittier's *Life of Brainard* occupies 29 of the 228 pages, is a good job of prose from every viewpoint, and shows his deep interest in New England literary color. In fact, the prose of this *Life*, and its elements of critical discernment, are far more mature than most Whittier work at this stage and far superior in treatment—though, of course, not in force or enthusiasm—to much later controversial writings. Brainard died in September, 1828, while Whittier was finishing his first term at the Academy, and therefore the personal impressions must all have come second-hand from friends in Hartford. Brainard wrote a little historical novel, usually known as the *Fort Braddock Papers*, first published in New York in 1824 and many times reprinted, which has become an outstanding rarity for Americana and early American fiction collectors and which assures the permanence of his name among authors of the epoch.

During 1832 Whittier published only seven poems in periodicals—two in the *Gazette*, one in the *Philadelphia Album*, one in the *New England Magazine*, and three in the *Hartford Iris*. Throughout the year he was at home in Haverhill or elsewhere in New England. With improved health, doubtless the result of less confining work, his political ambitions returned in full force. Though Andrew Jackson was elected president of the United States, Henry Clay carried Massachusetts, and Whittier felt he had contributed something to the local victory in defeat.

The story of how Whittier proved his political prowess only to foreswear all advantages it might bring to himself in favor of the Great Crusade of anti-slavery must be treated separately. Up to this point, though literally born into the anti-slavery movement, Whittier had published only one anti-slavery poem, the lines to Garrison.

As to Garrison: as will be shown presently, having already been in prison for the cause of Freedom, on January 1, 1831, he had cast aside all conservative partners and had founded *The Liberator*, with the aid of Isaac Knapp and no capital except courage. The paper was consecrated solely to the abolition of slavery. In the first number was this famous editorial announcement, "I am in earnest. I will not equivocate—I will not excuse—I will not retreat a single inch—and I will be heard."

It was not far from Boston, where Garrison was publishing *The Liberator*, to Haverhill; and Garrison, more than any man alive, knew the fighting power and persistence of a certain Yankee Quaker if he could only be thoroughly aroused.

8

TRANSITION

———

THE END OF THE YEAR 1832 seems a fitting date at which to draw the transition line between the first and second epochs of Whittier's life and work. It is true that one publication which should be grouped with his apprentice achievements—*Mogg Megone*—was not published until nearly four years later in the form of a tiny 16mo cloth-covered volume issued by Light and Stearns of Boston and copyrighted by them. But it is also true that Whittier, according to his own positive statement, began *Mogg* in 1830, though he put it aside for three years or more before completion. *Mogg Megone* is a kind of hang-over from the first period ˏcropping up in the second, and, for critical consideration, may properly be moved back to the place where it belongs. Whittier himself sanctions this treatment, for he relegated it to the appendix of the 1888 *Collected Poems*.

In his 1888 prefatory note to *Mogg Megone* Whittier says: "It deals with the border strife of the early settlers of eastern New England and their savage neighbors; but its personages and incidents are mainly fictitious. Looking at it, at the present time, it suggests the idea of a big Indian in his war-paint strutting about in Sir Walter Scott's plaid."

The scene is Castine, Maine. Mogg, the Sachem, is in love with the daughter of the white outlaw, etc., etc., etc. The death rate is about on a par with that of Shakespeare's *King Lear*. It is melodrama and heroics from start to finish. Cooper's characters are convincing by comparison.

The greater maturity which came to Whittier in 1833, the dawn of his second period, was the result of personal sacrifice and spiritual consecration, for and to the Abolition Cause. Garrison, who first urged him to seek education and first printed one of his poems, was again the prevailing influence.

The friendship between Whittier and Garrison had not been all one-sided. In 1830 Garrison had been imprisoned in Baltimore in default of $50 and costs with which to settle a fine for libeling a sea-captain from his home town of Newburyport engaged in transporting slaves between Maryland and Louisiana, and Whittier had obtained a promise of the necessary money from Henry Clay—only to have his good intentions nullified by the more speedy arrival of funds from the New York anti-slavery sympathizer, Arthur Tappan. The contact with Clay had undoubtedly been made through Prentice of the *New England Review,* who had gone South to write his life of Clay, leaving Whittier in Hartford as his editorial substitute.

The establishment of Garrison's new periodical, *The Liberator,* in Boston as of January 1, 1831, and Whittier's removal from Hartford back to Haverhill in the latter part of the same year had brought them so comparatively close together that they must have renewed personal contacts. Such renewed contact may well have been the immediate cause of Whittier's poem *To William Lloyd Garrison,* which appeared in November, 1831; and the year 1832, in which Whittier produced comparatively little for publication except *Moll Pitcher,* may well have been a period of incubation for the change of viewpoint—the interval between the intense activity of the apprentice period and the even more intense activity of the first propagandist period, which began with the publication of his prose anti-slavery manifesto, *Justice and Expediency,* in June, 1833. If Garrison's example and arguments pulled the trigger for this outburst, Whittier's own conscience and reflections probably had previously loaded and primed the gun—and the reverberations probably surprised them both.

Throughout the thirty years of crusading which followed

the 1833 decision Whittier, in search of relaxation, would now and again return to his first literary love of New England traditions, but not, of course, in the early immaturity of spirit. In later life he sometimes wrote sentimental verse such as *Memories* and the immortal *Maud Muller,* but in a vein of reminiscence and appreciation only. His unimportant attempt to be Byronic disappeared forever with his genuine and spiritual marriage to an ideal. His devotional verse acquired a new exaltation; his love for that land he meant all human beings to enjoy in equal freedom—its histories natural and supernatural—acquired the overtones of a deeper conviction; his verses of personal tribute disclosed a more profound concept of human relations.

Whittier was no born dreamer of dreams, no vision-inspired child reformer, no thwarted genius. Since the Quakers were the original American anti-slavery advocates, his Quaker birth made him susceptible to the abolitionist appeal, but his active participation in the movement he was to lead was founded on study and intellectual conviction as well as on ethical premises and righteous indignation. His life and his writings always had mental purpose—to promote welfare, arouse sympathy, excite opposition to tyranny in general and to slavery in particular, to punish treason, to memorialize the virtues of the dead, to perpetuate legend or history, to explain the beauties of nature or to expound the goodness of Omnipotence.

The poet himself is written authority for the fact that, even apart from Quaker convictions, anti-slavery sentiments "came natural" in East Haverhill. Says he, in an autobiographical fragment found after his death: "The standard reading book was the *American Preceptor,* liberally sprinkled with anti-slavery prose and poetry. One of the pieces rings in my memory even now. It was the story of an insurgent slave—a black Bruce."

Whittier's anti-slavery poems ranged from the most obvious propagandist melodrama to occasional bursts of very real genius. His development of the simple ballad form excelled anything of its type in modern English—less literary than Scott but more visual and more poignant. One might say that the vitality of his anti-slavery inspiration extended laterally through the whole field of his endeavor. The people of his fancy were imbued with the afflatus of real life drama, and his favorite subjects were those with foundations in fact. Whittier never again played at representing emotions he did not feel. The moral tags with which he ended so many poems were essentials as being the actual texts for the compositions.

A few samples of Whittier's first-period work before 1833 will provide sufficient general idea of pervading characteristics. *New England,* first printed in the *Review* in October, 1830, was incorporated into *Moll Pitcher* except for the last stanza, which Pickard, the official biographer, quotes to reveal "the high spirit of his youth." It is printed here to show how active was the early personal ambition which he smothered so thoroughly for the Emancipation Cause that in his mature writings self-advantage never appears as a motif.

The particular stanza reads:

> Land of my Fathers!—If my name,
> Now humble and unwed to fame,
> Hereafter burn upon the lip,
> As one of those which may not die,
> Linked in eternal fellowship
> With visions pure, and strong, and high;
> If the wild dreams, which quicken now
> The throbbing pulse of heart and brow,
> Hereafter take a real form
> Like spectres changed to being warm,
> And over temples wan and grey
> The star-like crown of glory shine!
> Thine be the bard's undying lay,
> The murmur of his praise be thine.

The much more familiar and frequently quoted portion of the same poem, Whittier's first spontaneous exhibition of something above modest talent, reads as follows:

Land of the forest and the rock—
Of dark blue lake, and mighty river—
Of mountains reared aloft to mock
The storm's career—the lightning's shock,—
My own, green land, forever!
Land of the beautiful and brave—
The freeman's home—the martyr's grave—
The nursery of giant men,
Whose deeds have linked with every glen,
And every hill and every stream,
The romance of some warrior-dream!
Oh—never-may a son of thine,
Where'er his wandering steps incline,
Forget the sky which bent above
His childhood like a dream of love—
The stream beneath the green hill flowing—
The broad-armed trees above it growing—
The clear breeze through the foliage blowing;
Or, hear, unmoved, the taunt of scorn
Breathed o'er the brave New-England born;—

From the famous failure of *Mogg Megone*, concerning which Whittier wrote to a friend, "After you have made a thing it persists in living and following you like Mrs. Shelley's *Frankenstein*," it will be enough to quote one of the better stanzas—one without any display of male or female scalps:

A cottage hidden in the wood—
Red through its seams a light is glowing,
On rock and bough and tree-trunk rude,
A narrow lustre throwing.
"Who's there?" a clear, firm voice demands;
"Hold, Ruth,—'tis I, the Sagamore!"
Quick, at the summons, hasty hands
Unclose the bolted door;
And on the outlaw's daughter shine
The flashes of the kindled pine.

Something of Whittier's mature force, in the process of unmistakable development, shows in the third stanza of *Bolivar*:

Asquam.

Holderness N.H.
7th mo 21 1883

Dear friend
        I am grateful for
thy generous estimate of my
writing in "Characteristics"
but I fear the critics will not
agree with thee. Why not
anticipate them, and own
up to faults & limitations which
everybody sees, and none
more clearly than myself.
Touch upon my false rhymes,
and Yankeeisms: confess
that I sometimes "crack the
voice of melody, & break the
legs of Time". Pitch into Mogg
Megone. That "big Injun,"
strutting round in Walter Scott's
plaid, has no friends and
deserves none. Own that
I sometimes choose unpoetical
themes. Endorse Lowell's
"Fable for Critics" that I
mistake occasionally, simple

excitement for inspiration.
In this way we can take
the wind out the sails of
ill-natured cavillers. I
am not one of the modern
singers & don't pose as one.
By the grace of God I am
only what I am. and
don't wish to pass for more.

I return the sheets, with
this note. Think of my suggestions
and act upon them if it
seems best to thee.

Always thy friend

John G. Whittier

How died that hero?—In the field with banners o'er
    him thrown,
With trumpets in his failing ear, by charging squad-
    rons blown?
With scatter'd foemen flying fast and fearfully before
    him—
With shouts of triumph swelling round, and brave
    men bending o'er him?˙
Alas—alas—he died not thus—no war-note round him
    rang,
No warriors beneath his eye in harness'd squadrons
    sprang:
Alone, he perished in the land he saved from slavery's
    ban,
The victim of unhallow'd wrong, a broken-hearted
    man!

As has already been pointed out, the poem *To William Lloyd Garrison* (November, 1831) was the earliest work retained by Whittier for the body (not the appendix) of his 1888 *Collected Poems* and was logically placed by him at the head of his anti-slavery writings. After the long turmoil had climaxed in the Civil War and victory, it was Whittier's habit to speak of his anti-slavery verses a trifle disparagingly or apologetically as "rhymes." The development of his own critical sense rendered him conscious of their elemental crudity; but he either over-estimated the defects or under-estimated the fire of these hot-off-the-bat effusions, which stand alone in the history of American versifying not only as a type of work but because of the electrifying effect they had on public sentiment and national events. *To William Lloyd Garrison,* a poem of deep personal and propagandist significance, is here quoted complete:

> Champion of those who groan beneath
> Oppression's iron hand;
> In view of penury, hate, and death,
> I see thee fearless stand.

Still bearing up thy lofty brow,
In the steadfast strength of truth,
In manhood sealing well the vow
And promise of thy youth.

Go on! for thou hast chosen well;
On, in the strength of God!
Long as one human heart shall swell
Beneath the tyrant's rod.
Speak in a slumbering nation's ear,
As thou hast ever spoken,
Until the dead in sin shall hear—
The fetter's link be broken!

I love thee with a brother's love,
I feel my pulses thrill,
To mark thy spirit soar above
The cloud of human ill.
My heart hath leap'd to answer thine,
And echo back thy words,
As leaps the warrior's at the shine
And flash of kindred swords!

They tell me thou art rash and vain—
A searcher after fame—
That thou art striving but to gain
A long-enduring name;
That thou hast nerved the Afric's hand
And steeled the Afric's heart,
To shake aloft his vengeful brand,
And rend his chain apart.

Have I not known thee well, and read ·
Thy mighty purpose long!
And watch'd the trials which have made
Thy human spirit strong?
And shall the slanderer's demon breath
Avail with one like me
To dim the sunshine of my faith
And earnest trust in thee?

Go on—the dagger's point may glare
Amid thy pathway's gloom—
The fate which sternly threatens there
Is glorious martyrdom!
Then onward with a martyr's zeal—
Press on to thy reward
The hour when man shall only kneel
Before his Father—God.

As has been explained, the Byron influence, if it ever existed as such, disappeared at this first big turn in the road. But the Burns influence remained traceable throughout Whittier's life in many of his nature and personal poems. The Milton influence, concerning which much has been written, was probably little more than an equal respect for human morals and holy writ, interpreted through the media of diametrically opposite literary gifts. Imagine the half nonsectarian but very conservative Quaker immersing himself in Miltonian images of Christian mythology! It must be recorded, however, that Whittier left a specific written statement concerning his admiration for Milton's prose.

Milton, the impressive and mighty, and Whittier, the humble yet humanly eternal, both gave the best years of their lives to public welfare as they conceived it—Milton to exploiting Cromwellian Puritanism, and Whittier to propaganda for the freeing of the American slave. Both men did their greatest purely literary work late in life—in the calm following the tempest. Milton transcribed a tapestry of glowing religious imagery against the background of darkening physical shadows. Whittier, more fortunate in seeing his aims achieved, described the objects and friendships of that common Yankee life and nature he had so well loved and must soon leave behind him, going to meet that Eternal Goodness he had served so faithfully. From 1832 onward he became the voice of New England nature and New England conscience.

9

DEDICATED TO
A CAUSE

Here is inaugurated the second phase of Whittier's career. That period, beginning in 1833—when he first irrevocably dedicated himself to the cause of Abolition by writing *Justice and Expediency* and publishing it at his own expense—and ending in 1840—when ill health forced his resignation from the editorship of the *Pennsylvania Freeman*—is the most active though not intellectually the most important segment of his life. For the first five years of this interval he seems to have been unusually well. In 1833, even after the defeat of Clay by Jackson, which might reasonably have depressed him, Whittier said in a letter to his old friend, Jonathan Law: "My health is vastly improved; the blues have left me; I go to husking frolics, and all that sort of thing. I have put the veto upon poetry; read all I can find—politics, history, rhyme, reason, etc., and am happy—at least, I believe I am."

During these years Whittier was especially active in anti-slavery politics, conventions, and lecture tours, especially those of the famous English abolitionist lecturer, George Thompson. Though there are no explicit confirming records available, he is said to have been a secondary speaker at various anti-slavery gatherings himself but evidently without notable success. During these years Whittier also had his few and not over-serious experiences with anti-abolitionist mob violence, and on at least one occasion seems almost to have enjoyed the adventure. And it was during this same period that he was for a time an active paid secretary of the

Anti-Slavery Society, performing the regular professional services of a trained publicist.

After the illness of 1831, which forced him to give up his control of the *New England Review,* Whittier seems to have made a comparatively quick and complete recovery. But it will be noted later that after the illness of 1839 and 1840, which resulted in his leaving the very center of anti-slavery agitation in Philadelphia and returning to the quiet of Amesbury, he seems to have regarded himself permanently as semi-invalid and to have begun systematically arranging all his numerous future endeavors so as to avoid grinding routine detail. Left to go his own gait, he could accomplish surprising results, because although he toiled with many brief rest intervals he was enormously persistent and wasted no time on recreations or side issues.

That a country boy of no towering genius, who finished an incomplete education before the beginning of his twentieth year in 1828 and began work in 1829, should have been able to establish within a single decade a reputation so substantial that it could be subsequently developed to fame of the first magnitude in the isolation of a country town like Amesbury is really astounding. Of course he did not remain continually in Amesbury or in Essex County, but his trips outside New England never took him beyond New York, Philadelphia, or Washington. He acquired the secrets of popular appeal, authorship, and of astute politics so thoroughly that from the humblest of small town cottages he could exert a dynamic force throughout the nation and beyond the seas.

The less Whittier traveled in the body the more his ballads traveled for him. By occasional quiet advice at the right moment; by an extraordinary judgment of men; by patient political conferences, usually at home or in Boston or in Philadelphia, on what seemed to be largely local issues, he greatly assisted John Quincy Adams in his fight to preserve the right of congressional petition and eventually placed Charles Sumner in the Senate, forcing forward the anti-slavery crusade not only as an ethical issue but as basic political doctrine.

Using his uncertain health as an excuse, he in no small degree forced the world to come to Amesbury instead of himself going to the world; and by not being too convenient of access he made himself the more sought for.

It has already been noted that Whittier's return in 1831 from Hartford to Haverhill brought him again in close propinquity to Garrison and the influence of his newly founded *Liberator*. During his convalescence, while supervising the activities of the Haverhill homestead farm and doing casual work for the *Essex Gazette* or other papers, Whittier had the spare time to analyze the whole slavery problem in enormous detail, and the deeper he delved the more indignant he became. With the growth of his righteous indignation came the natural instinct to declare himself publicly, though he was even then maturing entirely practical plans for his own entrance into party politics and public office and must have understood that the publication of his extreme anti-slavery views would blast all such schemes. The political position of the abolitionists in the 1830 to 1840 decade was that of irresponsible and dangerous extremists.

Ever since Whittier's birth in 1807, slavery had been growing more and more powerful, and many ambitious Southerners dreamed and even expected that their "peculiar institution" might spread to other parts of the Union. This feeling was exactly contrary to the sentiments of the Southern leaders of Revolutionary days, who had regarded slavery as an economic fallacy if not an ethical evil. Washington and Jefferson, at death, both freed their slaves, and John Randolph, who lived until 1833 but belonged to the older school of thought, not only freed his blacks but gave his executors such authority that they were able to spend $30,000 moving them into free Ohio and establishing them there.

Instead of trending toward manumission, many of the younger generation of Virginia and Carolina planters went quite openly into the slave-breeding business to supply the tremendous labor market which had developed in the Deep South through the increasing use of the cotton gin, and which was sustained through the fairly efficient enforcement of the law forbidding further slave importations. The value of able-bodied slaves, male or female, doubled and trebled and quadrupled. Blacks became the most valuable of all live-stock, and cotton was the ideal crop for them to "make" because it required constant but very rudimentary attention eight or nine months of the year. Slaves represented the most tangible assets in many large plantations and could always be mortgaged as chattels. Men of wealth and influence, North as well as South, regarded all abolitionists as communists, defended slavery as legalized ownership of private property sanctioned by the Bible, and insisted that ministers should ignore the subject or openly defend human bondage in their pulpits.

Here are a few salient facts, arranged in chronological order, to show the growth in might of the dragon Whittier determined to have a hand in slaying:

SLAVERY AND ANTI-SLAVERY SCHEDULE TO 1833

1793. Enactment of the Fugitive Slave Laws, based on Article 4, Section 2, of the Constitution, which remained in force until repealed in 1850.

1793. Invention, by Eli Whitney, of the cotton gin, which created enormous wealth in the South and a tremendous new demand for labor.

1808. Importation of slaves after this date positively forbidden. The numbers smuggled in were immaterial in the aggregate, and professional slave breeding resulted.

1816. Founding of the American Society for the Colonization of Free People of Color, of which the first president was Bushrod Washington and the second, Henry Clay. Organized to carry out a suggestion made by Jefferson in his *Notes on Virginia,* this society was later used in various attempts to sidetrack the anti-slavery movement.

1820. Missouri Compromise—the establishment of a permanent line between North and South, between free territory and slave territory.

1822. Appropriation by Congress of $100,000 for sending illegally imported slaves back to Africa and founding Liberia, working with the Colonization Society.

1822. Execution in Charleston of thirty-five blacks accused of plotting insurrection under the leadership of Denmark Vesey.

1830. Imprisonment, in Baltimore, of Garrison for libel; for attacking a ship captain who transported slaves between American coast cities.

1831. Election to Congress of ex-President John Quincy Adams, who aided the anti-slavery cause (with which he sympathized although he was no extreme abolitionist) by his extraordinary defiance of gag rules and his defense of the Right of Petition.

1831. Garrison founds *The Liberator*.

1831. Insurrection of slaves under the leadership of Nat Turner, results in the deaths of fifty-seven whites and several times that number of Negroes. Without proof, Southerners blamed the anti-slavery publications for this uprising.

1833. By the will of John Randolph, his three hundred slaves are freed and established in Ohio at a cost of $30,000.

1833. Composition and publication by Whittier, at his own expense, of *Justice and Expediency*, demanding immediate abolition and proving that the Colonization Society was being used as an ethical and political red herring.

1833. The first National Anti-Slavery Convention assembles in Philadelphia and the famous Declaration is signed.

The importance of the economic problem involved is summarized in the fact that the cotton crop of 1840 produced one hundred millions in cash for the South besides furnishing the staple raw stock for Northern and English mills. Able-bodied black field hands, worth $200 in 1798, were worth about $1,000 each in 1860, the price advancing almost every year so that the profit in slave-trading was virtually assured.

It may be well to anticipate a bit, extending the chronological table to cover essentials of the entire period under consideration:

SLAVERY AND ANTI-SLAVERY SCHEDULE CONTINUED TO 1840

1834. The appearance in *The Liberator*, edited by Garrison, of Whittier's first great anti-slavery poem, *Our Fellow Countrymen in Chains,* and its enormous circulation through broadside reprints.

1835. The mobbing of Garrison in Boston.

1836. The first "gag rules" passed by Congress in its efforts to muzzle J. Q. Adams and smother anti-slavery petitions.

1837. Whittier's *Poems Written during the Progress of the Abolition Question* published by Knapp, publisher of *The Liberator.*

1837. Mobbing and killing of the Western abolitionist publisher, Elijah P. Lovejoy, at Alton, Illinois.

1837. Extemporaneous defense and eulogy of Lovejoy in Faneuil Hall, Boston, makes Wendell Phillips the foremost orator of the cause.

1838. The burning of Pennsylvania Hall in Philadelphia by a mob, with the tacit consent of the civic authorities. This occurred on the third day of the dedication exercises. The Hall was intended to be the anti-slavery headquarters of the nation. In the building Whittier had established the editorial offices of the *Pennsylvania Freeman.*

1838. Disfranchisement in Pennsylvania of free Negroes.

1840. In February, after seeing the gag rule in more stringent form passed by Congress, Whittier has a physical collapse, gives up the editorship of the *Freeman* and retires again to Amesbury.

The political aspects of Whittier's career were representative of personal ambition only for a brief time before 1833, and then became merely part of an impersonal problem as to best means for bringing about abolition. The fact that he had, except at the very outset, no selfish aims to achieve probably accounted for his almost clairvoyant judgment of men and popular trends.

The first brief phase of personal ambition came largely through his work in Hartford as editor of the *New England Review.* In the course of campaigning for Clay against Jackson he was so thoroughly dosed with practical politics that he naturally thought of obtaining fame and financial independence through political success. And the natural place to start was his home town and Essex County.

As mentioned previously, influenza prevented Whittier

from attending the Republican Convention in December, 1831 (he had been named as a delegate from Hartford), but he watched the local developments in Essex County with an eagle eye because a sort of deadlock had developed between complicated opposing factions. Though there were seventeen congressional elections in the North Essex District (which included both Haverhill and Amesbury) between 1831 and 1833, according to Pickard, the seat was vacant most of the time—a strange situation made possible because a congressman, to be elected, had not only to defeat his opponents but to win a clear majority of all votes cast.

In the spring of 1832, friends urged Whittier to run for Congress himself. He had to explain that he was ineligible until he should have reached his twenty-fifth birthday on December 17 of that year—but he seems to have had an idea that he might foster the stalemate until he could take direct advantage of the situation. The outstanding candidate at the moment was Caleb Cushing, whose particular enemy was Whittier's old editor, Thayer. Harriman, editor of the *Haverhill Iris*, in which some Whittier contributions appeared from time to time, was one of the poet's good friends. Whittier seems to have really felt that, through Thayer and Harriman, he might unite opposing factions. In August of 1832 he wrote to Harriman: "It [election to Congress] would give me an opportunity of seeing and knowing our public characters and, in case of Mr. Clay's election, might enable me to do something for myself or my friends. . . . In this matter, if I know my own heart, I am not entirely selfish. I never yet deserted a friend, and I never will. If my friends enable me to acquire influence, it shall be exerted for their benefit."

The fact that Clay lost the national election did not appall Whittier because Clay triumphantly carried the state of Massachusetts, proving the efficiency of party work in the local field.

To make the situation absolutely clear, it must be repeated that it was at just about this time—in 1831—that John Quincy Adams, whose presidential career from 1825 to 1829 had been particularly colorless, startled America by accepting election to the House of Representatives and declaring that no position to which a man must be elected by his fellow citizens, even if it were that of selectman in Quincy, could be unworthy of a former Chief Executive. He proved to be more than correct—for he was certainly the greatest representative that ever lived. A fairly successful foreign minister, a notable Secretary of State under Monroe (being the real propounder of the Monroe Doctrine), an innocuous President, Adams found on the floor of the House the ideal opportunity to fight for the ethical ideals which were very real to him and to display the keen fighting intelligence which was the dominant trait in his unlovable but very honest personality. No more upright or stubborn defender of the Yankee theory of personal liberty in every form ever took the field. Though no abolitionist, he believed that the people who hated slavery had a right to speak and to be heard in the highest tribunal, and parliamentary rules stringent enough permanently to prevent him from introducing the flood of anti-slavery petitions had never been invented.

The typical abolitionist petition such as those promoted by Whittier and his fellow abolitionists urged that Congress should stamp out slavery where it had the right to do so without infringing on the prerogatives of the individual states—in the territories and, above all, in the city of Washington, which had become a sink of pro-slavery rottenness. It is a matter of record that free Negroes were repeatedly arrested there on the merest suspicion of being fugitives and sold back into slavery supposedly to pay the expenses of their own imprisonments but actually to the great profit of the jailers.

When Whittier came of congressional age in December, 1832—shortly after the election of Jackson as president—local situations and delays made his candidacy as national representative impossible. Six months later, when he had published *Justice and Expediency* in an edition of five hundred copies at his own expense, he must have known that his extreme abolitionism disqualified him as a political vote-getter however much influence he might have behind the lines. As a non-office-seeking political strategist, Whittier's successes were the result of logical Yankee horse-sense and skill in astute wirepulling. He might well have had less influence in office than coaching on the side-lines. After eight years of endeavor, Cushing became congressman from North Essex in 1834, but only after definitely pledging himself to Whittier as ready to introduce abolition petitions and oppose slavery.

Somehow, a poet had seized the balance of power in North Essex, Massachusetts.

10

JUSTICE AND EXPEDIENCY

The extraordinary pamphlet *Justice and Expediency*, though its somewhat over-emphatic characteristics of expression confess the youth of its author, ranks second only to Paine's *Common Sense* in the list of important individual American argumentative compositions of this type as distinguished from either books or printed speeches. For exhaustive study of detailed facts it may be compared even with the Lincoln Cooper Union Speech, which, though proved correct in every particular, literally took months to annotate with references and sources. As Lincoln had saturated himself with his subject—slavery and disunion thought in its more mature phases—so Whittier had steeped himself in all early slavery controversial data, completing by deliberate and exhaustive research the traditional knowledge imbibed during his Quaker youth.

The year 1833 was a year of destiny in the Emancipation movement. In that year, the final vote by which the English Parliament freed all slaves in the British dominions gave a fresh impetus to the anti-slavery movement in America just as it turned the attention of the British liberators to conditions in this country, growing not gradually better but rapidly worse. With English victory in the air, American abolitionists gathered fresh courage for attack. In that year John Randolph's death, with the manumission of his three hundred slaves—and their establishment in free Ohio—also provided ready ammunition with which to answer Southern arguments. In that same year, in the month of June, Whittier published in Haverhill five hundred copies of his own pamphlet, *Justice and Expediency*, probably as large an edition as he could finance. It was printed by his old friend Thayer, who doubtless sympathized. The bibliographical record of this pamphlet, which appeared just about two months before the English parliament finally voted to emancipate all slaves under British rule, reads as follows:

"Whittier, John Greenleaf. *Justice and Expediency;* or, Slavery Considered with A view to its Rightful and Effectual Remedy, Abolition. Haverhill; Printed by C. P. Thayer & Co., 1833. The leaf measures 9⅜ by 6¼ inches, untrimmed. The item consists of 26 pages, sewn but without covers of any kind."

A fair average copy of *Justice and Expediency* is now worth from $500 to $650, depending on details of condition. Thus have mighty little things risen while so many big things have fallen by the roadside.

Arthur Tappan, a wealthy merchant-philanthropist of New York, was one of the anti-slavery enthusiasts to whom Whittier sent copies of his pamphlet. Tappan—the same man who paid Garrison's fine when he was imprisoned in Baltimore for libeling a slave-carrying coastwise skipper—immediately recognized the power of *Justice and Expediency*. He financed an edition of 5,000 copies printed as No. 4 of the *Anti-Slavery Reporter*, issued in September, and distributed at a cost of postage only. T. F. Currier, most expert Whittier bibliographer, identifies a second issue of *Justice and Expediency* in this form, which establishes that the edition of 5,000 was only an initial printing. The second issue announces the price of the pamphlet as $25 per thousand or $3.00 per hundred— which would seem to assume the likelihood of extremely wide distribution. Moreover, Moses Brown, a rich Quaker, arranged to have the entire pamphlet reprinted in the *Providence Journal;* but most of the leading current periodicals closed their columns to a work then regarded merely as violent propaganda.

Whatever people might think of its literary qualities—or the lack of them—the compelling simplicity and logic of *Justice and Expediency* forced general recognition, and Whittier had the satisfaction of being attacked in the most virulent and threatening manner by pro-slavery editors and politicians. In 1834 Dr. Reuben Crandall of Washington, D. C., was actually arrested for the crime of lending a copy of *Justice and Expediency* to a fellow physician. He was confined in the unsanitary old City Prison until his health was broken, and his release was shortly followed by his death.

In the sense that it directly attacked the Colonization Society, of which he was president, *Justice and Expediency* was an assault on Henry Clay, Whittier's first political idol and the man whose presidential candidacy he had fostered while editing both the *Manufacturer* and the *New England Review*—the man to whose biography by Prentice he had added the final touches. It seems probable that Whittier had a vague hope that his attack might induce Clay to see the light, abandon the clumsy camouflage of the Colonization Society and come out for simon-pure liberation of the blacks. Nothing of the sort occurred and after waiting a decent interval Whittier made, in 1834, this point-blank written announcement: "We regret that truth and the cause of humanity, which he has betrayed, compel us to speak of Henry Clay as the enemy of Freedom."

It is difficult to see, in perspective, how or why the Colonization Society, organized in 1816 not to free slaves but merely to colonize free blacks in Africa, should have achieved the importance it did between 1820 and 1835. Its special appeal must have been that it represented the humanitarian middle of the road good-form—which is always something. Its members were supposed to have a benevolent attitude toward the black brother (which did not extend to spending money by purchasing his freedom), and possibly the more advanced thinkers among them really felt that this sentiment might mature and develop into something more practical, so that the Society would ultimately not only send free Negroes back to Africa, but, possibly with government aid, actually emancipate an increasing number of slaves to join that exodus. As has already been indicated, the mountain dwindled into a particularly tiny molehill—for scarcely more than a thousand slaves were colonized between 1820 and 1830, and only a fraction of this thousand survived return to their native shores.

The Colonization Society was popular not only in the North but in the South. From the average Southern viewpoint, sending any portion of the free 10 per cent of the Negro population anywhere out of the community on any excuse whatsoever was a brilliant idea, for the free Negroes were supposed to be the firebrands who inspired the slaves with a passion for freedom.

The text of *Justice and Expediency*, more impressive in substance than in over-emphatic composition, conveys the following basic line of argument: (1) All fine talk against slavery means nothing because the extent of slavery is constantly increasing; (2) New England is responsible even though New Englanders own no slaves because all states are legally bound to protect the slaveholder in the ownership and recovery of his property; (3) Such theories as binding the slaves to the soil (in the Russian manner) or gradual emancipation or boycotting slave-grown products are admittedly false and not practical, but the Colonization idea has become popular on the theory that, though organized only to colonize free slaves, it approaches the problem sympathetically and may somehow lead to setting slaves free.

Once Whittier has in this manner led up to the problem of the Colonization Society, he does not drop it until he has excoriated it for duplicity, hypocrisy, and failure of every sort, listing its main faults and providing extensive proof under each of these headings: (1) The Colonization Society excuses slavery and apologizes for the slaveholder; (2) it pledges itself not to oppose the system of slavery; (3) it regards God's rational creatures as property; (4) it boasts that its measures are calculated to perpetuate the detested system of slavery, to remove the fears of the slaveholder and to increase the value of his stock of human beings (through removing the free slaves who excite the appetite for freedom in their black brothers); (5) it denies the power of Christian love to overcome an unholy prejudice against a portion of our fellow creatures; (6) it strenuously opposes the education of the blacks in this country as being both useless and dangerous; (7) it positively does not prevent bootleg slave-trading from Africa—as proved by the society's own reports of atrocious slave raids in recent times.

After having annihilated the assumed worth of the Colonization Society, Whittier formulates his demand for immediate emancipation, beginning with the District of Columbia and the territories under direct federal control. This brings him to his two final propositions: (1) that immediate abolition can be safe and peaceful, which he supports with references to liberation experiences in Santo Domingo and South America; (2) that free labor, because more industrious and intelligent, is more profitable, which he proves with economic theories and with citations of specific comparative instances.

All in all, there is, never was, and never could be any real answer to *Justice and Expediency*, and this was its most exasperating quality from the opposition viewpoint. It left the bleached bones of the fastidious and fashionable church-endorsed and North-and-South-reconciling Colonization Society to whiten and crumble into dust.

Here it is appropriate to quote a sample argument, which must have stuck in many a high-collared throat:

"Let the facts speak. The Colonization Society was organized in 1817. It has 218 auxiliary societies. The legislatures of 14 states have recommended it. Contributions have poured into its treasury from every quarter of the United States. Addresses in its favor have been heard from all our pulpits. It has been in operation 16 years. During this period nearly one million human beings have died in slavery; and the number of slaves has increased more than half a million, in round numbers....................550,000.

"The Colonization society has been busily engaged all this while in conveying the slaves to Africa; in other words, abolishing slavery. In this very charitable occupation it has carried away of manumitted slaves..........613.
        Balance against the Society.................549,387."

When Whittier was bitterly attacked for *Justice and Expediency* by a writer of some capacity in the *Jeffersonian and Times,* of Richmond, Virginia, he wrote, in the *Essex Register*, a reply more than half as long as the original pamphlet. Pickard regards this as better than the original pamphlet (it is to be found in Volume III of Whittier's *Prose*) and it is a more closely knit, less emotional argument. But equal force and fervor are lacking—as indeed they should be in rebuttal. The most fanatical Whittier fan could not claim much in the way of literary merit or superior diction for *Justice and Expediency*, but the fighting Quaker said something important just the same, and in language that even a slave-trader couldn't fail to understand.

Justice and Expediency cleared the air like a clap of thunder. Whittier had said what a hundred other men had wanted to say, and what thousands knew to be basic truth. He had ruled himself out of politics as candidate in Essex County, Massachusetts, for national office; but, in exchange, he had suddenly become a national figure in the onsweep of the international attack against black bondage. He never repeated the violence of this un-Quakerly but very timely outburst in his future prose writings; but even *Justice and Expediency* is mild as compared with his more intense anti-slavery verses, which were obviously outbursts of his own pent-up emotions aimed at arousing similar emotions in other men and women, perhaps women in particular. In addition to treading out the grapes of wrath, like a good, practical Yankee farmer, Whittier deliberately set about pulling up the legal and political parasite growths which threatened to strangle the little freedom vines, struggling up to share the sunlight of liberty.

11

POETICAL WRITINGS
OF 1833-1834

THOUGH WHITTIER'S POETICAL OUTPUT was greatly reduced in quantity during the first few years of his concentrated anti-slavery activities, it took on new intensity, purpose, and maturity. The specific literary quality of conscious simplicity did not appear until later in life, but indications of it develop spontaneously from time to time.

After the Civil War, when his own taste had mellowed and when the exaggerations and melodramatic incidents of his anti-slavery poems must have seemed mawkish to him in retrospect, Whittier often referred to them slightingly as his "political jingles." He was doing himself a grave injustice. Though many of the anti-slavery compositions are poetry of a very special brand—for which poetry in the accepted sense may not be quite the just word—they are nevertheless very important and extraordinarily effective writing. In fact, nothing quite like them is to be found in eighteenth- or nineteenth-century literature.

The prose intensity of *Justice and Expediency* translated itself into perfervid verse; and these versified outbursts of indignation, satire, reproach, scorn, and exhortation, all mingled with specific arguments and supplications for divine aid, reached the ears and hearts of millions of sentimental women and lowly male toilers who would never have read prose pamphlets or have been influenced by them.

Though the most important poem of the *Justice and Expediency* year (1833) was not an attack on slavery, it was nevertheless a bold outcry for independence and freedom. This poem, which appeared first in the *New England Magazine* for June, 1833, was entitled *The Song of the Vermonters, 1779,* and could not have been more martial if written by Walter Scott instead of by a professed pacifist. In its first form subsequent to the magazine printing—a one-page broadside printed some ten years later in Windsor, Vermont—it is probably the rarest of all major Whittier items, for there are only five recorded copies. Undoubtedly there are rarer variants of other items which appear in several slightly altered forms of text or printing—and there are a handful of incidental minor items only one or two copies of which are known —but *The Song of the Vermonters,* because it is both so rare and so important, is the collector's chief unfinished nightmare.

Since Mr. Currier has proved that the broadside of *The Song of the Vermonters* did not appear until about 1843, it would be bibliologically sound to discuss it under that later date. But from the aspect of biography the subject undoubtedly falls into the period when it was written and was first printed in a current periodical.

For many years it was supposed that the actual writing of *The Song of the Vermonters* dated back to the time of Whittier's earliest compositions, and all the data concerning this delusion are gathered in the Currier Bibliography. However, apart from the facts as Mr. Currier marshals them—in manner to convince any reasonable man—and apart from the fact that it was published in 1833, internal evidence of the poem itself shows it to have been written at about that time. The characteristics of drama, melodrama, fervor, and versification bring it up to that period, when the furnace which burned beneath the Quaker exterior began to pour forth molten words.

Whittier did not sign *The Song of the Vermonters,* and it is true that the piece was read or recited as an authentic eighteenth-century composition at the Fourth Annual Meeting of the Vermont Historical and Antiquarian Society, on October 20, 1843, in Montpelier. Also it was reprinted three years later as an authentic document in connection with an address entitled *Deficiencies in our History*, delivered before the Vermont Historical Society.

That anybody should have mistaken this stirring ballad-song for a genuine eighteenth-century chant of Ethan Allen's Green Mountain Boys seems utterly incomprehensible to the most casual student of genuine American eighteenth-century verse. That the simple absence of signature and the most superficial imitation of antiquated forms worked this mystification is important because it may have suggested the more elaborate, semi-serious attempt at deception made by Whittier when he wrote and published *Leaves from Margaret Smith's Journal*, in 1849, as an actual colonial document.

The Song of the Vermonters did not appear in any gathering of Whittier verse until the edition of 1888, when it was included in the appendix. The composition consists of seventeen four-line stanzas. The first three and the last will show the spirit of the piece:

> Ho—all to the borders! Vermonters, come down,
> With your breeches of deerskin, and jackets of brown;
> With your red woolen caps, and your moccasins, come,
> To the gathering summons of trumpet and drum.

> Come down with your rifles!—let gray wolf and fox
> Howl on in the shade of their primitive rocks;
> Let the bear feed securely from pig-pen and stall;
> Here's two-legged game for your powder and ball.

> On our South came the Dutchmen, enveloped in grease;
> And, arming for battle, while chanting of peace;
> On our east, crafty Meshech has gathered his band,
> To hang up our leaders, and eat up our land.

> .   .   .   .   .   .

> Come York, or come Hampshire,—come traitors and
>   knaves;
> If ye rule o'er our land, ye shall rule o'er our graves;
> Our vow is recorded—our banner unfurled;
> In the name of Vermont we defy all the world!

It scarcely seems possible that anybody reading this eruption from a gentlemanly young Quaker should wonder why he didn't sign it or think that not signing it meant a hoax. He had trouble enough defending the belligerent spirit of his anti-slavery compositions, though they were fundamentally good Quaker doctrine. What would any Meeting say to sheer, downright lust of battle stuff like the *Song!*

In contrast to the *Song* is Whittier's first important hymn, *O Thou Whose Spirit [Presence] Went Before,* printed in the Order of Exercises for the Sabbath School Celebration of July 4, 1833—only two copies of which are known to exist. Though religious, the purpose is so distinctly anti-slavery that Whittier classified it under that heading. In final form, this poem has ten stanzas. The first and the last three will show the deep emotion which the author both feels and evokes:

> O Thou, whose spirit went before
>   Our fathers in their weary way,
> As with Thy chosen moved of yore
>   The fire by night—the cloud by day!

> .   .   .   .   .

> For broken heart, and clouded mind,
>   Whereon no human mercies fall,—
> Oh, be Thy gracious love inclined,
>   Who, as a Father, pitiest all!

> And grant, Oh Father! that the time
>   Of Earth's deliverance may be near,
> When every land and tongue and clime,
>   The message of Thy love shall hear!

> When, smitten as with fire from Heaven,
>   The captive's chain shall sink in dust;
> And to his fettered soul be given
>   The glorious freedom of the just.

Obviously, the genius of Whittier is yet only seeking its way to expression—but this is work of no mean talent conveying a message of high purpose.

In the sequence of Whittier separate publications, this hymn to freedom is followed by an anti-slavery poem with the vigor of *The Song of the Vermonters* plus an added withering sarcasm, beginning with that world-famous one-line dramatic exclamation, *Our Fellow Countrymen in Chains!* This absolute anti-slavery verbal war-dance was first published by Garrison in *The Liberator* for September 20, 1834, under the extraordinarily inadequate title of *Stanzas*. In the 1888 collected poems it still bears this same singular heading. Later it acquired the title of *Expostulation*. Thus, but less harshly, did Simon Legree "expostulate" with Uncle Tom.

Despite the title the American Anti-Slavery Society immediately sensed what Whittier had produced and lost no time reprinting the poem in large cheap broadside form, under a big cut of a kneeling Negro in chains, and with the direct-appeal heading, *Our Countrymen in Chains*. Garrison predicted that these lines would "ring from Maine to the Rocky Mountains" and he took good care to make sure that they re-echoed. Under the figure of the crouching serf appears the legend, "Am I not a man and a brother?" and under that the verses. Thousands and thousands of these broadsides—nobody knows how many thousand—were circulated over a period of years and the poem was reprinted in countless periodicals or newspapers. If *Justice and Expediency* was the blast of argument in the anti-slavery forum, this was an explosion of argument, drama, sarcasm, and invective destined to reach practically every Northern fireside. Condensed into one brief sentence, the unanswerable question which Whittier poses is this: "How can any American protest against any form of European tyranny when all European countries—even Russia—have freed their slaves while American slavery has become worse than ever?" Three of the fourteen stanzas—the first, tenth and fourteenth—summarize the thought and characteristics of this poem, one of the most dynamic pieces of verbal attack ever printed. It was not only read by millions but was recited from school and public-meeting platforms throughout all the states where the thought of abolition was spreading. It may not be great poetry—in the critical, literary sense it isn't poetry at all—or great oratory, or even great argument, but it proved itself to be stupendous propaganda.

> Our fellow countrymen in chains!
>   Slaves—in a land of light and law!—
> Slaves—crouching on the very plains
>   Where rolled the storm of Freedom's war!
> A groan from Eutaw's haunted wood—
>   A wail where Camden's martyrs fell—
> By every shrine of patriot blood,
>   From Moultrie's wall and Jasper's well!
>
>   .   .   .   .   .
>
> Just God! and shall we calmly rest,
>   The christian's scorn—the heathen's mirth—
> Content to live the lingering jest
>   And by-word of a mocking earth?
> Shall our own glorious land retain
>   That curse which Europe scorns to bear?
> Shall our own brethren drag the chain
>   Which not even Russia's menials wear?
>
>   .   .   .   .   .
>
> Prone let the shrine of Moloch sink,
>   And leave no traces where it stood—
> Nor longer let its idol drink
>   His daily cup of human blood:
> But rear another altar there,
>   To truth and love and mercy given,
> And Freedom's gift and Freedom's prayer
>   Shall call an answer down from Heaven!

The list of Whittier's other published poems for the *Justice and Expediency* year (1833) and the *Countrymen in Chains* year (1834) shows that every one of them except *The Female Martyr* (*New England Magazine*) dealt with the slavery subject which completely obsessed him. And the theme of self-sacrifice for others continues even in that poem—the story of a young nun who died voluntarily nursing cholera victims and was unceremoniously cast into the common grave. The list for these two years includes: *Randolph of Roanoke, Toussaint L'Ouverture,* and *A Lament,* in the *New England Magazine; To the Memory of Charles B. Storrs, To the Daughters of James Forten* (not published until 1836), *The Hunters of Men* and *Plead for the Slave* in *The Liberator; Apology to the "Chivalrous Sons of the South"* in *The Essex Gazette; The Slave Ships,* in *The Oasis.*

The Storrs and Forten poems and the *Lament* all have to do with anti-slavery personalities. *The Slave Ships* is almost as powerful—but not as strikingly picturesque—as *Our Countrymen in Chains* and should be read by every student of Whittier's verse propaganda.

12

THE FIRST
NATIONAL ANTI-SLAVERY
CONVENTION

As ALREADY INDICATED, the long deferred action of the British Parliament early in 1833, officially and permanently abolishing slavery throughout the Empire—including the West Indies—gave vast impetus to the emancipation movement in the United States, enlisting for the American cause experienced English anti-slavery lecturers and philanthropists. The rapid growth of the American movement, fostered by the blunt truths continually reiterated in Garrison's *The Liberator*, now in its third year, and by the violent popular reaction to Whittier's *Justice and Expediency*, culminated in arrangements for a National Anti-Slavery Convention to be held during December, 1833, in Philadelphia. Whittier, who was elected as a delegate to this convention by the Boston Young Men's Christian Association, found himself in the embarrassing position of lacking funds for the trip, but Samuel E. Sewall, Boston lawyer-philanthropist, supplied the necessary aid.

John Greenleaf Whittier, then just approaching his twenty-sixth birthday, was the youngest delegate. The eldest was the Reverend David Thurston of Maine. A group of twelve Massachusetts men—Garrison, Whittier, Joshua Coffin (Whittier's first schoolteacher and old friend), and nine others—made the journey to Philadelphia together, mainly by coach. Since Massachusetts influence undoubtedly dominated the convention, this trip must have been virtually one continuous steering committee caucus. Though various women had already attained a certain importance in the movement and were welcome to sit in this assembly, no woman was permitted to speak or sign the *Declaration*. The First National Convention seems to have been regarded as strictly a man's job, possibly a wise acknowledgment of the then still existent popular belief that serious thoughts necessarily wore trousers. Incidentally, nobody did as much as Whittier—with his distinctly emotional poetic appeals—to draw women into the movement and to win for them a full, fair share of later leadership.

Justice and Expediency had already given the baby delegate authority overshadowed only by that of Garrison himself. Despite his youth, Whittier was one of the secretaries of the convention and a member of the committee, under Garrison's chairmanship, selected to draft the *Declaration of Sentiments* which became the documentary corner-stone of all future abolition activities and which Garrison finished writing in the Philadelphia garret of a free Negro. Garrison was an excellent press agent for both the Cause and William Lloyd Garrison—and when he chose such a workroom for some part of his endeavors he doubtless had an eye wide open to the useful propaganda of the idea. No shrewder choice could possibly have been made.

The literal truth about the composition of the *Declaration* appears to be that Garrison wrote it, and this is well sustained by internal evidence of concept, construction, and phrase. But before it was submitted to the convention, both Whittier and S. J. May—most sage and conciliatory of the anti-slavery ringleaders—made sundry revisions acceptable to Garrison; and minor further revisions were made in open session by vote of the delegates. Though Whittier's direct written contribution to the *Declaration* was so slight, Currier includes the *Declaration* in his Whittier bibliography with good reason. It is quite impossible to imagine that he and Garrison traveled together from Boston to Philadelphia without having drafted it in outline before it was written in any formal manner. In fact, it seems impossible that Garrison should not have had some preliminary document with him—and pretty well advanced—for it appears that the Convention met on December 4 and the *Declaration* was submitted on December 6. Any such extended and intricate and exact and comprehensive and meticulously-worded pronouncement as this is far more probably the work of two months than of two days. The whole thing must have been more than just sketched out in Boston where Garrison's natural consultants would have been his self-effacing publisher, Knapp—who has never been accorded his full just credit in anti-slavery annals—and John Greenleaf Whittier.

Pickard states that there were sixty-two delegates to the convention but the signatures on the actual engrossed document count just fifty-eight, representing ten states—the six New England States, New York, New Jersey, Pennsylvania, and Ohio. True to tradition, a third of the delegates were Quakers, who exerted a very great influence although not in complete harmony because of the recent split between the orthodox members and the more demonstrative Hicksites. Whittier, in spite of the almost non-sectarian breadth of his fundamental convictions—one of the men he most revered in later life was Phillips Brooks, Episcopal Bishop of Massachusetts—belonged to the orthodox faction.

Of course, this National Convention was geared to endorse the Whittier-Garrison attack on the Colonization Society, not only by such references to that body as appear in the *Declaration* itself but by word-of-mouth. The abolitionists were in the position of having to eliminate the very scheme which many of them, including Whittier in his youthful editorial campaigns for Clay, had enthusiastically endorsed.

The Colonization Society, by taking the wind out of the sails of more direct efforts, had become the worst obstacle to any aggressive Northern anti-slavery movement. Respectable and conservative Northern people—who recognized slavery as an evil but did not feel called upon to root it up overnight—read into the Colonization Society aims and ultimate intentions which were simply non-existent. Though they knew that its present activities were limited to colonizing free Negroes—and with negligible results—they regarded it as humanitarian and they hoped that it might develop, in some mysterious manner, into a practical plan for gradual emancipation by due process of law. The fact that the Society was heartily endorsed by all Southerners—naturally glad to get rid of the troublesome free Negro population—was an enormous argument in its favor with people who were bound to the South by commercial ties and regarded any suggestion of disunion with horror.

Garrison and Whittier were right in sensing that their most immediate task was to disillusion Northern churches, humanitarian associations, and philanthropic individuals who had long believed in this government-approved society as the well-bred, safe-and-sane approach to the festering problem of human serfdom. In Garrison's own words they had to be shown that the Colonization Society was utter sham and the handmaid of slavery, and they were not likely to relish this unpalatable truth. The large money contributions heretofore raised for the Colonization Society must be charged off to total loss and new funds must be raised immediately for real fighting purposes.

It should always be remembered that the 1833 Convention was held twenty-eight years before Fort Sumter was fired upon. The peaceful settlement of West Indian slavery problems seemed to indicate that some similar solution was possible in the United States, though it is difficult to see just how the abolitionists—who declared that they wanted freedom with peace—meant to accomplish this since their *Declaration* outlawed compensation for the slaveholder and such compensation had been the very kernel of British adjustment. They may have feared to advocate compensation, not on the moral grounds which they professed, but on the far more practical basis that the North, faced with the prospect of having to raise money to buy slaves from Southern owners—to take hard cash from Yankee wallets and deliberately put it into cavalier saddle-bags—would turn a deaf ear to the entire controversy.

The idea that the slavery clash might ultimately result in Civil War was not unknown at that time or even novel, but was regarded as jingoism. Beverley Tucker's extraordinary novel, *The Partisan Leader*, purporting to record the events of a Civil War in 1856, was written and published in 1836, three years after the Convention. Though that interval had seen the three most intense years of anti-slavery agitation the country had ever known, *The Partisan Leader* was in no sense taken seriously by the public of the day.

The importance of the Anti-Slavery *Declaration of Sentiments* is much greater than is generally understood. Subsequent events undoubtedly made it one of the few supremely important non-governmental documents in American history. It crystallized thoughts and impulses that finally put a million and a half men under arms, caused huge sacrifice of human life, and wasted in war enough treasure to have purchased freedom for all the slaves many times over. Unquestionably a document based on the most impeccable Christian ideals, it preached a crusade to be accomplished solely by pacific methods, but it specified objectives that could be obtained only by war.

The most vital words in the *Declaration* are, in the final analysis, not those attacking colonization but the specific stipulation against paying slaveowners for the release of their property. As already indicated, this was probably prompted by a sane conviction that no sum the Southerners would agree to accept would ever be appropriated by Congress or provided by the Northerners who would have to bear the giant's share of the burden. The federal government was then almost literally without debt, and the wildest imaginations could never have conceived either the stupendous debt the North had shouldered by 1865 or such devastation as had then exhausted all Southern resources. Garrison was perfectly right in avoiding any campaign to free the slaves through purchase. However practical this appears in retrospect and despite the

English precedent, he could never have reached first base on such a drive.

Samuel J. May of Connecticut was chosen to read the *Declaration* to the Convention for its final passage. David Thurston, the senior delegate, was first to sign. The fifty-eight signatures constitute a roster of the anti-slavery old guard, but apart from Whittier, Garrison, and May comparatively few of the men are remembered today. As the movement gained momentum, marching toward its climax more than a quarter of a century distant, it attracted more brilliant and, generally speaking, younger adherents, who overshadowed the old-timers—men like Wendell Phillips and Charles Sumner.

The delegates most emphatically were in earnest and did as they had resolved. Immediately after the convention there was a tremendous stepping-up of anti-slavery activities. Scores of societies demanding immediate emancipation were organized not only in New England, New York, and Pennsylvania but in the Middle West. To use a modern phrase, hundreds of cells came into existence almost automatically and began the wider and wider propaganda that never relaxed until Lincoln's *Emancipation Proclamation* crowned its success.

The literary character of the *Declaration*—one hesitates to use the word quality—is rhetorical and bombastic to a degree. Garrison, composing his masterpiece with the aid of Whittier and May, was certainly no Jefferson or Alexander Hamilton—but neither was he writing a Declaration of Independence or framing a Constitution for government. He was a public exhorter attacking the Spirit of Evil and he expressed himself precisely as such, with excellent knowledge of how to do it to a turn, without overdoing it. The best aspect of the *Declaration of Sentiments* is its ring of patent sincerity. Its worst feature is its preachy prolixity. But had it been more terse and restrained it might have lacked that element of fervor by which long appeals make converts.

In a letter to Garrison, dated November 4, 1863, when war and emancipation had ended a long estrangement between them caused by different theories of action, Whittier wrote: "I set a higher value on my name as appended to the Anti-Slavery Declaration of 1833, than on the title page of any book." If Whittier meant this literally—as he was in the habit of meaning what he said—it surely does not tend to lessen any assumption that he was more than a little concerned with its composition.

A condensed summary of the *Declaration of Sentiments* follows:

"Preamble—The Convention, assembled in the City of Phila-delphia to organize a National Anti-Slavery Society, promptly seizes the opportunity to promulgate the following *Declaration of Sentiments,* as cherished by them in relation to the enslavement of one-sixth portion of the American people...."

Essential contentions: (1) That the slaves ought instantly to be set free and brought under protection of the law; (2) that all those laws now in force, admitting the right of slavery ... ought to be instantly abrogated; (3) ... that all persons of color, who possess the qualifications which are demanded of others, ought to be admitted forthwith to the enjoyment of the same privileges ...; (4) ... that no compensation should be given to the planters emancipating their slaves ... because slavery is a crime, and there-fore [a slave] it is not an article to be sold; and because, if com-pensation is to be given at all, it should be given to the outraged and guiltless slaves ...; (5) We regard as delusive, cruel, and dangerous, any scheme of expatriation which pretends to aid, either directly or indirectly, in the emancipation of the slaves or to be a substitute for the immediate and total abolition of slavery; (6) We fully and unanimously recognize the sovereignty of each State, to legislate exclusively on the subject of slavery which is tolerated within its limits.... But we maintain that Con-gress has a right, and is solemnly bound, to suppress the domestic slave trade between the several States, and to abolish slavery in those portions of our territory which the Constitution has placed under its exclusive jurisdiction; (7) We also maintain that there are, at the present time, the highest obligations resting on the people of the free States to remove slavery by moral and political action, as prescribed in the Constitution of the United States.

They are now living under a pledge of their tremendous physical force to fasten the galling fetters of tyranny upon the limbs of millions in the Southern States; they are liable to be called at any moment to suppress a general insurrection of the slaves; they authorize the slave owner to vote for three-fifths of his slaves as property and thus enable him to perpetuate his oppression; they support a standing army at the South for its protection; and they seize the slave who has escaped into their territories and send him back to be tortured by an enraged master or a brutal driver. This relation to slavery is criminal and full of danger. It must be broken up.

In the final paragraphs of the *Declaration* the organization pledges itself to organize societies, employ agents, circulate literature, purify the churches, give preference to the products of free labor, and spare no exertions or means "to bring the whole nation to speedy repentance."

What more could be said or was left unsaid?

13

THE NEW ENGLAND
ANTI-SLAVERY RIOTS

THE YEAR 1834 was a comparatively quiet interval for Whittier—an extension of the 1833 activities—the publication of *Our Fellow Countrymen in Chains* being the point of emphasis. He was unable to attend the annual January meeting of the New England Anti-Slavery Society but apparently wrote an open letter to the delegates which they received with enthusiasm. He must have regained very close contact with local politics, for the following year (1835), despite the handicap of his known extreme abolitionist principles, he was elected to the Massachusetts legislature for his first and only term in public office. As a matter of record, he was re-elected in 1836 but declined to serve because of recurrent ill health.

During the 1834-1835 winter, Whittier must have completed his long, Indian border warfare epic, *Mogg Megone*—started several years earlier and then laid aside—for it first appeared in the March and April issues of the *New England Magazine*, a year before the book publication in 1836. This composition has already been discussed and placed where, by all literary tests, it properly belongs—in the group of Whittier's apprentice efforts. Either the work was too far advanced for him to change the essential atmosphere and treatment or else returning to the old subject recalled the previous mood.

In the year 1835 Whittier items appeared solely in periodical publications, and apart from *Mogg Megone* only seven poems are recorded. Two anti-slavery pieces, *The Yankee*

Girl and *Stanzas for the Times,* and one other reform poem, *The Prisoner for Debt,* are all that have even the crude vital spark. Two of the seven shorter poems of 1835 were entirely excluded from the 1888 collected edition.

One of these incidental poems, *The Yankee Girl,* though its literary quality is decidedly of the less-said-sooner-mended variety, is important as marking a stage in the poet's development. His thesis is merely that a Yankee girl, performing tasks a slave would do in any prosperous Southern household, is better off than she would be as the pet and pride of a wealthy slaveholder, but the treatment is of special interest. Instead of merely making this statement and elaborating upon it, Whittier translates the idea into action and composes a genuine ballad to make his point. *The Yankee Girl* is just as much a ballad as *Skipper Ireson* or *Barbara Frietchie* or *Maud Muller,* and is the first Whittier item utilizing the pure narrative ballad verse form in which he was to excel all contemporaries. Though *The Slave Ships* is told in a half-way narrative style—and is both better verse and more valuable propaganda—it is no genuine ballad. The trite but catchy last stanza of the *Yankee Girl* reads:

> Full low at thy bidding thy negroes may kneel,
> With the iron of bondage on spirit and heel;
> Yet know that the Yankee girl sooner would be
> In fetters with them, than in freedom with thee!

Whittier's 1835 session in the Massachusetts legislature produced no sensational results but enabled him to make a host of useful friends for subsequent operations behind the lines. For instance, while in Boston he roomed with Robert Rantoul, representative from Gloucester, who became one of his stanchest allies. Though Whittier was no speech-maker he was no idler. He sponsored a movement to do away with capital punishment, he had his finger in every anti-slavery pie, and he was constantly in touch with ex-President John Quincy Adams regarding the various anti-slavery petitions with which Adams was beginning to bombard the House of Rep-

resentatives in Washington. While Whittier was in Boston
for the legislative sittings he must naturally have seen more
of Garrison than at any time for years.

It will be recalled that Garrison brought George Thompson—very sane and very eloquent English abolition advocate
—to this country in 1834 as lecturer-in-chief for American
anti-slavery meetings. Garrison had the discretion, at first, to
arrange meetings for Thompson only in the secondary New
England cities, where he knew the emancipation element was
well represented. But as Thompson's reputation grew and
the meetings he addressed naturally became more important,
this British agitator became a target not only for the pro-
slavery advocates but also for the neutral conservatives, who
were against all deliberate exploitation of a problem for which
they knew no rational solution. Someone hit on the idea of
representing that Thompson was no mere reformer but was
actually an English *agent provocateur* whose real object was
to foment trouble between the North and the South. This preposterous calumny, catering to old American anti-British
prejudices and antagonisms, spread like wildfire.

Thompson began to have trouble at his meetings, not mob
violence in any imminently dangerous degree but disturb-
ances and interruptions which sometimes made it impossible
for him to speak. In August of 1835 he came to the Whittier
house in Haverhill for a few days of rest, which he sorely
needed. According to the official Pickard biography, Thompson delivered an address in Haverhill (at the end of his rest
period) without any unpleasant incident and then went to
Salem, where Whittier and his mother were attending a
Quaker quarterly meeting. For some unknown reason,
Thompson's friends became worried about his personal safety
in Salem and sent him back to Haverhill, where he arrived
on August 26, accompanied by Samuel May. On the morning
of August 27, Thompson and Whittier left for a short trip
into New Hampshire. That same evening, Mr. May, who had
remained behind, attempted to deliver an address in the
Haverhill Christian Church (the First Parish Meeting House

had closed its doors to him) but was thwarted by a crowd of some two hundred men and boys who threw large stones through the windows. Mr. May, who left the meeting with Elizabeth Whittier on one arm and Harriet Minot (the Judge's daughter) on the other, was not assaulted.

Thompson and Whittier, who had never imagined there would be any trouble about the May lecture—it is probable that the mob assembled under the impression that the Englishman was still in town and that he, rather than May, would make the main speech—proceeded first to Plymouth, New Hampshire, where they arrived on August 28 and where Thompson delivered three addresses which were appreciatively received. To reach Plymouth they had passed through Concord, spending Sunday night at the home of Mr. George Kent, and they arranged with him for an anti-slavery meeting in Concord on their return from Plymouth. Kent printed handbills announcing this meeting, which was scheduled for Friday, September 4, at the Court House.

Whittier and Thompson returned without incident from Plymouth to Concord on the appointed day, but when lecture time arrived a hostile crowd of such size had gathered in front of the Court House that the selectmen refused to open the doors. Instead of dispersing, the crowd headed for Kent's house, where it was assumed Thompson would be found. On its way, the mob ran into Whittier and Kimball, editor of a local paper, and in spite of Kimball's protests pelted Whittier with mud and stones and rotten eggs on the theory that he was Thompson, spoiling his clothes but doing him no serious injury. In their retreat, Whittier and Kimball passed by the house of Kent's brother, William, who opened his door for them to slip in and then flatly defied the crowd to force entrance. By the time the crowd sensed its mistake and reassembled at George Kent's house, where Thompson had gone, Thompson and George Kent had been warned and had left by a back way. A General Davis, who was present, managed to convince the crowd that only women were in the house and sent it about its business.

The next stage of this strange upheaval in the strangest of all towns for such an excitement to occur was a general adjournment to the saloons; a celebration of the victory achieved in preventing Thompson from speaking, with fireworks and cannon; and the burning of Thompson's effigy in State House Park. Finally, the remnants of the crowd, suspecting that Thompson must have returned to George Kent's, gathered in front of his house again and kept up a howling rumpus from two o'clock in the morning until dawn.

At a matter of fact, Thompson had gone back to George Kent's, and Whittier, disguised by changing his Quaker hat for that of a clergyman, had also made his way there. Early in the morning they made their escape by having their carriage brought to a side door, jumping in, and driving right through the crowd before anybody appreciated just what was happening, and then driving out of town over the one bridge that had been left unguarded.

On their way back to Haverhill, Whittier and Thompson stopped to eat at an inn, where they overheard the landlord giving an exaggerated account of the manner in which May's Sunday night lecture there had been stopped, much to the evident satisfaction of a group of rough customers. When Thompson and Whittier had finished and had climbed back into their carriage ready to drive off, Whittier could not resist the temptation to identify Thompson and himself, just for the fun of observing the innkeeper's astonishment.

It is said that the extreme purpose of the Concord mob was nothing more serious than a dose of tar and feathers for Thompson. There was certainly no tremendous hue and cry, because Thompson went home with Whittier and spent a week there entirely undisturbed. The excitement, however, must have been a considerable strain for a man of Whittier's fragile physique, habitual nervous tension, and customary placid life. Though Whittier endured such experiences philosophically, he found them most distasteful. He used to say drily that he had never been in danger of losing his life, but that he felt he could have faced such a risk better than the prospect of being maltreated and made ridiculous in the manner of his own Floyd Ireson.

The popular anti-abolitionist characterization of Thompson at that time was "The English Incendiary"; and it must be remembered that these events all happened only twenty-one years after the conclusion of our second war with England. It is easier to believe that the New Hampshire folk hated the Britisher—good old Yankee word—for meddling with American affairs, more than they seriously disapproved of what he had to say. Even today, an Englishman who tried parading around this country to give gratuitous public advice about a crisis in our domestic affairs as vital as the slavery issue, might not be received with universal love and kisses—and it is certain that a German—our war with Germany being about as recent as the War of 1812 was in 1835—would be lucky to escape with a whole skin if he tried anything of the sort. Calling Thompson into the controversy was certainly a diplomatic error; but it is doubtful if Garrison even understood the meaning of the word diplomacy, and it was certainly an effective way of stirring things up.

On October 21, 1835, a more serious demonstration, at which Whittier was present only as a witness, occurred in Boston, where the Female Anti-Slavery Society had scheduled a meeting. Business-men, not rowdies, headed the mob which broke up this meeting and, failing to trap Thompson (who seems to have acquired some special technique for evading violence) laid hands on Garrison and led him through the streets of the Modern Athens with a rope around his neck, according to tradition, though, according to some eyewitnesses, the rope was around his waist.

Whittier was attending a session of the legislature at the State House and when he got news of the riot was much concerned for the safety of his sister Elizabeth, who had come to town to attend the meeting. First he satisfied himself that his sister and all the other women were safe, and then he worked his way through the mob until he got a glimpse of Garrison just as he was being rescued by the police and rushed off, as one would say today, under protective arrest to the Leverett Street Jail. Whittier followed along and managed to see Garrison in jail, glad to learn that he was not much the worse for wear.

This Boston incident was the most noted of the New England anti-abolitionist riots and, because substantial men were involved, was a more responsible expression of opinion, by far, than the small-town demonstrations. However, it was a tame affair as compared to the Illinois riot two years later which resulted in the death of Lovejoy (the only real abolition martyr) or as compared with the burning of Pennsylvania Hall three years later, an event in which Whittier was a leading figure.

These events signalized the beginning of the persecution era for abolitionists, when the best people regarded them as rabble-rousers and the best magazines refused even the non-political compositions of foremost authors who believed in freedom for the slave and said so. Professor Follen was discharged from Harvard; Arthur Tappan's house was sacked; the school of Prudence Crandall—a sister of the physician who was arrested for circulating *Justice and Expediency*—was wrecked; and Lydia Maria Child was excluded from the Boston Athenaeum as an undesirable!

14

GETTING BACK INTO
HARNESS

WHITTIER's 1833-1835 free-lance period of propaganda, politics, and public meetings—made possible by improved health and the inspiration of a life-task acknowledged and undertaken—had as its background the Haverhill homestead of his ancestors, which he still tried to farm for the support of his family. Returning there from his legislative trips to Boston, his Convention trip to Philadelphia, his numerous other brief wanderings to meetings and conventions as agent of the American Anti-Slavery Society, he avoided the heavy desk work which he must already have learned from bitter experience to dread. But it developed that his other vital interests and continual absences made operation of the farm on a profitable basis a virtual impossibility.

The extent of Whittier's absorption in politics and active propaganda is in no manner more clearly demonstrated than by the way he tied Pegasus up in the stable and mounted him only on rare occasions, generally for the good of the cause. The man who, in the dawn of his career, had produced almost a poem a week regardless of other demands on his time, now merely tinkered over old efforts or took a flight at rather less than monthly intervals. In 1834-1835 he had no established editorial connection; yet he produced even less prose than verse at a time when he might reasonably have been expected to follow up the success of *Justice and Expediency*. An account of a lecture in *The Liberator;* an article on Daniel O'Connell in the *Iris; The Opium Eater* and *Passaconaway* in the *New England Magazine;* and *The Riot at Concord* in the *Essex Gazette* are merely casual contributions.

Whittier's temporary semi-retirement from the literary field may not have been one hundred per cent voluntary. He was now a red-hot abolitionist—from the viewpoint of all upper class editors, a jingo and leader of jingoes. The magazines with money to spend, to which Whittier by this time might normally have aspired with every prospect of success, wanted no contributions from wild-eyed agitators even if they did call themselves Quakers. *The Liberator,* which survived by the decree of fate and the ingenuity of Knapp (Garrison's publisher) literally had no cash. Publications such as the *Essex Gazette,* the *Haverhill Iris* and the *New England Magazine* must have paid very little, the last named somewhat better than the other two. More than occasional gratuitous or nearly gratuitous writing is almost impossible for a man in definite straits for money.

In 1836 Whittier published only eight poems—two in *The Liberator* and six in the *Essex Gazette,* of which he became editor for the second time during that season. He also wrote a ninth poem which did not get into print until he included it in the 1838 issue of his collected verse. In 1837 he again published just eight poems—three in *The Liberator,* one in *The Emancipator,* one in *The Knickerbocker,* one in the *New York Mirror,* and two in the *United States Magazine and Democratic Review.* Again he wrote an unpublished ninth poem—and this remained in manuscript until 1934!

None of the 1836 poems merits special attention. But *The Pastoral Letter,* published in *The Liberator* on October 20, 1837, is verse invective of the most unusual ability directed against the ministry for seeking to exclude from the pulpit all anti-slavery arguments, especially speeches by women abolitionists. Of the sixteen poems actually first published in 1836-1837, ten were anti-slavery, though one of these, *Lines on the Death of S. Oliver Torrey* (an emancipation advocate) was eventually classified by the poet himself under the heading of personal. *The Fountain,* printed in the *Mirror,* is the only nature verse of the period. The other five are all religious.

The Pastoral Letter outburst is well worth study, for, whatever its deficiencies, its power is undeniable. When he got down to brass tacks, Whittier was the kind of Quaker who forgot to quake himself but knew how to make his antagonists quake in sober earnest. The immediate cause of the church ukase attacked by Whittier in this poem—not the climax of his melodramatic denunciatory power but perhaps his greatest piece of sarcasm—was the anti-slavery lectures of Angelina and Sarah Grimké, two South Carolina women who had freed their slaves and joined the emancipation movement.

Three stanzas will convey the spirit of the composition:

> So, this is all,—the utmost reach
>   Of priestly power the mind to fetter!
> When laymen think—when women preach—
>   A war of words, a "Pastoral Letter!"
> Now, shame upon ye, parish Popes!
>   Was't thus with those, your predecessors,
> Who sealed with racks, and fire, and ropes
>   Their loving-kindness to transgressors?

> When, for the sighing of the poor,
>   And for the needy, God hath risen,
> And chains are breaking, and a door
>   Is opening for the souls in prison!
> If then ye would, with puny hands,
>   Arrest the very work of Heaven,
> And bind anew the evil bands
>   Which God's right arm of power hath riven—

> What marvel that, in many a mind,
>   Those darker deeds of bigot madness
> Are closely with your own combined,
>   Yet "less in anger than in sadness"?

What marvel, if the people learn
To claim the right of free opinion?
What marvel, if at times they spurn
The ancient yoke of your dominion?

The separate publications of 1836 were only a possible pamphlet issue of *The Summons* and *Mogg Megone,* already more than sufficiently discussed. But it must be noted, as will presently appear, that for six months of that year Whittier was actively editing the old *Gazette,* not merely supplying occasional contributions.

The separate publications of 1837 were: (1) *The Letters from John Quincy Adams to His Constituents,* edited by Whittier and with an introduction by him; (2) *Poems Written during the Progress of the Abolition Question*—the first collection of Whittier verses; (3) preface to Harriet Martineau's *Views of Slavery and Emancipation.* The collected poems had all been previously published, and the two prefaces—though that in the Adams book had much special significance—were slight compositions. These three publications will be treated more fully in the next chapter.

Whittier's income, always very small until after the close of the Civil War, must have fallen to an almost irreducible minimum. He had no capital other than his farm. Obviously he must either work it or dispose of it. The only practical course was the second alternative, and in April of 1836 Whittier finally sold the homestead to Aaron Chase for $3,000. He invested $1,200 of the proceeds in purchasing the cottage in Amesbury Village from which he was buried fifty-six years later, this being a far more suitable dwelling for the women of the family during his absences, and conveniently near the Quaker Meeting House.

On May 7, 1836, Whittier resumed full editorship of the *Essex Gazette,* after having refused a pressing invitation from his old friend, Thayer (former owner-editor of the *Gazette*), to undertake a new publication venture with him in Philadelphia. At the moment, the *Gazette* was the property of Erastus Brooks, who had printed various Whittier contributions and now wanted to move from Haverhill to Washington as correspondent for a group of newspapers. It seems probable that when Brooks employed Whittier to edit the *Gazette* for him he was already negotiating for its sale to Whittier's brother-in-law, Jacob Caldwell, who took formal possession on June 2; and it is reasonable to assume, though no documents are available, that there was some practical connection between these three events—Whittier's move into town, Brooks's employment of Whittier to edit the paper, and Caldwell's purchase of the paper. The circumstances have all the earmarks of a three-cornered Yankee deal—and it didn't turn out much better than most family trades.

Whittier obviously intended to use the *Gazette* primarily as an anti-slavery medium. His very first number, in his *Notice to the Public,* contained this slogan: "I regard the present struggle as the closing one between Liberty and Slavery in this Republic." To support the extremist anti-slavery movement of which Whittier was an accredited leader meant to support the emancipation petitions being presented to Congress by John Quincy Adams and to oppose the policies of Edward Everett, now Governor of Massachusetts. Everett, who was always a good bit of a stuffed shirt as one might guess from his pompous oratory, was a natural conservative and rather less than lukewarm on the slavery problem. He could then never have imagined that he would one day make that long and tedious oration at the Consecration of Gettysburg Battlefield which contemporaries regarded as showing the ridiculous inadequacy of Lincoln's few world-famous words spoken on the same occasion.

The slavery question simply had become white-hot, for the first attempted gag rule to prevent Adams from introducing abolitionist petitions in the House of Representatives was passed this very year (1836) and Adams had already undertaken his historic fight to ignore it and have it repealed —not so much because he favored immediate emancipation as because he was against any attempt by Congress to barricade itself against the force of public opinion.

Whittier went anti-slavery in the *Gazette* hammer and tongs. For the only time in his life, he overplayed his hand and antagonized a large proportion of his subscribers. The situation must have become really serious, for on September 15, Caldwell sold a half interest in the publication to Jeremiah Spofford of near-by East Bradford and made Spofford senior editor in charge of policies and politics. Whittier himself made this announcement in a cautiously worded notice explaining that Spofford was assuming joint editorship because of his wide influence in the rapidly growing neighbor towns and that he (Whittier) would be junior editor, in charge of the miscellaneous and literary departments. The abolitionist headlines and articles thereupon disappeared.

Obviously it was impossible to throttle down Whittier's enthusiasm in this manner and have him either useful or contented. For a time he thought of buying Caldwell's interest in the paper, but his sober common sense restrained him from purchasing the fruit of his own error. He must have known that he was no longer the practical political editor he once had been but solely a propagandist, and his resignation was announced in the issue of December 17 as strictly a business arrangement. This release must have been an enormous emotional relief and not much pecuniary loss, for in a letter quoted by Pickard, Whittier asserts that all he received for his work on the *Gazette* was $90 and the expenses actually incurred in circulating petitions.

From May to September, the *Gazette* printed forty-six editorials, all presumably by Whittier. The authorship of the editorials after September is naturally uncertain. This home-town project was Whittier's one and only downright editorial failure, and the family complications must have been most unpleasant.

Whittier spent the month of March, 1837, in Boston, not as a legislator but virtually as a lobbyist at the State House. The occasion for this was the general dissatisfaction caused by Van Buren's inaugural address, which had been unexpectedly pro-Southern and which Whittier hoped might lead

to the adoption of definitely abolitionist resolutions, especially one for the jury trial of fugitive slaves. Van Buren had
flatly declared that he was against abolishing slavery in the
District of Columbia, which was one of the cardinal objectives named in the anti-slavery *Declaration of Sentiments*.
The result of the antagonism created against the slave power
by Van Buren's submission to it and of the pressure brought
by the abolition forces—largely under Whittier's guidance—
was the passage of the jury-trial-for-fugitives bill by overwhelming majorities in both houses of the Massachusetts
legislature.

During the next few months Whittier can be traced back
in Amesbury, in Portland, in Boston—for the New England
Anti-Slavery Convention—and in Newport. Not later than
June 17 he reached New York for a stay of some two and a
half months, the longest he was ever to make in the metropolis. He was then one of the regular paid secretaries of the
American Anti-Slavery Society and he is supposed to have
been drafted to help temporarily with the editing of two of
the society's six publications—*The Emancipator* and *The
Anti-Slavery Record*. One of his famous hymns, *O Holy
Father*, first appeared in *The Emancipator* for August.

Whittier worked in Manhattan at the publication offices
of the Society, 143 Nassau Street, side by side with James G.
Birney, Theodore D. Weld, Henry B. Stanton, Elizur Wright,
and Joshua Leavitt. He did not keep hard and fast office hours
but lived in Brooklyn, coming and going as he saw fit. He was
troubled with "my old complaint of palpitations."

In addition to editing the regular anti-slavery publications,
this group of publicists composed various tracts, kept in touch
with wealthy supporters—such as Lewis and Arthur Tappan,
Gerrit Smith and Joseph Sturge of England—and carried on
all the activities incidental to a colossal publicity campaign.
Dissensions between this group—with which Whittier found
himself in accord—and Garrison had already begun to develop. To insure abolition in the North, Garrison was willing
to defy the Constitution or even to split the Union. Whittier

and the New York associates were too sagacious to entertain any such hair-brained schemes.

While Whittier was working in New York, mainly bridging the gap between *The Emancipator* editorships of Phelps and Leavitt, a movement was initiated to start an anti-slavery paper under his absolute editorship in Portland, Maine. This seems to have been abandoned only because of bad business conditions prevailing Down East as the aftermath of too much land speculation. By the latter part of August, 1837, Whittier was back in Boston with his plans for the future very vague.

It was during his stay in New York that Whittier made the acquaintance of Lucy Hooper, then only twenty years of age but ambitious to develop her modest poetical talents. Though a native of Whittier's own Essex County in Massachusetts, she now lived with her parents in Brooklyn, not too far from where the poet boarded, and he was a frequent visitor at her house. He sympathized with her literary aspirations and printed some of her poems a year or two later while he was editing the *Pennsylvania Freeman*.

That Whittier found real joy in Lucy's presence is proved by a charmingly ingenuous note which he wrote to her on August 17, 1837, saying in part: "I really had no idea it was so late when I left your house last evening. I never carry a watch—the only time I ever did such a thing I was too careless to take care of it—and gave it up to my sister after a three months' trial."

The New York visit, otherwise unimportant, gave Whittier direct and minute insight into all the mechanics of the propagandist mill operated by the Anti-Slavery Society at the home office. This was to be essential indeed to him and a great permanent advantage. From that time onward, he knew what made the wheels go round.

15

THE YEAR 1837

BRIEF MENTION HAS already been made of Whittier's three non-periodical publications during the year 1837: his preface to *The Letters from John Quincy Adams to His Constituents* issued in May; the unauthorized *Poems Written during the Progress of the Abolition Question,* released in June; and his preface to Harriet Martineau's *View of Slavery and Emancipation,* which appeared in July or August.

The Letters from John Quincy Adams, which had previously been printed only in four numbers of the strictly local *Quincy Patriot* and Adams's *Speech in the House on Feb. 9, 1837, in Defense of the Right of Petition,* made up the bulk of the volume, which was published by Knapp—Garrison's associate in the conduct of *The Liberator*—for its obvious propaganda value. Whittier was doubtless glad to write the preface, as much to come into closer contact with Adams as to spread the doctrine. This introduction, though it occupies only three pages in the collected prose works and only one page in the original seventy-two-page pamphlet, is splendid, dignified prose, infinitely superior to the work of three years previous. In addition to the Adams letters, Adams's speech, and Whittier's preface, the pamphlet includes the first printing in book form of Whittier's vivid anti-slavery poem, *The Summons,* under its original curiously exact title of *Lines Written on the Passage of Pinckney's Resolution in the House of Representatives and of Calhoun's "Bill of Abominations" in the Senate of the United States.* This poem is supposed to have been printed as a separate leaflet in 1836, but as no copy can be found the printing in *The Letters from John*

Quincy Adams is the virtual first. The Adams pamphlet concludes with a reprint of another of Whittier's violent anti-slavery poems, *Stanzas for the Times.*

Courageous, arbitrary, unlovable but able and generally invincible, John Quincy Adams always denied that he was an abolitionist in the sense of demanding immediate emancipation and said he was merely the defender of every citizen's right to be heard in legislative conclave. However that may be, Knapp and Whittier certainly tucked him into their anti-slavery bed when he let them publish his *Letters* and *Speech* with a Whittier introduction preceding his works and a double dose of Whittier poetry at the end.

The Martineau *Views of Slavery and Emancipation* is a pamphlet of about the same size as the Adams item and also without covers of any kind. It consists of extracts from Miss Martineau's two-volume *Society in America.* The brief and unimportant Whittier preface explains that the material is reprinted in this form so that it may be available to the general public at very modest cost.

The circumstances concerning the publication of the first book collection of Whittier poems (third of the special publications in 1837), entitled *Poems Written during the Progress of the Abolition Question,* have always been more or less in dispute. The traditional view is that the publication was without the author's consent or knowledge, arranged by Knapp of *The Liberator* as just another anti-slavery propaganda volume—for that was always his essential reason for publishing anything. The first issue has ninety-six pages and includes twenty-one poems—twenty by Whittier and one by his sister Elizabeth—the interest being about 80 per cent anti-slavery. The two poems added for the second issue were violently abolitionist, thus increasing the percentage of propaganda value. The items of any importance have already been covered.

The arguments as to whether Whittier had any advance knowledge of this publication are reducible to mere hair-splitting. It is announced in the advertisements of the Adams

Letters, which appeared in May, and Whittier did not go to New York until after the advertised publication date of the *Poems* in June. It is true that he made various short trips at about this time, but he was then on terms of the utmost friendly intimacy with both Garrison and Knapp and in constant touch with them. There is and never was any earthly reason why they should have put anything over on him.

Of course, Currier is right when he contends that Whittier obviously did not edit the book, for the poems are reprinted verbatim as published in periodicals, without corrections or alterations. And he is right in saying that Whittier would probably have objected to the over-eulogistic introduction. If it is silly to assume that Whittier didn't know the book was to be issued, it is just as silly to imagine that he supervised the publication. He knew what was being done but decided to let it ride. He may have thought that an unauthorized issue of this sort was a good way to find out how collections of his poems would be received without making himself a target for the critics by sponsoring the book himself. Though there is no actual proof that Garrison wrote the fulsome introduction it sounds like his diction, and there is every reason to think that Garrison himself threw the volume together for its propaganda value—and that Whittier knew it was being done for precisely that purpose.

The mere fact that two editions of *Poems Written during the Progress of the Abolition Question* were issued proves that it was not too badly received, and in the sense that it probably encouraged Whittier to regard his literary future a bit more seriously, Garrison and Knapp did him a good turn when they put it to press. In his introduction the anonymous editor (Garrison?) characteristically hit the nail on the head despite exaggerations. For instance he says: "The wish to bind them [Whittier's fugitive poems] together is strengthened in the editor's mind by the knowledge that the author is himself but too careless of preserving their form."

Also, note the true comment on Whittier's dwindling poetical output: "It is to be regretted, as a loss to American literature, that one so highly gifted as a poet should devote so little time to poetic labours."

It seems possible that Garrison edited the volume which his own *Liberator* partner published, not only as direct-appeal literature for the cause but also to boost Whittier, partly from friendship and partly because he felt he could use a steadier supply of red-hot abolitionist verse. In any event, this first haphazard collection—literally pitch-forked together— was the forerunner of a long line of carefully prepared collections of poems by John Greenleaf Whittier.

Whittier's return from his temporary work at the American Anti-Slavery New York Headquarters to New England occurred between August 21 and August 27, 1837. This is proved by two letters from Whittier to Lucy Hooper, both printed by Pickard: the one written in New York on August 21 and the other in Boston on August 27. Since in the second letter he says that he is going home to Amesbury for a fortnight, he was probably there when he received the call to Philadelphia, which was apparently more or less unexpected. This summons came from Benjamin Lundy, the old Quaker emancipator who discovered Garrison and then parted from him because of his extremist methods. Lundy, who was editing the emancipationist *National Enquirer* in Philadelphia, evidently knew that his physical forces were at the point of exhaustion. That Quaker Lundy should have designated Quaker Whittier as his successor was the most natural sequence of events possible; and that Whittier could scarcely refuse is obvious. Pickard, who is always meticulous in the matter of dates when this is possible, says merely that Whittier went to Philadelphia to work with Lundy in the late autumn; and this is probably all that Whittier himself could recall.

Whittier must have been already installed in Philadelphia when two momentous events happened which did not bear directly on his personal life but which had a profound effect on the anti-slavery movement. Elijah P. Lovejoy, persistent and indomitable abolitionist publisher, was murdered by a mob in Alton, Illinois, forcing the nation to see that the opposition to abolition had become more extreme than abolition itself. And young Wendell Phillips, gifted, wealthy, and socially prominent Bostonian, became most famous of all abolition orators over night because of his inspired extemporaneous speech in Faneuil Hall, on December 8, 1837, defending poor Lovejoy's work and hallowing his memory.

The Faneuil Hall meeting began with a speech by James T. Austin, not praising Lovejoy but insisting that he had died "as the fool dieth." Phillips, who had not intended to speak and had been graduated from the Harvard Law School only three years earlier, was urged forward by his friends and opened his retort with a sentence that has become world-famous—

"When I heard the gentleman lay down principles which placed the murderers of Alton side by side with Otis and Hancock, with Quincy and Adams, I thought those pictured lips [indicating their portraits] would have broken into voice to rebuke the recreant American, the slanderer of the dead."

One of Whittier's earlier biographers, Kennedy, first pointed out that this famous phrase, attributed almost universally to Phillips, was in basic thought a plagiarism from Whittier's five-column letter to Edward Everett, printed in *The Liberator* for February 20, 1836. The letter in question bitterly upbraided Everett for his coolness toward the cause of abolition and cited a denunciation of Washington once made in Faneuil Hall on the ground that he was a slave-holder. In defending the memory of Washington (who freed his slaves at his death) Whittier did undeniably refer to the possibility of Washington's portrait opening its lips to deny the charge. Nothing is more probable than that Phillips got his cue from Whittier unconsciously, under the stress of excitedly searching, without notice, for just the right thing to say.

If this idea of plagiarism ever occurred to Whittier he never mentioned it. And if he had known it to be a fact he would only have been gratified, for he would have given much more than a phrase to bring this ideal recruit into anti-slavery ranks. Wendell Phillips was the first of the Boston Brahmins to come out flatfootedly for abolition, and his conversion raised the whole social status of the movement. What this young man did, just couldn't be bad form for other young men and their sisters to do. Five years later young Professor Longfellow of Harvard published his *Poems on Slavery,* and before long, the rich, the aristocrats, and the intellectuals were adopting Whittier's waif as their child.

The cause had needed martyr blood and Lovejoy had been the sacrifice. The cause had needed a silver-tongued Knight in Shining Armor—and there stood the magnificent Phillips for the whole world to see and admire. Abolition was emerging from the shadows to contend for its place in the sun so vigorously that it overshadowed all other issues for a generation of American life.

Somewhat earlier in this same eventful 1837, probably in the late spring, Whittier himself had another taste of mob violence. The scene was the Newburyport garden of Mrs. Charles Butler, which was being used at the moment for an Essex County Anti-Slavery Convention, no hall or church being available. The meeting was broken up by a gang of local roughs blowing horns, beating tin pans, and throwing rotten eggs. One of the speakers, Stanton, had the buttons torn off his coat. Whittier was not harmed but says in one of his letters that he left the place "at an undignified trot."

Whittier's move from Amesbury to Philadelphia did not mean that he was going into exile among strangers. He had visited the city at least once—and probably two or three times—since the National Anti-Slavery Convention in 1833. He had relatives and friends living there, and the whole city was a sort of headquarters for the fraternity of Quaker abolitionists. As a matter of fact, when Whittier first arrived in Philadelphia he took quarters with the Thayers, the very people with whom he had boarded when at the Haverhill Academy.

After four or five months of breaking Whittier in, Lundy

retired completely from active editing of his *National Enquirer*. On March 15, 1838, Whittier assumed full charge of
the paper, which had been renamed the *Pennsylvania Freeman*. He pledged his entire efforts to anti-slavery work and
was as industrious as a beaver, writing continually and attending innumerable meetings. He must have felt both the
honor and the responsibility of wearing the mantle of Chalkley, Woolman, Benezet, and Lundy; and he doubtless bore
his share of all duties incidental to the building of the Pennsylvania Hall as a Temple of Liberty and permanent meeting
place for anti-slavery gatherings. Though this project was
far advanced before Whittier came into the situation at all,
his position as editor of the *Freeman* brought him into close
contact with every aspect of the enterprise. As it neared completion he even transferred the office of the *Freeman* into
the building, the total cost of which—entirely raised by sub-
scription—was $43,000, a figure which would be very modest
today but which was then considered a very respectable sum
of money.

Even while Whittier was working under great pressure,
editing the *Freeman* and making preparations for the inauguration of Pennsylvania Hall, he contrived to visit New
York early in May, 1838, for the annual meeting of the
American Anti-Slavery Society, at which he offered a resolution against the use of force to protect members or agents
against mob violence—and lost it. He returned immediately
to Philadelphia for the ill-fated opening of Pennsylvania
Hall, which was burned to the ground by a mob on the night
of May 17, destroying the office of the *Freeman* with the rest
of the structure, as narrated in the next chapter.

Even this appalling catastrophe in Philadelphia could not
stop Whittier or deflect him from his appointed rounds of
anti-slavery meetings. After a single week devoted to establishing new publication headquarters—the *Freeman* was fortunately printed outside the Hall—he went to Boston for the
annual meeting of the New England Anti-Slavery Society.
The last week in June he returned to Philadelphia, and mean-

while had edited the *Freeman* by mail, as he was well able to do from past experience.

Whittier never became a jingo. He was a temperance man and a personal abstainer; he was an early advocate of women's suffrage; and he was interested in labor reform. But no problems such as these could claim his time or lead him astray from his job as Press Agent of Liberty. He stuck to his last, and let others take the lead in other movements. Also, however intense his interest might be in any one particular activity, Whittier never failed to see the abolition movement as a whole and to regard each branch as only part of that whole. If he worked his political schemes mainly in Boston, that was because he knew the local situation best on his home ground. If he worked at the New York headquarters, that was because he wanted to understand the functioning of the home office. If he entered into the Philadelphia situation with eagerness, that was because he knew it to be at the time the forefront of the battle line. He regarded himself as a sort of special delegate at large. He was and wished to be a one-man shock division.

He was the ideal practical crusader, writing for public appeal verses that were hot-off-the-bat, uncompromising, and melodramatic; and at the same time employing endless patience and shrewdness in his political combinations for getting liberty-men into controlling offices. He was no exhibitionist and never paraded the sacrifices he made to propagandize for the faith as he saw it. On the contrary, in later life he resented the idea that the pecuniary loss and the jettisoning of other ambitions had been a sacrifice at all, insisting that the satisfaction of the work itself had been ample compensation. Never, until war began to seem inevitable, did he even consider the views of the extremists who were ready to divide the Union to solve the slavery muddle. He meant to have his cake and eat it—to have Liberty and Union both.

16

THE BURNING
OF PENNSYLVANIA HALL
MAY 17, 1838

HOSTILE SPECTACULAR EVENTS recruit sympathizers and bring out the fighting spirit in all important reform movements. Thus the destruction of Pennsylvania Hall by a mob in the City of Brotherly Love, supposedly the anti-slavery stronghold and the most orderly large city in America, gave more impetus to emancipation than a hundred meetings within its walls could possibly have done. The anti-anti-slavery organizers, by resorting to crude violence under such circumstances that the whole world must recognize the obvious gangsterism, confessed its moral weakness and its dread of the rising tide of abolition sentiment. It proved that the murder of Lovejoy was not just a rough Western accident but was in keeping with the true spirit of the Northern pro-slavery elements.

The bloodless riot in Philadelphia and the burning of the brand-new Temple of Emancipation on the night of the fourth day of its opening exercises, made possible only by the connivance of police and municipal authorities, was a direct challenge to the forces of law and order in all the Northern states. The conservative elements which had opposed emancipation largely from pacifist and business motives had no wish to claim brotherhood with great-city scum turned incendiaries.

Though it is natural to think of Pennsylvania as strictly a Northern state one must remember that, before the establishment of West Virginia in 1863, it actually bordered on Virginia, one of the greatest slave states, and the fugitive slave problem was consequently more vital there than in New York or New England. Also, there were probably more free blacks in Pennsylvania than in any other Northern state —perhaps more than in any other state of the Union. It was far simpler for the Southern pro-slavery groups to exert influence across the Pennsylvania state line than to invade the veritable rock-ribbed North; and the direct routes of the Northern anti-slavery Underground Railway for smuggling runaway slaves to Canada and freedom were necessarily through Pennsylvania and the other great border state of Ohio.

The much advertised building of Pennsylvania Hall, with its announced purpose of concentrating anti-slavery sentiment and fostering immediate emancipation, provided the pro-slavery advocates with every possible motive to organize in opposition. For months before the inauguration there seems to have been a deliberate whispering campaign against the blacks, particularly on the unpleasant charge of miscegenation. It was commonly alleged that abolitionists of both sexes were "nigger lovers" in the most literal sense. These insinuations were founded on the truth that intelligent Negroes were admitted to a degree of formal social intercourse with white abolitionists in Philadelphia more freely than elsewhere in the United States, for various phases of liberation activities made this inevitable.

Every now and again the Philadelphia conflict between serfdom and liberty would break out in some unexpected highlight. The spectacle of a particularly intelligent Negro being tried as an escaped slave in Independence Hall, judged to be a fugitive on the mere word of the manhunters, and manacled on the spot—all reported faithfully by Whittier in his *Pennsylvania Freeman*—is startling enough to satisfy the most melodramatic soul.

Pennsylvania Hall was officially opened on May 14, 1838. The auditorium was crowded at every session. An ode by

Whittier was one of the features of the dedication exercises. During the first three days, addresses were delivered by a long list of anti-slavery celebrities and letters were read from John Quincy Adams, Gerrit Smith, William Jay, Thaddeus Stevens (the scourge of the Confederate States after the Civil War), and other notables who either were unable to be present or still hesitated at personal participation in such affairs. From the list of speakers Pickard picks the names of William Lloyd Garrison, David Paul Brown, Arnold Buffum, Angelina Grimké Weld, Maria Chapman, and Abby Kelly— which graphically illustrates the growth of female influence and participation since the National Convention of 1833. Whittier's emotional appeals and his entire willingness—and Garrison's also—to let the women share the limelight as well as the labor and financial burdens, were beginning to bear fruit.

Mrs. Weld—born Angelina Grimké—and her sister Sarah, thirteen years her elder (both already mentioned in connection with Whittier's *The Pastoral Letter*) were easily the most picturesque of all abolitionist platform speakers. Born of wealthy, aristocratic, slaveholding South Carolina parents, they had freed their slaves to become Quakers and emancipationists. After they had both published anti-slavery appeals to Southerners, Elizur Wright—corresponding secretary of the Anti-Slavery Society—had persuaded them to lecture together, first privately and then in large halls. Their enormous success in Massachusetts in 1837 had brought them into close contact with Whittier, who sensed all the potentialities at a glance and sustained them in every possible manner, perhaps with a bit of added personal interest because Angelina's husband, Weld, was one of Whittier's abolitionist friends.

From the moment of the first opening of the doors of Pennsylvania Hall there were signs of unrest, but no overt acts until the evening of the 16th (the third day of the exercises) when some windows were broken during an address by Garrison. At the end of the meeting there was no serious disturbance, and the inner shutters had protected the audience from harm while the trouble was on.

On the morning of the 17th, however, a larger and more threatening crowd assembled outside the building. The management, through its president, Daniel Neall, demanded protection from the city authorities. The Mayor replied: "It is public opinion that makes mobs, and ninety-nine out of a hundred of those with whom I converse are against you." Though posters calling for an illegal attack on the meeting in Pennsylvania Hall were conspiciously posted all over town, the City Solicitor, siding with the Mayor, deliberately ordered the police not to make any arrest in connection with this agitation.

By the evening of the 17th, the mob counted some fifteen thousand people. The Mayor finally stated that he would restore order if he were given the keys to the Hall, and they were handed over to him at once. His method of fulfilling his promise was to address the crowd in a manner which it correctly interpreted as endorsing its intention. His words were:

"There will be no meeting here this evening. This house has been given up to me. The managers had the right to hold their meeting; but as good citizens they have, at my request, suspended their meeting for this evening.

"*We never call out the military here!* ... I would, fellow-citizens, look upon *you* as my *police,* and I trust you will keep order.

"I now bid you farewell for the night!"

After cheering the Mayor, who promptly disappeared, the mob got down to the business for which it had assembled—ransacked Whittier's editorial office, piled combustibles on the speaker's desk, turned on the gas and applied the torch. Fire companies which appeared on the scene were permitted only to prevent the flames from spreading to other buildings.

According to Pickard, who had the story direct from Whittier—already not entirely without experience in the use of disguise as a safeguard against mobs—the poet saved some of his valuable papers by going to the house of his friend, Dr. Parrish, donning a wig and long white overcoat, and joining the crowd that invaded his sanctum. The issue of the *Freeman* for May 18 appeared as usual, with this laconic announcement from the pen of its editor:

"18th of 5th Month, half past seven o'clock,—Pennsylvania Hall is in ashes! The beautiful temple consecrated to Liberty has been offered a smoking sacrifice to the Demon of Slavery. In the heart of this city a flame has gone up to Heaven. It will be seen from Maine to Georgia. In its red and lurid light, men will see more clearly than ever the black abominations of the fiend at whose instigation it was kindled. . . .

"Let the abhorred deed speak for itself. Let all men see by what a frail tenure they hold property and life in a land overshadowed by the curse of slavery."

Whittier struck while the iron was hot—and he knew that the burning was better than the talking! Also, he took a leading part in the meeting of the 18th, held in the open street in front of the ruins and in the presence of an angry crowd which, however, did nothing more than threaten. This was a political meeting, urging votes against all candidates who opposed freedom of press and speech, abolition in the territories and District of Columbia, and the franchise for free Negroes. In connection with this third stipulation, it is interesting to note that the Negro citizens of Pennsylvania were disfranchised in this very year of 1838—proof sufficient that the growing abolition sentiment of the state had not then become majority opinion.

The only violent local aftermath of the Pennsylvania Hall conflagration was the burning of a colored church and an incomplete building intended to be a Negro orphanage. A contemplated attack on the office of the *Public Ledger* for advocating open discussion of the slavery problem was abandoned because the newspaper openly armed its employees for resistance.

Ritner, the emancipation-minded governor of the state—

to whom Whittier had written a commendatory poem in 1837—was furious at the events in Philadelphia. He offered a futile reward of $500 for the identification of each and every member of the mob. Then the Mayor tried to save his face by doing the same thing, but so worded his proclamation that it would actually apply only to the one unknown person who lighted the fire. Damages to the extent of $33,000 for the burning of Pennsylvania Hall were finally collected from the county in 1841. The site was purchased by the Odd Fellows, who erected a new hall for their own purposes in 1846.

Pickard quotes a Whittier letter written in Philadelphia on August 4, one sentence of which is illuminating and shows how clearly he always summarized local situations. He says, "You, in New England, have got pro-slavery to contend with; we have got into a death grapple with slavery itself."

As might have been expected, the strain of labor and excitement made a combination beyond Whittier's slight reserve of physical endurance. By October his semi-invalid condition of nerves and heart drove him back to the refuge of his cottage in Amesbury and the care of mother and sister, who best knew how to help him overcome these collapses. But he was not entirely idle in Amesbury. While there he managed to re-cement his political connections during a long congressional campaign, and continued to control the *Pennsylvania Freeman*, which he edited by mail with amazing dexterity. The simple comforts of his home and relief from confining desk work apparently brought the natural recovery in just about the usual interval, for Whittier was back on the Philadelphia job in April, 1839.

The first six months of the year 1838, when John Greenleaf Whittier was in the thirtieth year of his age, represented the dramatic climax of his active life. Though that life was to continue for more than another half century, though all of its more important literary achievement lay ahead, though the climax of his behind-the-scenes political power was yet unapproached, Whittier was soon to recognize that his

PENNSYLVANIA HALL IN FLAMES

From an illustration in the *History of Pennsylvania Hall* (Philadelphia, 1838) showing the burning of the Hall on May 17, 1838, "drawn from the spot and engraved by J. Sartain."

CHARLES SUMNER

The "dyed-in-the-wool-yard-wide-and-unshrinkable abolitionist"
whom Whittier, in 1850, drafted for the United States Senate.

continued usefulness depended upon sedulously guarding against the intensities of routine work. Little by little he built up a sort of shadow existence which left his mind and spirit an active force in the world but which sheltered his body from all needless contacts with exterior fact. Though he was able to take up his task again when he returned to Philadelphia in April of 1839, he must have done so with a feeling that he could not permanently carry the load. The experience was so similar to what he had been through in Hartford that no penetrating mind could have failed to recognize the pattern of events.

It is futile to speculate on what Whittier might have been had his fire of soul been matched by force of body. He might well have been America's greatest journalist or a noted politician or militant reformer-in-chief, but it seems most unlikely that he would ever have produced *Snow-Bound* or any other literature for the ages. In him, the limitations of life bred comprehension of nature and soul. Like a hermit of old, he could emerge from seclusion for temporary duty among men, to inspire and direct his Great Crusade; but he had need of his cell for composure, continued self-education of the artistic senses, and the development of his highly individual, slow-maturing, wholly indigenous and unique literary gift.

17

CONCLUSION
OF THE PHILADELPHIA
ENGAGEMENT

_____

When Whittier returned to Amesbury in the autumn of
1837 after making himself very useful as editor and propagandist at the anti-slavery headquarters in New York—and
incidentally meeting Lucy Hooper in Brooklyn—he was, so
to speak, in direct line for an independent command. He
wrote to Thayer, in Philadelphia, that he had been offered
$2,100 a year to edit the Portland paper—which was never
started—but that he preferred going to Philadelphia because
he was acquainted there and because it was the center of
the struggle between mobocracy and liberty. From a letter
quoted by Pickard, it appears that Whittier visited Philadelphia during the winter of 1836-1837, staying with his
Philadelphia cousins, the Wendells; so it is apparent that he
would indeed be no stranger in the community. This Wendell
family consisted of Ann and Margaret, an older brother
named Isaac and a younger brother, Evart. The call from
Lundy was probably most welcome, not only because it
opened the doors to wider opportunity but because Philadelphia seemed the logical place for Whittier to make his
mark.

When Whittier first arrived in Philadelphia to work with
Lundy he went to board with the family of his old friend
and teacher, A. W. Thayer. A little later—possibly for the
sake of business convenience outside office hours—he moved
into the household of Joseph Healy, publisher of the _Penn-_

sylvania Freeman, financial agent of the Anti-Slavery Society
and leading anti-slavery printer of Philadelphia. As at the
very outset of his career, he literally lived with his job. A
fellow-boarder in the Healy establishment was Sarah Lewis,
a very much alive young woman who coöperated with Healy
in publishing an edition of Whittier's *Moll Pitcher and The
Minstrel Girl* in the spring of 1840, just after the poet's ill
health had compelled him to abandon the Philadelphia venture.

The coterie of Whittier's friends, allies, and co-workers
embraced the Wendells; Healy and Miss Lewis; the Thayer
family; Lucretia Mott and her son-in-law Edward M. Davis;
Daniel Neall, chairman of the Pennsylvania Hall enterprise,
and his daughter Elizabeth; John Dickinson and his two
young daughters, Anna E. (later a noted speaker) and Susan
E. (later a writer of some consequence); Thomas Shipley,
noted abolitionist; various other earnest workers; and Elizabeth Lloyd—of whom more anon.

Joseph Sturge, president of the English and Foreign Anti-
Slavery Society, visited Philadelphia during Whittier's stay
there and is known to have inspected the portrait of Whittier
by Bass Otis in the parlor of the Wendell house, and to have
told the poet that he was not entirely pleased with it. From
contemporary correspondence Pickard brings out an anecdote about Whittier and Margaret Wendell—how, sleigh-
driving out to her brother Isaac's house, they got dumped in
the snow and were very merry about it. Also, Whittier's favorite cousin Joseph Cartland—at whose house in Newburyport Whittier spent much of his time in later years, after the
death of his sister Elizabeth—also joined the Philadelphia
group in the early spring of 1838, for it is recorded that
Cartland and Whittier visited Healy's farm in Bucks County.
These incidents and facts, trivial in themselves, provide a
picture of normal life which is not without importance. Undoubtedly Whittier overworked with characteristic concentration, but he was certainly no nostalgic recluse.

In addition to all his public activities, Whittier seems to

have interested himself in the practical workings of the so-called Underground Railway—a system by which anti-slavery enthusiasts smuggled escaping slaves by night, from station to station, and finally across the Canadian border. Two of the leaders in this field were Edwin H. Coates and John P. Burr (said to have been an illegitimate son of Aaron Burr). Whittier seems specifically to have shared some of the responsibility with Coates in arranging for the escape of a Negro family by the name of Douglas.

While editing the *Pennsylvania Freeman* Whittier published in periodicals ten new poems, the long *Pennsylvania Hall,* read at the dedication exercises, and nine of more modest proportions. One of these, *The Farewell of a Virginia Slave Mother to her Daughters Sold into Southern Bondage,* is the greatest of all his anti-slavery versified tirades—is unquestionably an inspired work of its type. Early in 1838, before taking full charge of the *Freeman,* he had done a superlative job of hack publicity work by writing *The Narrative of James Williams, An American Slave,* intended to be authentic narrative but ultimately discredited in part and a subject of so much controversy that it must presently be treated at some length. And in the summer of 1838 the first authorized edition of Whittier's *Poems,* edited by Whittier and published by Healy, had made its appearance, containing fifty-one poems, fourteen of which were omitted by Whittier from the definitive 1888 collection and all but two of which had been previously printed, eighteen of them in the 1837 edition. Twenty-four of these subjects were distinctly anti-slavery and the other twenty-seven covered a wide range of thought.

In January, 1839, Whittier's poem, *The New Year,* a terrific anti-slavery onslaught under this harmless name, was reprinted from the *Freeman* as a separate leaflet; and in December, 1839, Whittier appeared as editor of *The North Star,* a gift book published for the benefit of an anti-slavery fair opening that month in Philadelphia. In this anthology Whittier included only two of his own compositions, *The Exile* and *The World Convention,* both new.

If the extent of Whittier's activities as editor, prose peri-odical writer, and propagandist are to be judged by the paucity of his poetical output, it is obvious that the intense realities of his burdensome routine in 1838 and 1839 nearly crushed the muse to death and that she spoke only when spe-cial occasion demanded or when the heat of indignation made silence unbearable.

Though Whittier's work on the *Freeman* was continuous in spirit, it was in fact intermittent in much the same manner as his Hartford editorship of the *New England Review*. His recuperative trip to Amesbury between October, 1838, and April, 1839, has been dwelt upon. On his return to work he scarcely had a chance to get things into some semblance of order before Joshua Leavitt and Henry B. Stanton lugged him off in June to the Albany Anti-Slavery Convention, where it was his problem to broaden a movement which showed a perilous tendency to over-concentrate. That job out of the way, he took a brief breathing space at Saratoga Springs, nursing himself and visiting with friends from both North and South.

About this time Whittier and Stanton were authorized by the Society to hire seventy speakers if possible and to stir things up in Pennsylvania at any cost. So Whittier hastily installed his cousin Moses Cartland as temporary editor of the *Freeman* and started off with the indefatigable Stanton on a tour of Western Pennsylvania towns, Stanton speaking and Whittier organizing. About the only pleasure Whittier got out of the whole trip was his visit to old Governor Ritner, now in retirement but still mindful of the fine poem Whittier had written about him.

Cartland, with the help of Whittier's letters, ran the *Free-man* well enough; so, when that dreadful siege of speaking and organizing was over, Whittier quietly returned once more to Amesbury, where he had some political fish to fry while resting. Caleb Cushing, Whittier's candidate, who had to toe the chalk-line to retain the poet's support, had finally been elected to Congress; and Whittier devoted himself to piling up congressional petitions against inter-state slave trade and slavery in Washington, for introduction or attempted introduction by Cushing and ex-President Adams.

The authorized edition of Whittier's *Poems* was on the market and the poet's star so definitely in the ascendant that Healy advertised in the *Freeman* likenesses of Whittier with his facsimile autograph to be sold for the benefit of the cause.

When Whittier returned to Philadelphia in October, 1839, he was accompanied by his sister Elizabeth. He immediately began writing and publishing in the *Freeman* a series of trenchant prose editorials, urging that every possible pressure should be brought to prevent congressmen from voting for the passage of the gag rule which had been introduced and which would automatically table all anti-slavery petitions. In January, 1840, anxious to follow every detail of this contention, Whittier traveled to Washington and was present in person when the dreaded gag rule was passed. This was a terrible blow, but he was no more really down for the count than that old veteran fighter, John Quincy Adams, who could not recognize defeat even when it stared him full in the face.

However, he was completely worn out, and the resultant nervous breakdown was so serious that his friends insisted upon his consulting the very best physicians. The consequence was that he resigned from the *Freeman* as of February 20, 1840, and returned to Amesbury with Elizabeth, making the trip in about one week. His second attempt at active, full-blooded, vital participation in public life was at an end.

During his residence in Philadelphia, the young poet-editor, champion of a favorite cause, had become a bit of a social lion in those Quaker-Abolitionist circles with which he had most intimate contact. He was just over thirty, unmarried, good-looking, meticulous in dress, poor but enjoying the friendship of men to whom he might appeal for advancement if he only would. How could young women fail to be conscious of the appeal of his unique and very strong personality, especially when he forever said them "nay"?

The fact seems to be that despite his expanded social life, Whittier remained attached primarily to Lucy Hooper, the young poetess from Essex, Massachusetts, at whose Brooklyn home he had spent fleeting hours while working in New York. He wrote her about her work, published some of her verses in the *Freeman,* included one of her poems in his anti-slavery anthology, *The North Star,* and doubtless saw her whenever that was possible. She was about twenty and many people thought them engaged. The difficulty was probably not so much the religious obstacle (Miss Hooper was an Episcopalian) or even the financial problem of Whittier's dependent mother and sister, as it was the physical condition of them both. In 1840, Whittier was certainly unfit for marriage, and Lucy had tuberculosis, the cause of her death in 1841, within four years of her first meeting with Whittier and about eighteen months after he surrendered his position on the *Freeman.* It seems clear that Whittier saw Lucy after leaving Philadelphia, for in his letter of condolence to her sisters after her death, he states explicitly that they met not only in Brooklyn but back home in Essex County. He wrote and published a poem to her memory.

Most important among the female acquaintances he made in Philadelphia was Elizabeth Lloyd, an attractive and intelligent young woman whose people were of the prosperous Quaker class. She was also a poetess and had written one poem then considered notable, *Milton on His Blindness.* Pickard mentions her only once, speaking of her by name and quoting a letter from Susan Dickinson: "There was a special glamour attached to her because she was supposed to be one of the very few with whom Whittier was really on terms of warm, personal friendship."

This friendship merits more than casual attention not only because Miss Lloyd, who had real intellectual appreciation of Whittier's then undeveloped talents, urged him to more

distinctly literary efforts but because it lasted for many years
and came nearer to culminating in actual marriage than any
other provable experience in the poet's life. A book of letters
from Whittier to Miss Lloyd, published nineteen years ago
under the title of *Whittier's Unknown Romance*, has recently
been supplemented by another booklet, edited by Mr. Currier, entitled *Elizabeth Lloyd and the Whittiers*, giving, in
the main, Miss Lloyd's letters to Whittier and his sister.
When these two series of letters are arranged chronologically
a reasonably clear picture emerges. Until after the death of
Lucy Hooper there is not the slightest indication of romantic
attachment. The poet announced Miss Hooper's death to
Miss Lloyd by letter in these words: "Dids't thou get a paper
from me containing a notice of the death of Lucy Hooper?
She was one of my dearest friends—a noble girl *in heart as
well as intellect.*" It was some fourteen months later, on
October 1, 1842, so far as the record shows, that Miss Lloyd
wrote her first letter to the poet in intimate and affectionate
vein, unmistakably suggesting a response in kind—which she
did not get. In 1844, Miss Lloyd, in the arch manner of the
day, wrote the poet chiding him for being cold and a month
later wrote a second epistle frankly urging him to visit her—
still with no romantic response. Then came a lapse of five
years, and a purely matter-of-fact letter, as if the question
of more significant friendship had been dropped.

In 1853 Miss Lloyd quite sensibly married a man named
Howell, became an Episcopalian—and invited the Whittiers,
Greenleaf and his sister, to visit her. But there is no evidence
of any such family gathering.

In another three years the former Miss Lloyd was a
widow; and in the autumn of 1858 Whittier was positively
in Philadelphia and on a footing of much greater intimacy
with Mrs. Howell than had ever been the case with Miss
Lloyd. A letter written to her by Whittier in Philadelphia on
November 2, 1858, plainly states how much he wants to see
her and, referring to some eye-trouble which she is having,

says, "I wish I could cure them as thee did my head the other day." Another epistle, written the very same day, asks about a picture of her "which, I assure thee, will be worth more to me than a whole gallery of Old World Madonnas and Saints."

No facts are available to explain precisely what occurred between November, 1858, and May 17, 1859, under which date Whittier wrote to Mrs. Howell the important letter reproduced in facsimile in *Whittier's Unknown Romance*. Explaining that she must not write him if it hurts her eyes to do so but that he will be satisfied to receive from her a blank sheet of paper, he says, "The very blank paper which thy hand has folded for my sake will be dear to me. . . . The sweet memory of the past few weeks makes me rich forever . . . etc." He makes it perfectly evident that he has been in love; that, in a sense, he is still in love; but that he already sees the experience in retrospect. In the letters that follow, the breaking off is completed with care and courtesy but positively. And in August of 1859 he writes candidly of their unfitness for each other and that he will not thrust himself between her and the memory of her husband. Later letters, on both sides, revert to friendly correspondence.

If it is true, as Thomas Wentworth Higginson explicitly states, that, in later life, Mrs. Howell sometimes spoke unkindly of Whittier, this is certainly not altogether incomprehensible. Even granting that she was the aggressor, her favors had obviously been rejected after she had every reason to believe them appreciated. On the other hand, the instinct that led Whittier to escape was one of spiritual self-preservation and was basically right. It is hard to imagine that Whittier, married to Mrs. Howell, would ever have written *Snow-Bound*.

There is most certainly nothing discreditable to either in this long-time episode. A man would have to be devoid of all common sense and humanity to blame Mrs. Howell for a romantic attachment to Whittier and for trying to break through the armor of his bachelorhood with the weapons of feminine charm. As for Whittier, it makes him a bit more human, less "too good to be true," to know that he had his times of need and could write a downright love letter and mean it.

18

THE PERENNIAL
INVALID

WHITTIER'S DEFINITE PHYSICAL weaknesses appear to have first developed during early adolescence, though he had always been less robust than his younger brother, Matthew. Whatever they were, they reached a first climax in 1831, when he collapsed while editing the *New England Review* in Hartford, traveled home in charge of a physician, and was unable to be present at the Republican Convention of 1832, which he must certainly have desired to attend. The history of this breakdown has been narrated and attributed primarily to years of combined intensive study and habitual overwork plus the severe emotional strain caused by his father's death.

In 1840 another period of particularly strenuous work and excitement, this time in Philadelphia, culminated in his second serious collapse. He was obliged to give up the editorship of the *Pennsylvania Freeman* and again return home to New England; and his plans to attend the International Anti-Slavery Convention in London were cancelled on the explicit orders of Dr. Henry I. Bowditch, of Boston, who insisted that his heart might become seriously affected if he did not have absolute rest. Bowditch was no alarmist; on the contrary, he was one of the ablest physicians of his generation.

Whittier's attitude toward his ailments may always have been more neurotic than heroic, but he was surely never "hypo" enough to have remained away voluntarily either from the 1832 Republican Convention or the 1840 International in London. The exhaustion which overpowered him in Philadelphia was the culmination of a long-sustained effort, precisely as in the earlier Hartford experience. No personal tragedy such as his father's death had occurred, but the emotional atmosphere of his anti-slavery activities had been tense throughout, beginning with the destruction by mob violence of Philadelphia Hall, almost at the outset of his career in that city.

Mordell's persistent idea that sex-repression accounted for Whittier's ill health is equally far-fetched whether applied to the circumstances in Hartford or in Philadelphia. Not a scintilla of evidence—including all the array of minor incidents introduced by Mordell—exists to show that there was anything hectic in any affair of the heart or in all of them lumped together—surely nothing to undermine the physical health of a man 90 per cent absorbed in editing and reform activities.

The internal evidence as to the exact nature of Whittier's illness is scanty. In a letter dated July 4, 1837, he states specifically that he is suffering from his "old complaint of palpitation." If this was an old complaint before he was thirty there must have been some positive justification for the bad heart diagnosis. Anybody who has ever had heart palpitations or seen others suffering from acute attacks knows that the seizures are more terrifying than dangerous. The throbbing of the heart can produce a visible shaking of the body. The definite cause given for Whittier's resignation from the *Freeman* in 1840 was "heart trouble," and this represented not one doctor's viewpoint but a consensus of expert professional opinions. In the century which has elapsed since this diagnosis, no science, previously known for centuries, has changed as much as medicine. The discovery of ether, which came just a little later, revolutionized surgery in particular, making examination and surgery of the living brain and heart possible. In Whittier's early life a man suffering from readily observable heart palpitations manifestly had "heart trouble," but the nature of that trouble, and whether it came from nervous or organic causes, might never be known.

Despite lifelong complaints of ill health, Whittier lived to be about eighty-four and a half years old, and died of a mild stroke of apoplexy. In relation to his age, he appears to have enjoyed better health in the last twenty years of his life than ever before. But it must be noted that those last twenty years passed in calm and comfort. When the conclusion of the Civil War had fulfilled the purpose of his thirty years' struggle to free the slave, Whittier, who had scarcely ever had a thousand dollars to his name, wrote *Snow-Bound,* was suddenly recognized at his full artistic stature, and began a belated financial harvest which piled up to more than $100,000 before his decease. The relaxation of nervous tension and the absence of worry naturally improved the old poet's physical condition. No life of storm ever entered upon a more peaceful twilight. He still complained habitually of ill health but one cannot avoid the conviction that he used this excuse to shield himself from the public functions he detested attending and to avoid at least some of the prying pilgrims who pursued him from all four corners of the globe.

A physician by the name of Gould wrote an article some years ago in which he undertook to prove that Whittier's sickness was due almost entirely to eye-strain, caused by defective vision never properly rectified. Dr. Gould assembles his symptoms convincingly and even takes care to point out that this eye condition could not have been in any way related to that color blindness which made the poet see all reds as yellows of varying shades and intensities. But in the two volumes including this Whittier article—which is only one of many such analyses—Gould proves to his own complete satisfaction that a long list of other celebrated authors in the always-ailing category were also exclusively victims of eye-strain. The inescapable reaction after reading Gould is that he claims so much for his theory of optical troubles as applied to so many men that he weakens his entire case and sacrifices the right to anything beyond very much qualified belief. That Whittier had some ocular difficulty seems entirely plausible as an element in his sicknesses but hopelessly unsatisfying as a sole explanation.

In various letters, Whittier mentions pains in the head and in the chest, by which latter term he probably means the cardiac rather than the lung cavity. Again and again he states that he cannot concentrate for more than half an hour at a stretch. Excruciating headaches follow any severe or long-continued mental exertion, especially under emotional stress. In other words, he seems to have had heart palpitations and some sort of persistent migraine headaches, still a painful and elusive malady by no means thoroughly understood. It is an established fact that he worked best in a most peculiar manner—short periods of concentration separated by interludes of deliberate relaxation. It is also true that at public functions which he could not avoid attending, he tried always to have himself seated so that he could inconspicuously retire and return after an interval. Even in intimate gatherings under his own roof he would find excuses to withdraw for a few minutes now and then.

Obviously a man working under such limitations could accomplish much more as a free lance and in the sheltered, understanding atmosphere of his own home than he could when tied down to the laborious routine editorial jobs involved in the control of such publications as the politically minded *New England Review* or the ardently propagandist *Pennsylvania Freeman.*

An idea seems to exist in many lay minds that extreme nervous headaches of the migraine type result from lack of sexual relief, which would bolster up Mordell's theory of sex starvation as the basic cause of Whittier's sicknesses. However, according to the best current thought, this idea is false. The unrest which comes to naturally ardent types of both men and women deprived of sexual contact is something entirely different and, incidentally, something that will generally if not invariably find expression unless physically restrained. Moreover, such lack of relief can become physically serious

only when there is insistence of demand, and this was not
evident in Whittier at any time.

Gould contends that the particular form of eye-strain
which he attributes to Whittier would normally have les-
sened in later life; it is rather to be expected that migraine
will decrease with age; and lack of fatigue and nervous tension might well have improved the conditions responsible
for heart palpitation. Thus, if these were the basic ills, improvement in later life would have been logical enough.

It is well known that Whittier always suffered more or less
from insomnia—another essentially nervous problem—and
this was the only one of his miseries that increased as the
years rolled by. On one occasion he claimed specifically to
have been awake for 120 hours or five days—a very real trial
if literally true. He always left the curtains in his bedroom
raised because he knew that he would be awake before sunrise and that the dawn would come as a relief. However, the
tendency to exaggerate sleeplessness is particularly insidious
and many aged men sleep very little or have a tendency to
"cat naps" for short periods. Many old people live with not
more than four hours of actual sleep in the twenty-four and
need no more.

We all know two widely divergent types of human beings
—those who dilate upon small ills but face major operations
with stoical courage and those who are cheerful in bearing
minor woes but shiver with dread when even approaching
the highways and byways of death. Whittier belonged to the
former of these types and knew it, for he himself said, speaking of his experiences with mob violence, that he was more
afraid of indignities than of serious injury. As a matter of
fact, his death was a sublime example of cheerful courage,
welcoming the inevitable and proving his belief in Eternal
Goodness to have been no Quaker lip-service or poetic sham.

It seems clear that Whittier was a high-strung, ethically
idealistic nature in a comparatively fragile body; that he
was unable to endure the grind of continuous overwork and
study; that his collapses were nervous breakdowns from ef-

forts beyond his strength. Palpitations are both nerve and heart manifestations; violent headaches of any nature are surely not altogether divorced from the nervous system, and eye-strain would contribute to them; palpitations and head-aches might both be emphasized by insomnia—in itself an-other nervous development. As a last and realistic word to the sex starvation hypothesis, it might be noted that if he suffered in that manner there was no reason on earth why he shouldn't have taken some little part of what was so abun-dantly available. He was no fool—and Bowditch would have talked plain English.

Whittier was undoubtedly more than a bit pampered by the adoring women who constituted his small household—and minor physical heroism was not his rôle in life. Just be-cause he was sickly, he took such good care of himself that he lived to four score and four. If he had continued to burn himself up with repeated over-exertions he would never have lived to do his best poetical work. His illnesses were real—but they were also convenient excuses for avoiding futile distractions.

Annie Fields (Mrs. James T. Fields), wife of Whittier's publisher during the successful years of his life, wrote a little book of anecdote and comment about the poet shortly after his death. Her description of his physical appearance, as a comparatively young man, reads in part: "His lithe, upright form, full of quick movement, his burning eye, his keen wit, bore witness to a contrast in himself with the staid, controlled manner and the habit of the sect into which he was born."

This certainly does not sound like the description of an in-valid! Yet, in the same little book, Mrs. Fields says, humor-ously but not unkindly, that Whittier and his sister Elizabeth worried so continuously about each other's health that it was a question which would die first from worrying about the other.

And here is a remark made by Whittier himself on the sub-ject of sex, in anything but a morbid Mordellian spirit. In a friendly letter he wrote: "Were I an autocrat I would see to it that every young man over twenty-five and every young woman over twenty was married without delay. Perhaps, on second thought, it might be well to keep one old maid and one old bachelor in each town by way of warning, just as the Spartans did their drunken helots."

The best story of all, with a real Yankee dig in it, is Annie Fields' report of an exchange between Emerson and Whittier when she finally achieved the triumph—after the customary series of excuses and delays from Whittier—of getting them both to her house at the same time.

Said Whittier to Emerson: "I had to choose between hearing thee at thy lecture and coming here to see thee. I could not do both."

Said Emerson to Whittier: "I hope you are pretty well, sir. I believe you formerly bragged of bad health."

19

EMOTIONAL ONSLAUGHT
ON SLAVERY

WHITTIER'S TERM of first-line service in the anti-slavery cause, beginning in 1833, covered a scant seven years before he retired from editorship of the *Freeman* and planted himself behind the foremost trenches, where he was less conspicuous but got a more useful view of the battle. His work for the cause—which he regarded as his sole purpose in life and which he pursued to the exclusion of all other interests—continued for another twenty years but, so to speak, on his own time. Even while acting as co-editor of the *National Era* of Washington—1847 to 1859—he worked at home in Amesbury "at his own gait" and sent his voluminous contributions by mail.

At this time Whittier was probably the most widely read young poet in America (Longfellow's *Ballads* did not appear until 1842), but he had not produced a single poem of distinctive literary excellence or written a single one of those ballads by which he is known to the average well-read man or woman of today. It is obvious that the popular-appeal quality in his work preceded the emergence of conscious art.

Whittier's first recognition had come as the result of a veritable deluge of newspaper and magazine verse prior to his 1833 anti-slavery consecration. But it was the impetus of his anti-slavery convictions, expressing itself in such prose as *Justice and Expediency* or in such verse as *Our Fellow Countrymen in Chains,* that compelled the public really to watch, look, and listen. The absence of strictly literary appeal was more than amply compensated for by a contagious emotional throb and a certain ring of deep sincerity in almost everything he wrote. Whittier was writing secondary poetry as such, but primary verse propaganda so extraordinary that there is nothing in the nineteenth century with which its effect can properly be compared.

On the whole, eliminating *Justice and Expediency*, Whittier's prose was less important than his verse and less effective than Garrison's hammer-and-tongs method of attack. However, his one prose emotional appeal, *The Narrative of James Williams, An American Slave*, occupies a niche that is all its own.

This booklet, issued anonymously by the Anti-Slavery Society in 1838, was intended to be a biographical sketch based on verified fact, showing how slaves were maltreated by even the more intelligent overseers on plantations in the Deep South. There was a real James Williams and he was a fugitive slave and Whittier doubtless wrote the story as Williams told it to him and a group of other sympathizers. The only trouble seems to have been that the ex-slave was doing a bit of propaganda himself by touching up the highlights of his tale. There is no doubt about the authorship because Whittier acknowledged the book in later life and one of the footnotes in the original issue virtually identifies him as the writer.

The Narrative of James Williams, which appeared in February, was at once mailed to Southern editors as a challenge. An instant storm of indignation broke loose below Mason and Dixon's line. The executive committee of the Anti-Slavery Society investigated all charges brought by the Southerners in detail and published a long defense of the booklet in *The Emancipator;* and then investigated some more, and went over the ground step by step with Whittier. Discontinuance of the publication was announced in *The Emancipator* for October 15, not admitting any essentials of the story to be false but conceding that there were sufficient minor inaccuracies to throw suspicion on the whole narrative.

This explosive little volume purports to narrate the exact

experiences of James Williams, who, reared as his master's personal servant on a prosperous Virginia estate, was sent as a "driver" with the overseer employed to take charge of a new plantation in Alabama, it being understood that he should presently be reunited with his wife and children, whom he never saw again. He was one of 214 slaves transferred from the Virginia plantation. The overseer fed his slaves well and worked them only the recognized harsh and exhausting hours, but he got drunk periodically on peach brandy and was a devil in his cups. During the period covered by the narrative, the Master from Virginia visited his Alabama plantation just once, promised to reform all abuses, and left without doing anything at all.

James, in his capacity of driver (a sort of Negro gang boss under the white overseer) had to inflict extreme punishments on his own brothers and sisters in misery for a period of three years, from 1833 to 1836. Successive main incidents of slave punishments are as follows: "Little John," trying to escape, is literally torn to death by dogs; another runaway is captured, pinned to the ground with forked stakes, his back terribly lacerated by enraged cats, is whipped most frightfully, then put in the stocks—and found dead on the third day; "Big Harry," a good worker but somewhat defiant, is shot by the overseer for no real reason; Sarah, a daughter of the "Old Master" by one of his slaves (therefore half sister to the plantation owner) while pregnant is strung up by her wrists, with her ankles tied, and slashed with the whip so as to cut her abdomen and cause her death; Priscilla, also pregnant, is tied to a tree and whipped until she gives birth to a dead child literally under the lash; James himself is tied naked to a tree and terribly whipped because he only pretended to lash one of the women he had been ordered to punish. At last, the overseer and two neighbors, after beating a runaway nearly to death and making James prepare a salt and pepper wash for the wounds, tell James they are going to give him at least 250 lashes for being too lenient—and James escapes.

Between the publication of *The Narrative of James Wil-*

liams in February and its withdrawal in October, the following known printings occurred: two impressions of the first New York edition, a second New York edition so announced, a bound Boston edition, an unbound New York edition, and an unbound Boston edition. The protesting voice of James Williams as recorded by Whittier had certainly been heard in the land.

The controversial articles about this item point out that Williams seemed sincere, not animated by any spirit of revenge and with no hope of making money by repeating his tale. As a matter of record, the Southern denials, though most emphatic, were not really proved, and the withdrawal—after the sensation had been duly registered by six editions in eight months—seems to have been less a formal retraction than a gesture of fair play. Nobody really knows who fathered the idea of having Williams' account of his captivity published; but Whittier did the job and it was the emotional type of publicity in which he believed. The book was powerful in itself and still more powerful by suggestion. If such things happened under the rule of a comparatively sensible overseer, reputed to be a good manager, what must have happened to the poor Negroes under the control of illiterate tyrants?

Whittier's verse was not only more effective than his prose —perhaps more effective than anybody's prose could have been—but more conspicuous because in that field he had no competitor of anything like equal caliber. Although, in the authorized 1888 collection of his poems, Whittier includes under the general heading of Anti-Slavery such diverse items as hymns, eulogies in honor of various emancipation leaders, songs and poems incidental to the Kansas strife in the fifties, and Civil War poems, it is best for the purposes of this immediate analysis to consider only such poems as were genuine attacks on slavery and were published before the end of 1839—with the single exception of *A Sabbath Scene*. This one miniature piece of melodramatic verse propaganda is excepted because although it was not published until 1850, it was a reversion to Whittier's earlier type of work. Printed first in the *National Era*, then as a broadside, and then as a pamphlet, its sensational if somewhat low-grade appeal puts it in the class of the earlier anti-slavery onslaughts, with the difference only that the startling incidents turn out to be a dream, showing the tendency of the propagandist to become merged in the conscious poetic craftsman.

We have already quoted from *To William Lloyd Garrison*, 1833 anti-slavery poem number one, read at the famous Philadelphia Convention; *Expostulation* (*Our Fellow Countrymen in the Chains*); Hymn—*O Thou Whose Presence Went Before*; and *The Pastoral Letter*, that terrible flaying of the ministers who tried to bar anti-slavery lectures from their churches. Particular mention has been made of *The Slave Ships*, which must be read complete to be appreciated. And it has been pointed out that *The Letters from John Quincy Adams to His Constituents* included two Whittier verse attacks on slavery—*Lines Written on the Passage of Pinckney's Resolution*, later known as *The Summons*; and *Stanzas for the Times*. The first two stanzas of each poem will give the keynote idea, and these compositions, obviously suitable for the Adams pamphlet, are excellent examples of Whittier verses inspired by political events. The opening stanzas of *The Summons* read:

> Now, by my father's ashes! where's the spirit
>   Of the true-hearted and the unshackled gone?
> Sons of old freemen, do we but inherit
>   Their names alone?
>
>
> Is the old Pilgrim spirit quenched within us?
>   Stoops the strong manhood of our souls so low,
> That Mammon's lure or Party's wile can win us
>   To silence now?

The initial lines to *Stanzas for the Times* are:

Is this the land our fathers loved,
  The freedom which they toil'd to win?
Is this the soil whereon they moved?
  Are these the graves they slumber in?
Are we the sons by whom are borne
  The mantles which the dead have worn?

And shall we crouch above these graves
  With craven soul and fetter'd lip?
Yoke in with marked and branded slaves,
  And tremble at the driver's whip?
Bend to the earth our pliant knees,
  And speak—but as our masters please?

Throughout all these poems runs the intense local pride in Massachusetts leadership as distinguished even from that of the other New England states. And it was this same Yankee pride which eventually put so many Massachusetts men into the forefront of the battle during those terrible months when the Confederates were teaching the Army of the Potomac the art of war, and which made Massachusetts' volunteer service proportionately the largest of all the Northern states. This glory in specific place-origin, running through so many of Whittier's early abolition poems, found its full expression three years later in *Massachusetts To Virginia*, which is the point of transition between the poet's first and second propagandist styles, with the fire undiminished but with careful writing apparent.

The 1839 New Year's number of the *Pennsylvania Freeman*, then edited by Whittier, carried, under the innocuous title of *The New Year*, a poem of towering denunciation into which the poet wrote his opinion of Atherton, the New Hampshire congressman who had made himself the tool of the Southerners by attempting to gag the anti-slavery petitions pending before Congress. Four short stanzas will show just what Quaker John Greenleaf Whittier could do to an enemy when righteous indignation boiled over in the strangest Quaker heart that ever beat. Here they are:

And he—the basest of the base—
  The vilest of the vile—whose name,
Embalmed in infinite disgrace,
  Is deathless in its shame!—

A tool—to bolt the people's door
  Against the people clamoring there,—
An ass—to trample on their floor,
  A people's right to prayer!

Nailed to his self-made gibbet fast,
  Self-pilloried to the public view—
A mark for every passing blast
  Of scorn to whistle through;

There let him hang, and hear the boast
  Of Southrons o'er their pliant tool—
A new Stylites on his post,
  "Sacred to ridicule"!

It is to be remarked that no name was named—and none was needed. The identification was inescapable.

Fragments of poems, at the best, are only fragments. That is why *The Farewell of a Virginia Slave Mother to Her Daughters Sold into Southern Bondage* is here quoted entire. This poem, published in 1838, combined the most potent qualities of Whittier's sentimental and melodramatic appeals, making a composite emotional force so powerful that it brushed aside all obstacles of economics and politics and spread throughout the North the fire of freedom from the torch of Liberty.

The Farewell is not great poetry and does not even pretend to be. But it is essential truth dispensed as stupendous propaganda before which all students of that veiled mystery —the plunger which will set off the dynamite of national emotional response—should bow with due respect.

THE FAREWELL
OF A VIRGINIA SLAVE MOTHER TO HER DAUGHTERS
SOLD INTO SOUTHERN BONDAGE

Gone, gone—sold and gone,
To the rice-swamp dank and lone.
Where the slave-whip ceaseless swings,
Where the noisome insect stings,
Where the fever demon strews
Poison with the falling dews,
Where the sickly sunbeams glare
Through the hot and misty air,—
Gone, gone—sold and gone,
To the rice-swamp dank and lone,
From Virginia's hills and waters,—
Woe is me, my stolen daughters!

Gone, gone—sold and gone,
To the rice-swamp dank and lone.
There no mother's eye is near them,
There no mother's ear can hear them;
Never, when the torturing lash
Seams their back with many a gash,
Shall a mother's kindness bless them,
Or a mother's arms caress them.
Gone, gone—sold and gone,
To the rice-swamp dank and lone,
From Virginia's hills and waters,—
Woe is me, my stolen daughters!

Gone, gone—sold and gone,
To the rice-swamp dank and lone.
Oh, when weary, sad, and slow,
From the fields at night they go,
Faint with toil, and racked with pain,
To their cheerless homes again—
There no brother's voice shall greet them—
There no father's welcome meet them.

Gone, gone—sold and gone,
To the rice-swamp dank and lone,
From Virginia's hills and waters,—
Woe is me, my stolen daughters!

Gone, gone—sold and gone,
To the rice-swamp dank and lone,
From the tree whose shadow lay
On their childhood's place of play—
From the cool spring where they drank—
Rock, and hill, and rivulet bank—
From the solemn house of prayer,
And the holy counsels there—
Gone, gone—sold and gone,
To the rice-swamp dank and lone,
From Virginia's hills and waters,—
Woe is me, my stolen daughters!

Gone, gone—sold and gone,
To the rice-swamp dank and lone—
Toiling through the weary day,
And at night the Spoiler's prey.
Oh, that they had earlier died,
Sleeping calmly, side by side,
Where the tyrant's power is o'er,
And the fetter galls no more!
Gone, gone—sold and gone,
To the rice-swamp dank and lone,
From Virginia's hills and waters,—
Woe is me, my stolen daughters!

Gone, gone—sold and gone,
To the rice-swamp dank and lone.
By the holy love He beareth—
By the bruised reed He spareth—
Oh, may He, to whom alone
All their cruel wrongs are known,
Still their hope and refuge prove,
With a more than mother's love.

Gone, gone—sold and gone,
To the rice-swamp dank and lone,
From Virginia's hills and waters,—
Woe is me, my stolen daughters!

20

FRUSTRATIONS AND NEW
FOUNDATIONS

THOUGH THE PERIOD of transition before Whittier's formal emergence as a conscious literary artist, signalized by the publication of *Lays of My Home,* occupied nearly three years, 1840 marked the beginning of a new epoch in his life.

The illness, disappointment, disillusionment, and mental pause which followed his resignation from the *Pennsylvania Freeman* and ended with his starting off on a new tack, must necessarily be paralleled with his sickness-retirement from the *New England Review* in 1831, his mental and political fumblings back home thereafter, his yielding to the sympathetic abolition impulse crystallized by Garrison's new *Liberator,* his publication of his own *Justice and Expediency* and his joining the American Anti-Slavery Society. But the second physical and nervous retreat was much worse than the first, for it was coupled with a sense of defeat.

Early in 1840 Whittier's health seems to have reached an all-life low, sufficiently serious to alarm experienced physicians. This condition, which because of the warnings of sane, sensible, and expert Dr. Henry Bowditch prevented him from attending the 1840 World Anti-Slavery Convention in London, must have been a real cross in itself. He had undoubtedly looked forward to the English trip as affording opportunities to increase his prestige and service; and remaining behind while many others made the voyage must have been unmistakable frustration for the leader who had published his poem on the subject—*The World Convention* —the preceding August. The problem of the trip's expense

156

was not really too important, for that would doubtless have been solved by Sturge or Sewall or Smith or one of the Tappans. Whittier, who would take nothing from friends for strictly personal needs, never had the least hesitation about accepting expense money for the good of the cause he advocated.

In addition to the depression of illness and the loss of the trip abroad, Whittier was in a slough of political despondency. The final adoption of the congressional gag rule against those very anti-slavery petitions to which he had devoted so much time and energy had been a crushing blow. He could not then foresee that in another two years he would be preparing the veritable mastodon of all Essex County petitions, and that in four years stubborn old John Quincy Adams would triumph over his adversaries and preserve the right of petition for generations unborn. Moreover, to cap his troubles, there was a more personal sorrow—the obviously impending split in the anti-slavery ranks and the inevitable disagreement with his oldest friend, Garrison. This was the unkindest cut of all—that he should be obliged to choose between what he believed to be the good of the cause and his affection for the man who had helped him at every stage of his career, literally from before the beginning.

Whittier never lost his temper and could not be induced to speak evil of Garrison or anyone else who was fighting honestly for the cause of abolition in any way. But blunt Garrison made no bones about expressing himself. He said openly in a *Liberator* editorial that Whittier's retirement might be anything but an unmitigated misfortune for the movement.

Though Whittier traveled from Amesbury to Philadelphia for the annual Spring Meeting of the Pennsylvania Anti-Slavery Society he deliberately absented himself from the slightly later New York Convention of the American Anti-Slavery Society. He knew that the quarrel must come to a head then and there; and he wished to avoid clashes with old fellow-workers even if he was out of harmony with their

extreme views. As he foresaw, the actual split occurred at
that time. Garrison and many of the original workers, especially of the New England group, continued the old American Anti-Slavery Society. The insurgents, more recently
recruited from New York and Pennsylvania, formed the new
American and Foreign Anti-Slavery Society. Whittier, the
most absolute Yankee of them all, found himself by deep
conviction allied with the new group, even though
he avoided executive participation by pleading ill health.

Garrison and the Garrisonians put no faith in reform by
political manipulation. They saw the problem as a simple
issue of right or wrong, and were ready to disrupt the Union
rather than longer tolerate the humiliations of pro-slavery
dominance. Whittier favored a broader viewpoint. He shared
the belief of the less fanatical element—that abolition could
be brought about within the framework of the Constitution;
that aggressive and persistent political action might produce
results; that emancipation must somehow be attained without splitting the Union. These opposed viewpoints were utterly irreconcilable.

Handicapped by invalidism, defeated in politics, at odds
with his oldest friends, Whittier was also without visible
means of support. Every time he entered the little Amesbury
cottage he must have passed the wolf sitting at the door.

What Whittier used for money between his resignation
from the *Freeman* in February, 1840, and his becoming editor
of the Lowell *Middlesex Standard* in July, 1844, has always
been a puzzle. He dabbled in unpaid politics, he had odd
jobs of editing, and he published prose and poems from time
to time in papers that paid little or nothing. When he sold
the Haverhill farm and bought the Amesbury cottage in
1836 he had a balance of $1800, from that transaction, and
as he was more or less steadily employed from 1837 to 1840,
at least part of this may have been saved and have been
still available. In any event, his financial worry must have
been most pressing. His bread-and-butter problem was how
to support his mother, his aunt, his sister, and himself by

exertions which would not so exhaust him by routine editorial or executive labors as to beget fresh physical infirmities.

In situations as black as these, the coward and the fool crack up for life. The courageous and wise man turns the searchlight inward on himself and thinks. Whittier was courageous and Whittier was long-headed. He must have had the sense to see that man cannot live by enthusiasm alone or by propaganda work that pays but little for a grind beyond his strength. And, because he was no fool, from somewhere in his inner consciousness he evolved the thought that he would make his writing more worth while, so that it should be salable for its literary merit, if this were indeed within the scope of his ability.

A shrewd observer of everything about him, Whittier must have been cognizant of the fact that literature as such had become a definite American profession from which not only men but women earned their livelihoods and that this had developed largely during the years of his recent complete immersion in anti-slavery propaganda. During the thirties, not only Cooper and Irving but a host of lesser novelists or story-tellers—Neal, Kennedy, Paulding, Thompson, Bird, and Miss Sedgwick among the best—had created a rousing market for American fiction. A troop of poets—Bryant at their head—were getting real money in exchange for verses. Holmes was becoming a familiar name; young Professor Longfellow's *Psalm of Life* in *Voices of the Night* had created a downright sensation in 1839; an irresponsible but unmistakable genius by the name of Poe was publishing almost incredible stuff in various magazines and being taken seriously. Literary men and women were sprouting up everywhere and every year, while he—beyond all doubt the most widely read of American verse writers—was grinding out propaganda (mostly unpaid except for scant editorial wages) for a cause as close to his heart as the bloodstream, but now divided against itself.

Then, as in later life, Whittier—whose analyses of other people's work, as shown by his literary essays, was surprisingly eclectic—undervalued the spontaneous energy and vivid imagery of his anti-slavery poems. Then, as to his dying day, his estimate of his own talents was most modest and his desire to improve thoroughly sincere. He reflected—he must have reflected—that his early poetry, before he began his assault on slavery, had not been without popular appeal despite its crudity; that his non-political poems in his 1837 and 1838 collections had not been unfavorably received; that what he lacked in education might have been in some considerable degree equalized by his wealth of experience. Perhaps, if he tried hard enough—and if he had the time to try in his own puttering way—he could write literature as well as propaganda. And literature, if it could be made to produce any tangible income, had for him the enormous advantage of something one could create at home, when the spirit moved, when the headaches and the palpitations didn't intrude. He could do plenty of work if only he could toil in his own home, in his own way, at his own intermittent, hop-scotch gait.

Whether the premises and details of this explanation are right in every respect or not, the conclusion is positively correct, for the simple and undeniable fact is that from 1840 onwards Whittier's work shows unquestionable evidence of conscious literary self-editorship. And that effort at self-instructive discipline continued for many years until what had originally been deliberate became so natural and unconscious that, at the late age of fifty-nine, he first appeared before the world in *Snow-Bound* as the complete master-poet of welded art and inspiration—an almost if not absolutely unique development to occur long past life's meridian.

This effort at intensive self-criticism had its effect even on Whittier's later anti-slavery poems. It was the direct cause of that pause in his propaganda writing which was only long enough for him to get his second wind but which vitally changed his manner of composition. On two or three occasions—as in *Massachusetts to Virginia*—this new literary impulse raised propaganda into the class of peculiarly forceful and dramatic verse; but in more instances it sapped the crude fury which had made such poems as *Our Fellow Coun-trymen in Chains* and *The Farewell of a Virginia Slave Mother* battle cries of freedom. In other directions, his work showed enormous improvement.

From 1840 to 1842 Whittier actually published only fifteen poems, all in periodicals. They appeared in a variety of maga-zines or newspapers—the *Pennsylvania Freeman, The Friend* (Philadelphia), *The Knickerbocker, Democratic Review, Boston Notion, The Lady's Pearl* (Lowell), and the *Amer-ican and Foreign Anti-Slavery Reporter,* which he at one time edited for a couple of numbers. Of these fourteen published poems only one—the very first, *Freedom's Gathering*—is anti-slavery and that is not preserved in the 1888 collection. The others all deal with persons, nature, or themes of labor and reform. For the moment, the Bard of Freedom, clearly fed up with organization bickerings, was tuning his harp to other melodies, listening to his own strummings as he sought out new themes and more correct expression.

Because objective actualities are more comprehensible than subjective abstractions, biographers and students have made the most conscientious efforts to identify exterior in-fluences redirecting Whittier's energies into more literary channels.

As previously noted, the poet's two most intimate feminine comradeships of the period preceding the change were Lucy Hooper—who died in 1841 and was clearly not critic but ad-miring pupil—and Elizabeth Lloyd. Though Miss Lloyd was assuredly no passionate sweetheart, it is true that she was critically minded and well educated and corresponded with Whittier on literary matters, but perusal of their letters com-pletely negatives any theory of special influence. Like Pro-fessor George Lyman Kittredge's famous answer to the Baconian theory of Shakespeare authorship—"Read Bacon" —the answer is simply "Read Miss Lloyd." However, Miss Lloyd and other feminine members of the Philadelphia circle must be credited with implanting in Whittier's mind a sense of distinctly literary achievement.

As to men: When Whittier, in 1842, wished to publish the collection of poems issued under the title of *Lays of My Home*, he applied for help to James T. Fields, then an employee but not yet a partner of the Ticknor publishing company in Boston, which had already identified itself with the best New England writers; and it is to be assumed that he must have had some previous personal contact with Fields as early as 1839, because Fields contributed a poem to *The North Star*, an anti-slavery anthology edited by Whittier at that time and already mentioned. After 1843 and for the remainder of his life, Fields was Whittier's preëminent guiding and encouraging critic-publisher in the very highest sense, but there is not the faintest evidence that he had anything whatever to do with the immediately preceding period of transition. The letter written by Whittier to Fields regarding the publication of his poems—printed by Currier—is an almost formal and diffident request for coöperation; most certainly not a letter from an author, seeking a higher level, to his established intimate adviser.

Next to Fields, the man who did most for Whittier in later years was James Russell Lowell, while editor of *The Atlantic Monthly*. Lowell was twelve years younger than Whittier and seems to have been in no literary contact with him until the very year *Lays Of My Home* was published—well after the essential poems had been written and most of them published in periodicals. And then it was Lowell who made the approach, asking Whittier to contribute a poem to his first magazine venture, *The Pioneer*, which existed for only the first three months of 1843 and which carried the Whittier poem in its second number.

Incontestably, Whittier's later guides were not his discoverers in the sense of "scouting" his genius and urging him to do himself justice. The truth is simply that John Greenleaf Whittier, by persistent delving, unearthed the poet within himself when a breathing space in the rush of affairs left inspiration free to burgeon.

In all this analysis, one must not forget the Quaker inner

light to which Whittier always held fast as a religious tenet, and one must remember that this was the very essence of highly sensitized introspection. That self-examination should have revealed the possibilities of his own creative temperament is not astounding. A certain mysticism of thought and practicality of life were curiously intermingled not only in Whittier and Mrs. Stowe (with her spiritualist leanings) and in many of their friends, but even in the High Priest of the Cult, Ralph Waldo Emerson himself, who told Whittier that he concluded prayer every morning with thanks that he lived so near Boston.

If there was any outside influence one must consider the claims of Greenleaf's sister Elizabeth—so much a part of him that she always seemed to many people the other side of his own personality—who must have been closer to him during the tedious days and sleepless nights of his 1840 invalidism than for some time previous. If he thought aloud to anybody or showed abortive attempts at better work, she was most probably the one human being completely in his confidence. During the dreary winter of 1840-1841 in Amesbury, there was ample time for communion between the searching soul of Greenleaf and the incisive mind of Elizabeth; ample opportunity to reflect on the criticisms and urgings of his Philadelphia friends.

Whittier's own explanation seems to have been that he had always wanted to write many forms of poetry but that this instinct—indulged so broadly and so crudely in early youth—had been restrained for years by the intensity of his self-dedication to the anti-slavery cause; that, with some moderating of his abolitionist activity, his poetic inspiration overflowed its narrow propaganda channel as the water, escaping from a millrace, flows back into the wider stream. But, to continue the comparison, the water flowing back from the millrace into the stream below speeds up the current to a pace far more rapid than that in the pond above the dam. The intensity of his propaganda verse had endowed Whittier with the power to feel more deeply and to

speak with the directly forceful simplicity which became his
peculiar gift.

No better explanation of Whittier's idea of Whittier can be
given than to quote his description of himself in *The Tent
on the Beach,* published a quarter of a century later:

> And one there was, a dreamer born,
> Who, with a mission to fulfil,
> Had left the Muses' haunts to turn
> The crank of an opinion-mill,
> Making his rustic reed of song
> A weapon in the war with wrong,
> Yoking his fancy to the breaking-plough
> That beam-deep turned the soil for truth to spring
>   and grow.
>
> Too quiet seemed the man to ride
> The winged Hippogriff Reform;
> Was his a voice from side to side
> To pierce the tumult of the storm?
> A silent, shy, peace-loving man,
> He seemed no fiery partisan
> To hold his way against the public frown,
> The ban of Church and State, the fierce mob's
>   hounding down.
>
> For while he wrought with strenuous will
> The work his hands had found to do,
> He heard the fitful music still
> Of winds that out of dream-land blew;
> The din about him could not drown
> What the strange voices whispered down;
> Along his task-field weird processions swept,
> And visionary pomp of stately phantoms stepped.

Perhaps the very fact that Whittier's poetic inspiration,
instead of being consumed in the fiery furnace of propaganda, was only tempered and purified, is the surest proof
that what lay so long under the surface of facile talent was
the veritable gold of genius.

21

THE ANTI-SLAVERY MOVEMENT
FORMALLY ENTERS
POLITICS

In 1840 the politically minded anti-slavery organizers—those who had formed the American and Foreign Anti-Slavery Society—thought that the movement had grown to such a point that it could found a party of its own instead of merely endorsing or rejecting the candidates of other parties. Whittier did not immediately concur, for he believed that the strongest political action would be advertised inaction in the form of refusal to vote for any ticket whatever. As already stated, he did not attend the convention held in Albany for the establishment of the Liberty party and overwhelmingly controlled by New York delegates, but he came into line a bit later and earnestly supported the candidate, James E. Birney, whom he liked and respected.

In many ways, Birney was really the ideal leader. A Kentucky slaveholder, he liberated his own slaves in 1834. He then founded and persisted in publishing, despite mob violence and widespread opposition, a very able abolitionist paper, the *Philanthropist,* in Cincinnati. He distinguished himself as a convincing platform orator and always insisted that slavery could be abolished under the Constitution. Birney and his supporters did not imagine that the Liberty party would poll a very serious vote at the outset, but they saw clearly that it would form a rallying point for thousands of men determined to prevent the further spread of slavery and irrevocably opposed to the fugitive slave laws.

A glance ahead at the national elections from 1840 to the Civil War will clarify the situation and make subsequent narrative more understandable if a trifle repetitious.

The Whig nominee for president in 1840 was William Henry Harrison; the Democratic nominee was Martin Van Buren, seeking reëlection—and Whig Harrison won. Birney ran for the Liberty party, as already explained.

In 1844 Democrat Polk defeated Whig Clay, who had lost many of his old Northern supporters. Birney ran a second time on the Liberty party ticket, and the party began to be a political force.

In 1848 both candidates, Whig Zachary Taylor and Democrat Lewis Cass, were pro-slavery men. This astounding situation gave added impetus to the little Liberty party and led to the formation of the more important Free Soil party, which was a combination of the Liberty party with anti-slavery Whigs and Democrats. Van Buren accepted the Free Soil nomination. Though Whig Taylor became president and the Democrats remained the chief opposition, Free Soiler Van Buren polled 300,000 votes and two Free Soilers were elected senators—Seward of New York and Chase of Ohio.

In 1852 Northern Democrat Pierce annihilated Whig Winfield Scott by 254 electoral votes as against only 42, virtually putting the old Whig party out of existence. This led to the formation of the Republican party which was a combination of anti-slavery Whigs (the pro-slavery Whigs had all voted for Democrat Pierce), anti-slavery Democrats, and Free Soilers. The Republican party was formally organized at a convention held in Michigan in July, 1854, with the publicly announced purpose of opposing the extension of slavery and the Kansas-Nebraska bill.

In 1856 Democrat James Buchanan defeated the first Republican candidate, John C. Frémont, later one of Whittier's closest friends.

In 1860 the Republicans elected Abraham Lincoln—and abolition was achieved under the Constitution and without division of the Union—through the fiery ordeal of Civil War.

The basic political strategy of the anti-slavery leaders—among whom Whittier exercised much authority—is obvious. Once having formed a party, they fought through two elections with as much determination and enthusiasm as if they expected to win. The moment they found they could get recruits by combining with the disaffected elements of the older parties, they coöperated first in forming the Free Soil party and again in forming the Republican party. Party identity and personal ambitions were not allowed to complicate the situation in any manner. The sole object was to assemble the largest possible group of anti-slavery voters under any banner and any respectable leadership.

The minor details of Whittier's local political activities in North Essex, Massachusetts, are often amusingly astute but are actually less important in retrospect than his services as a self-appointed and widely accepted general adviser. His calmly perceptive advice on practical measures to be taken in any situation and his almost x-ray judgments of men and motives were admitted by all the more active political leaders. A bit apart from the more robust, bustling world, he saw life-at-large in such perspective that even little North Essex was not a corner by itself but a part of the United States just as the United States was for him just part of a Free Universe.

Whittier spent the summer of 1840 mainly recuperating and visiting friends. He was well enough to attend the regular annual Quaker Meeting in Newport, and he returned for a time to the vicinity of Philadelphia, where he visited with his cousin Joseph Cartland at Healy's Spring Grove Farm and doubtless listened in on many abolition plans. He had dropped his connection with the *Freeman* entirely because of the refusal of the editor, C. C. Burleigh, to print one of his articles concerning the exclusion of women from the London Anti-Slavery Convention. For the moment, he rested on his oars.

Even though Whittier took special care to reiterate his anti-slavery convictions in the most public manner at the

Newport Friends Meeting, his refusal to be on the Birney electoral ticket or on the executive committee of the American and Foreign Anti-Slavery Society seems to have been misconstrued as a desertion even by many of his old associates. An indication of how generally Whittier was under suspicion of forsaking the Cause is to be found in a letter to him from Elizabeth Lloyd, dated December 6, 1840, and recently published by Currier. In this letter Miss Lloyd enclosed a copy of some verses by Elizabeth Nicholson (another member of the intimate Philadelphia anti-slavery group) already mentioned in previous correspondence.

These verses bear the title *A Lament*. The first and last stanzas will show clearly enough what the straight-forward Miss Nicholson thought and did not hesitate to say. Here they are:

> Furl, furl your proud standard! Let Liberty mourn,
>   And in silence and sadness your banners be borne!
> For the foremost among ye—the pride of your field—
>   Crestfallen and wary, now rests on his shield.
>
> And they gathered from near—and they hastened from
>   far—
>   Like the Magi they followed one glorious star;
> But the poet from all his high visions came down
>   To a Quaker Convention at old Germantown!

In the same letter, which was not written until the winter, when Whittier had begun to reconsider the situation and some months after the probable writing of *A Lament* (clearly referring to the London Convention), Miss Lloyd also encloses a continuation of the effusion from Miss Nicholson, entitled *The Rejoicing*, in exactly opposite vein, welcoming Whittier back into the movement. The last of the four stanzas is so unexpectedly discerning that it surely merits recording—

Then "weary" perhaps, but "crestfallen" never,
The Lyrics of Freedom they flourish forever!
And Liberty's harp-strings, they gather no rust,
Till the hand that awakened them is cold in the dust.

Evidently enough, even the inner circles had been puzzled
by Whittier's efforts to avoid the partisan warfare within the
anti-slavery camp, and had doubted whether his illness was
serious enough to keep him away from the London Convention—if he had really wished to go. However, there can be
no real question that, as stated in the preceding chapter,
Whittier remained at home instead of going to the World's
Convention because of Dr. Bowditch's advice; for, with all
his foresight, he can scarcely have surmised that this enormously advertised affair would end as a bit of a fiasco and
would be eventually remembered not as an important step
in the emancipation of Negro slaves but as an initial effort
in the direction of woman's rights.

It seems advisable at this point to simplify the succeeding
story of Whittier's participation in public affairs by inserting
here a schedule of important events from 1840 to the Civil
War. These events, supplementing the list of presidents for
the same period already given, bear exclusively upon matters
of anti-slavery interest and were therefore of special significance for Whittier.

1842 (Tyler, succeeding Harrison). Haverhill petition to dissolve the Union forces test of gag rule in Congress.
1843 (Tyler). The fugitive slave Latimer is refused jury trial
in Massachusetts, on the ground that the law which Whittier
helped to pass in 1836 was unconstitutional.
1844 (Tyler). J. Q. Adams finally triumphs and the gag rules
of Congress in the matter of petitions are revoked.
1845 (Polk). Texas is admitted to the Union, thus greatly increasing slave territory.
1846 (Polk). The Mexican War tends still further to increase
the territory that might naturally be pro-slavery.

1848 (Polk). California and New Mexico are acquired for the United States, involving still further problems of dividing the Union into anti-slavery and pro-slavery sections.

1850 (Taylor-Fillmore). Taylor, though a large plantation owner and slave-holder, favors the admission of California as a free state, but dies after less than six months in office, being succeeded by Fillmore, a New York moderate, who tries to restrain sectional antagonism by aiding the Compromise of 1850, abolishing slavery in the District of Columbia but making the fugitive slave laws still more stringent. This same year Calhoun dies at sixty-eight years of age and Whittier rouses the anti-slavery anti-fugitive-law spirit by writing his famous *Sabbath Scene*.

1851. Thomas Sims, a fugitive slave, is virtually kidnaped by the Boston Sheriff acting against widespread public opinion, and forcibly returned to bondage.

1852 (Fillmore). Sumner is elected to the Senate largely at Whittier's suggestion and through his political manipulation. In his first speech, he takes an uncompromising stand against slavery, asserting, "Freedom is national—slavery sectional."

1854 (Pierce). The pro-slavery elements conspire without success to acquire Cuba as a means of expanding their influence. The old Missouri Compromise fixing the North-South dividing line between slavery and freedom is revoked and the Douglas-sponsored Kansas-Nebraska bill adopted. This makes slavery a local option issue and centers the struggle in Kansas. The Republican party is organized this same year. Anthony Burns, alleged fugitive slave, is returned to bondage by the Massachusetts authorities, outraging general public opinion still further, and Theodore Parker, greatest of New England Unitarian clergymen, is put under indictment for speaking against the arrest of Burns.

1855-57 (Pierce and Buchanan). Decisions in the case of the fugitive slave, Dred Scott, uphold slavery from every viewpoint and arouse bitter hostility in the free states.

1856 (Pierce). Sumner is brutally assaulted on the floor of the Senate by a Southern congressman named Brooks and almost fatally injured.

1859 (Buchanan). Pro-slavery men attempt to enact legislation which will revive the importation of slaves.

1859-1860 (Buchanan). John Brown attempts to establish an organized refuge for slaves, attacks and captures the arsenal at

Harpers Ferry, is seized with his men by a detachment of troops under Robert E. Lee and is hanged for treason.

1860 (Buchanan). Abraham Lincoln is elected president.

During the pause in Whittier's more active life, in the period of 1840-1842—which corresponded with the pause in national affairs before the storm of stupendous events—and while he was incubating his new more literary poetical ideals, he seems to have undergone something of a spiritual rebirth in the strictly religious sense. His call to free the slave acquired a new quality of control, patience, and complete confidence in ultimate achievement. Liberty became veritably part of Whittier's religion, and the unshakable depth of all his religious convictions is beyond question.

Whittier's almost saintly existence (and perhaps there is no need of the qualifying adverb), his religious poems, and his brief farewell to life when he knew his hour had come— *Love to the World!*—are evidence conclusive that for him Eternal Goodness was a pervading presence no less real because mystically inscrutable. Whittier's illnesses, because they continually thwarted his most treasured plans, may well have seemed more critical to him than to the world at large and have urged upon him the contemplation of immortality. Anyone who has suffered from severe heart palpitations knows how difficult it is to believe that the spasm will pass and that every thump is not a hoof-beat of Time galloping straight for the one-way gate of Eternity.

Whittier's spiritual awakening occurred at the Newport Quaker Meeting of 1840—the same meeting at which he took occasion to reiterate his anti-slavery principles. He had gone to call on J. J. Gurney relative to anti-slavery activities and had found one Richard Mott there. After the discussion with Gurney ended, Mott asked permission to accompany Whittier back to his lodgings. The gist of what then occurred is quoted from a letter written by Whittier on July 13, 1840, to his cousin Ann Wendell in Philadelphia:

"During our walk he [Mott] told me he knew not how it

was or why, but that his mind had been drawn into a deep and extraordinary exercise of sympathy with me; that he had been sensible of a deep trial and exercise in my own mind; and that he had felt it so strongly that he could not rest easy without informing me of it, although he had heard nothing and seen nothing to produce this conviction in his mind. He felt desirous to offer me the language of encouragement, to urge me to put aside every weight that encumbers, and to look unto Him who was able to deliver from every trial."

Whittier regarded this as a positive, direct manifestation of the Quaker inner light.

The Amesbury winter of 1840-1841 was perhaps Whittier's most profound interlude of self-communion; of reconstruction through self-revelation. From this Quaker novena he emerged more of the prophet and less of the exhorter; not less determined but more disciplined; not less powerful in expression but with power restrained and directed. In the course of eighteen months of physical inactivity his mind and soul had matured at least a decade.

22

BACK IN
THE ANTI-SLAVERY
CONFLICT

In April of 1841 Whittier emerged from his mental and physical seclusion. He went to New York and there met Joseph Sturge, the wealthy and sagacious English abolitionist-philanthropist.

Pickard, in the official life, states that Whittier now met Joseph Sturge for the first time. Earlier in the same volume Pickard quotes Ann Wendell (under the date of 1836), as being present when the Bass Otis portrait of Whittier was shown to Sturge, and Sturge commented, "John, I do not quite like it." This incident is told expressly in relation to "Greenleaf's first visit to us in the Winter of 1836-37"—before he became editor of *The Freeman*. The inconsistency is obvious, and it is certainly likely that the two men met on Sturge's previous visit to America.

Be that as it may, the friendship of Sturge and Whittier now became firmly cemented and endured until the day of Sturge's death in 1859. Whittier traveled with Sturge, at Sturge's expense, almost but not quite continuously from April until Sturge's departure for England in August. It was in the company of this kind, powerful, and very sensible man that Whittier re-surveyed the anti-slavery political arena before making his personal reappearance. With Fellow-Quaker Sturge, Whittier visited Slaughter's slave-market in Baltimore and attended, in that city, the Baptist convention which proposed to remove all abolitionists from its missionary

board. Then poet and millionaire traveled together to Philadelphia and Wilmington—at which point an increase in
Whittier's indisposition forced him to return home temporarily.

In June Whittier rejoined Sturge at Wilmington and together they attended an anti-slavery meeting of men who
had formed a project to buy freedom for Delaware slaves
through the imposition of a land tax. They next went to Washington and were present in the House during one of the great
gag rule debates. They called on John Quincy Adams and
President Tyler and Henry Clay. When Clay rebuked Whittier for having deserted him, the poet turned the tables on
the politician by explaining just why he had done so. They
went from Capitol Hill to a near-by slave pen, and thence
to the foul prison where Dr. Crandall had been confined for
giving Whittier's *Justice and Expediency* to a friend—and
from which he had been released only to die.

Still together, Whittier and Sturge attended the Quaker
Meeting in Newport, only to have their anti-slavery activities quietly ignored, but despite this fact they had a fruitful
meeting with William Ellery Channing, one of the great New
England intellectual forces of the day, who urged the filing
of petitions to relieve the free states of any duty that might
tend to enforce slavery. From Newport, Sturge and Whittier
journeyed to Amesbury and spent a few days at the poet's
little cottage, after which they returned to Boston for a long
conference with Garrison, aiming to reunite the two wings
of the anti-slavery movement. Garrison, with the London convention still fresh in mind, thrust the woman's rights dispute
too much into the foreground, whereas Whittier—though
always sympathetic toward that cause—refused to accept it as
a prime factor in the situation, thereby sticking fast to his
resolution never to let any side issue swerve him from the
one basic purpose of his life.

The tour was interrupted a second time by Whittier's illness and resumed in July, continuing virtually to the hour
of Sturge's reëmbarkation in August. This extended tour,

with such a companion, must have added greatly to Whittier's personal prestige with men of experience and substance. It is true that the two travelers did not accomplish much toward Sturge's specific purpose, which was to arouse the American Quakers to a more active interest in abolition. But the calm, astute, rich English Quaker—who had done more than any other one man to free British slaves—clearly imbued Whittier with the courage to resume his anti-slavery work along the patient, realistic, political lines which seemed logical to both of them. Though the Liberty party, with Birney as candidate, had polled only an immaterial vote in the political contest which had just elected Whig Harrison president over Democrat Van Buren, it had established a certain amount of political machinery which could be turned to practical account.

So far as can be judged, President Harrison's death after only a few months in office and the installation of Vice-President Tyler in his place was to the advantage of the pro-slavery elements. The schemes of the slavery advocates for gaining a permanent upper hand in the federal legislative chambers by the addition to the United States of further Southwestern natural slave territory were perfectly apparent. Men like Whittier and Sturge cannot have been deceived for a moment.

Sturge was so genuinely concerned about Whittier's personal health and financial problems—which he must have seen at close quarters while visiting in Amesbury—that before he embarked for London he left $1,000 with Lewis Tappan of New York for Whittier to use in virtually any way he saw fit for his own needs, with a provision that any unused surplus should be used for the anti-slavery movement. Apparently Whittier declined the assistance, though illness and personal need must have been grievous problems. After Whittier's death, Pickard found among his papers a letter from Tappan asking how he should spend a $400 balance remaining from Sturge's $1,000 contribution toward work for the cause!

In August of 1841, Lucy Hooper, the consumptive young poetess already mentioned, died, and a personal attachment which might well have developed into something permanent and beautiful was removed from the range of human possibility.

In this same autumn of 1841, Whittier got back into editorial harness for a few weeks, preparing the September and October issues of the *Anti-Slavery Reporter*. This paper was the not very successful attempt of the new American and Foreign Anti-Slavery Society to rival Garrison's thundering *Liberator*. And it was at about this same time that Whittier gave striking evidence of just how expert he had become in the game of practical politics and of how dangerous it might be to cross the purposes of a saintlike Quaker from Amesbury.

In 1840 Whittier had himself run as congressman in North Essex on the Liberty party ticket just as a matter of form. His old protégé and unwilling ally, Caleb Cushing, running on the Whig ticket had been swept into office on the Harrison landslide without having been obliged to give Whittier the customary pledges of anti-slavery support. At last Cushing imagined he was free to shape his career strictly on the profit-and-loss personal basis. But—he had reckoned without his Quaker! Three times in succession Tyler nominated Cushing to be Secretary of the Treasury and three times in succession Congress refused to confirm. And this was all because Whittier, knowing that Congress would never confirm a Secretary of anti-slavery sympathies, published broadcast the anti-slavery pledge he had himself written years before and forced Cushing to sign. The impoverished poet, in retirement at Amesbury, could still balk a President of the United States and inflict terrible discipline upon a traitor. Nor penury, nor distance, nor illness, nor discouragement could veil Whittier's vision or numb his infallible instinct for choosing the strategic moment.

In 1842 Politician Whittier was confronted with a fresh puzzle—that he could force no anti-slavery pledge from either the Democratic or the Whig congressional candidate in North Essex. So he repeated the same tactics he had used in obtaining pledges a decade earlier, and the regularly organized Liberty party, entitled to a candidate of its own, was a handy implement. This strategy was made possible by the fact that the election law was still the same—a candidate, to be elected, was obliged to obtain not merely the largest number of votes but a majority of all votes cast.

Whittier forced a stalemate by himself remaining the Liberty party candidate throughout 1842-1843, always polling at many elections enough votes to prevent a victory by either Whig or Democrat. Then a terribly embarrassing thing happened. He began to get more votes than necessary for his purpose. Finally, in December of 1843 Daniel Webster—ready to do almost anything rather than let a Democrat win—suggested to the Whigs that they accept Whittier as their candidate. Despite local Whig opposition, this advice seemed to be on the verge of acceptance and the combined Whig-Liberty party endorsement would have been tantamount to election. Now the very last thing that Whittier had intended to do or felt his health would permit him to do was to win the election. He hastily withdrew his name, the substitute Liberty party candidate was ineffectual, and the Whig was returned at the polls.

Whittier's uncompromising political creed is magnificently summarized by his letter accepting the Liberty party nomination of 1842. This is quoted from the *Haverhill Gazette* of that year, October 10:

"So long as our cause is an unpopular one—I am willing to stand in any position in which my friends assign me, and which does not conflict with my ideas of duty. I therefore cheerfully accept the nomination of the Convention, promising, however, that whenever our cause shall have gathered about it the elements of complete success, I shall be ready with still greater cheerfulness, to give my support to some person better able than myself to represent the friends of impartial freedom in the national councils. . . .

"I can only say in the words of the lamented William Leggett, when his name was proposed by his Democratic friends as candidate for Congress:—'I am an abolitionist.' Let other men twist themselves as they please, to gratify the present tastes of the people; I choose to retain undisturbed the image of my God. I hate slavery in all its forms, degrees and influences, and I deem myself bound by the highest moral and political obligations not to let that sentiment of hate lie dormant, and smoldering in my own breast, but to give it free vent and let it blaze forth, that it may kindle equal ardor through the whole sphere of my influence. I would not have this fact disguised or mystified for any office the people have it in their power to give."

Whittier lost this round of the local political battle by not gauging the growth of his own popularity. However, he had become definitely a figure to be reckoned with in local and state politics and also, under special circumstances, in the national arena. The youth who had ruled himself out of politics at twenty-six—when political office had really been his essential ambition—by writing *Justice and Expediency* had now, only eight years later, despite all his dangerous convictions proclaimed from the housetops in prose and verse, become of such stature that only by retiring could he prevent himself from becoming congressman in Washington.

Whittier's third political achievement of this period was the strangest of all, and, unfortunately, must be attributed to him rather than absolutely identified as primarily his work. This episode is the so-called Haverhill Petition of 1842, which almost precipitated an actual riot in Congress. This petition, signed by forty-three citizens of Haverhill (Whittier not being among them) was clearly a sarcastic rejoinder to the many threats of secession already made by Southern leaders.

It was very brief and read as follows:

"The undersigned citizens of Haverhill, in the Commonwealth of Massachusetts, pray you will immediately adopt measures, peaceably to dissolve the Union of these states: First, because no Union can be agreeable or permanent which does not offer prospects of reciprocal benefit; second, because a vast proportion of the resources of one section of the Union is annually drained to sustain the views and course of another section without any adequate return; third, because (judging from the history of past nations) this Union, if persisted in, in the present course of things, will certainly overwhelm the whole nation in utter destruction."

Pickard merely says, "Haverhill and Amesbury did more than their share in petitioning, and Mr. Whittier's hand is to be seen in the whole movement in that part of Massachusetts."

John Quincy Adams introduced this petition and doubtless relished the row it stirred up. For four days Congress debated whether ex-President Adams should not be unseated for offering to the House and to the American people an insult smacking of high treason. And obviously this burlesque petition gave old Adams the ideal opportunity for driving home his distinction between the basic right of citizens to have any petition considered by their representatives in Congress and the substance of the petitions offered. He voiced his disagreement with the text of the petition even while insisting that it must be heard.

How can Whittier's part in this subtle move be reasonably questioned? For years he had been supplying petitions; he knew Adams well and every angle of Adams' political strategy. He had groomed Cushing for Congress only when Cushing signed the anti-slavery pledge and agreed to present petitions and defend the Right of Petition. The year previous he and Sturge had discussed with Channing the possibility of petitions designed to relieve the Northern states from all obligations to support slavery. The satirical Haverhill petition to break up the Union was only a step beyond the Channing idea and, in truth, the only means by which the Channing idea could be carried out in actual practice—another way of showing that the continuation of slavery and permanent Union would prove impossible. It is inconceivable that Whittier did not know the plan for this petition right in his own district. The fact that he—the leading anti-slavery figure of the entire locality—did *not* sign it, points to him as the originator or at least one of the originators much more emphatically than if he had put his name to it, for, by signing it, Whittier would have injured its semblance of sincerity by branding it as an obvious political snare.

The touch of grim humor in the Haverhill Petition is typical of Whittier's mentality in every possible aspect. If, by chance, this specimen of truly Homeric satire was not first conceived by Whittier, nothing in this life is more certain than that it could never have reached Washington without his knowledge and would never have been sponsored by Adams without his approval.

The bitter arguments started by this petition and the attempts to expel Adams revived the whole subject of the gag rules and finally started the definite movement for their repeal, which occurred two years later, in 1844. The triumph of Adams in thus unholding the personal rights of citizens as against their own legislative bodies is a unique chapter in American history and established him as one of the permanently illustrious figures in the history of democratic government.

By the end of 1842, Whittier had definitely assumed his new political rôle—the invisible and almost invincible force behind the scenes.

23

THE REBIRTH OF
A POET

As THE YEAR OF 1842 merged into 1843, John Greenleaf Whittier, now self-relegated to general staff politics rather than to the front-line trenches, again became articulate in verse. And the verse he now wrote was of such serious poetical excellence as to indicate an inspiration of entirely new caliber in every emotional and intellectual dimension.

The Whittier of 1842-1843 is not yet the Whittier of *The Barefoot Boy, The Eternal Goodness,* and *Snow-Bound* but it is Whittier displaying a master talent all the same. From discouragements, disillusionments, and inner questionings of mind and spirit he has acquired dignity, authentic poetical expression, unpretentious confidence in his own ability, and classic simplicity. He has discovered how to utilize fully his somewhat limited and untutored but very potent indigenous gifts.

This emergence of the new Whittier was no sudden and exhausting outburst of genius such as the year 1848 produced in the life of James Russell Lowell when, in one season, he gave to the world *The Vision of Sir Launfal,* the second series of his *Poems, The Biglow Papers,* and *A Fable for Critics.* But it was the long-maturing decisive step upward and forward. At least three poems of this period, all first printed in book form in one little volume entitled *Lays of My Home* (1843), belong among the New England classics —*Cassandra Southwick,* a legendary ballad; *Memories,* a sentimental poem of youth in retrospect; and *Massachusetts to Virginia,* an entirely new species of propagandist anti-slavery poem. These three poems, it will be noted, represent three of the main facets in Whittier's genius. The only slender thread that binds them to his earlier compositions is the fact, already stated in another connection, that Whittier borrowed the first two stanzas of *Memories* from *Moll Pitcher,* published eleven years earlier.

None of the poems in *Lays of My Home* had appeared in either the 1837 or 1838 Whittier collections. All except two or three, however, had appeared in magazines, and some half dozen had been printed in verse anthologies.

Whittier was fully conscious that he was doing better work than ever before and was determined to make the transition complete. Elizabeth Lloyd and other friends had noted the improvement in his 1840-1842 periodical printings of poems and had discussed it with him. When he decided to publish these recent verses, he did not turn to his old and every-ready anti-slavery publishers but sought contact with Ticknor & Co., already the publishers of Emerson, Longfellow, and Holmes. In current vernacular, he thought he had something and wanted it presented to the public in proper dress and by influential sponsors.

As has already been mentioned, Whittier had come to know James T. Fields in 1839 by including one of Fields' poems in his Philadelphia abolition anthology, *The North Star.* Fields was now employed by Ticknor, the very man Whittier wished to reach. His feeling-out letter to Fields, quoted by Currier, reads:

Amesbury, 24th 1st mo. 1842

MY DEAR FRIEND FIELDS:—

I suppose there is already abundance of poetry in the market, but a wish to preserve a few floating pieces of mine, & to favor some personal friends, induces me to think of publishing a small collection under the title of "Legends of the Merrimack" &c., including the following pieces, some of which thee might have seen, "The Exiles," "The Merrimack," "The Norsemen," "The Fountain," "Pentucket"—and other poems; "St John," "The Funeral Tree of the Sokokis," "The Cypress Tree of Ceylon," and three or four other pieces as yet in MS making in all about 100 pages.—I want it printed in first rate style or not at all. I am wholly unacquainted with booksellers, having never published anything of any consequence, and would be greatly obliged to thee if thee would take the trouble to negotiate for me, and let me know as soon as convenient the result of thy inquiry. I wish it to be done well or not at all.

Believe me very truly thy friend,
John G. Whittier.

Despite lack of immediate practical returns, Ticknor & Co. and its successors published virtually all later Whittier authorized volumes printed in America to the day of his death—with abundant though long-delayed ultimate returns that were amazing.

The bibliographical record of this first important verse volume by Whittier is:

Whittier, John G. Lays of my Home, and Other Poems, by John G. Whittier. Boston, William D. Ticknor. 1843 (June)

The booklet contains 122 pages of text and a total of twenty-three poems, in addition to the verse dedication to John Pierrepont.

Of these twenty-three poems (all considered sufficiently important by their author to be included in the definitive edition of 1888) only two were ultimately classed as anti-slavery—*The Relic* and *Massachusetts to Virginia*. The relic referred to was a cane made from a fragment of the Pennsylvania Hall woodwork and presented to the poet; and the poem that it suggested, though containing the usual forceful demand for freedom, is naturally reminiscent and not an exhortation. *Massachusetts to Virginia* may well be regarded as the very climax of Whittier's unique verse talent for propaganda—substituting for the overt melodrama of *Our Fellow Countrymen in Chains* and *The Farewell of a Virginia Slave Mother* a profound dramatic conflict expressed in vital but restrained poetic phrase, picturing the two states not only as places but personifying them to represent the sentiments of their inhabitants.

Before proceeding to detailed analysis, it is to be noted in passing that among the *Lays of My Home* are *Democracy, The Gallows, The Human Sacrifice* and *The Reformers of England,* all later classified as *Songs of Labor and Reform. The Gallows* and *The Human Sacrifice* are direct, emphatic attacks on capital punishment—the first of Whittier's mature assaults on evils other than human bondage.

In the next ten years, Whittier wrote and published more than a hundred poems—works of high average interest and excellence—but not until 1854 did he produce an essentially new collection to equal or surpass *Lays of My Home.* Then came *The Panorama,* with *Maud Muller* and *The Barefoot Boy,* establishing the author as a household and schoolroom favorite so continually quoted that the very extent of his success made him trite to an entire generation of Americans over-exposed to him in unappreciative childhood days.

Massachusetts to Virginia, in which Massachusetts explains the New England point of view to her sister commonwealth, has not the quaint Yankee genius that makes Lowell's dialogue between Concord Bridge and Bunker Hill Monument in *Mason and Slidell* unique among the world's versified political controversies, but it reaches a point of contagious intensity entirely beyond the range of Lowell's patrician personality. As a poem written for a special occasion it has surely never been surpassed in America except possibly by Emerson's *Concord Hymn.*

Massachusetts to Virginia was the result of the tremendous excitement in 1842-1843 caused by the plight of an escaped slave named George Latimer, to whom the Chief Justice of Massachusetts refused jury trial as guaranteed by the law which Whittier had himself done much to pass in 1836. In making this decision he was following a Supreme Court ruling that the Massachusetts law was unconstitutional. Latimer's personal situation was saved by the simple expedient of purchasing his freedom for the sum of $400, but the entire fugitive slave controversy flared up again as one of the burning questions never really to be quenched until drowned in the blood of civil war.

Simultaneous conventions of protest were called by the anti-slavery leaders in each county of Massachusetts for January 2, 1843. Whittier's thrilling poem was written specifically for the Essex County convention, read there to great applause, and published by Garrison in *The Liberator* on January 27. Garrison's personal argument with Whittier regarding ways and means of freeing the black man did not for one moment stay his hand in reaching out for this timely verse thunderbolt. *Massachusetts to Virginia* consists of twenty-four stanzas of four lines each.

The writer will have achieved no small part of his purpose if at this point the reader will pick up his copy of Whittier's *Poems*—or buy one if he have it not—and read *Massachusetts to Virginia* once a day for three successive days. He will then understand the mental or educational deficiencies of any man who tries to dismiss Whittier as a nice old man who wrote pretty pieces for schoolrooms and just happened once to hit the nail on the head with *Snow-Bound*.

Stanzas 1, 3, 6, 10, 23, and 24, though necessarily disconnected, display the inception, progression, and conclusion of the poem:

> The blast from Freedom's northern hills, upon its
>   Southern way,
> Bears greeting to Virginia from Massachusetts Bay:—
> No word of haughty challenging, nor battle bugle's
>   peal,
> Nor steady tread of marching files, nor clang of horse-
>   man's steel.
>
> We hear thy threats, Virginia! thy stormy words and
>   high,
> Swell harshly on the Southern winds which melt along
>   our sky;

Yet, not one brown, hard hand foregoes its honest
        labor here;
No hewer of our mountain oaks suspends his axe in
        fear.

What means the Old Dominion? Hath she forgot the
        day
When o'er her conquered valleys swept the Briton's
        steel array?
How side by side, with sons of hers, the Massachu-
        setts men
Encountered Tarleton's charge of fire, and stout Corn-
        wallis, then?

Thank God! Not yet so vilely can Massachusetts bow,
The spirit of her early time is with her even now;
Dream not because her pilgrim blood moves slow and
        calm, and cool,
She thus can stoop her chainless neck, a sister's slave
        and tool!

We wage no war—we lift no arm—we fling no torch
        within
The fire-damps of the quaking mine beneath your soil
        of sin;
We leave ye with your bondmen—to wrestle, while ye
        can,
With the strong upward tendencies and God-like soul
        of man!

But for us and for our children, the vow which we
        have given
For Freedom and humanity is registered in Heaven:
No slave-hunt in our borders,—no pirate on our strand!
No fetters in the Bay State—no slave upon our land!

The Latimer case led to the drafting of a monster petition
from the people to the Massachusetts legislature, signed with
62,791 names of citizens, against the future arrest of fugitive
slaves within the borders of the state. The unexpected

strength shown by the Liberty party in 1844 with Samuel Sewall as candidate for governor put the legislature into a receptive frame of mind. This petition was handed along to Congress, calling (in Whittier's own words) "for such laws and amendments to the constitution as should relieve the Commonwealth from all further participation in the crime of oppression."

Of course no such laws were made and no such constitutional amendments considered, but a petition of these immense proportions riding on a surging wave of popular indignation was a two-edged sword in the skillful hands of John Quincy Adams, first grim grenadier on the battlefield for the rights of the people in their own legislative conclaves. This and the Haverhill petition were two of the very last steps leading to the ultimate success of Adams in repealing the gag laws—already variously mentioned. For better or worse, the controversy was in the open at last. All efforts to smother public debate on the slavery issue were abandoned as futile. The wonder is not that the conflicting ideals and economic situations of the North and the South took yet another sixteen years to be translated into armies but that the moderate thinkers on both sides so long held back the inevitable appeal to arms.

In all these events—and in the greater events now pending —appeared from time to time the weaving hand that belonged to a politically minded, impoverished, semi-invalid Quaker poet of Amesbury, Massachusetts. But though the hand worked as a shadow, scarcely traceable, the voice spake as a trumpet to all the world, for it had a special endowment for saying true and terrible things in simple and homely rhyme which echoed and reëchoed in the minds of average men and women.

LEGENDS AND REMINISCENCES

CONSENSUS OF OPINION establishes *Cassandra Southwick,* a ballad, and *Memories,* a poem of sentimental retrospection, as the best non-propagandist poems in *Lays of My Home.* *Cassandra Southwick* had previously appeared, only three months before the publication of *Lays of My Home,* in the *Democratic Review,* which had printed much of Whittier's best verse since 1837. *Memories,* though listed by Pickard as written in 1841, seems never to have been printed—except for the few introductory lines borrowed from *Moll Pitcher*— previous to its inclusion in this collected group.

Since correspondence very recently unearthed by the noted collector, C. A. Wilson, shows that Whittier not only succeeded in getting Fields to arrange publication of the *Lays of My Home* by the Ticknor firm which employed him but immediately recognized Fields' critical instinct by consulting him about the poems to be gathered into the volume, it is evident that Whittier at last had the benefit of competent and sympathetic editing. *Cassandra* and *Memories* are not merely the highlights of this particular volume but vastly the best poems of both types produced by Whittier up to this time.

It will be remembered that Whittier, in his first letter to Fields on the subject, suggested the title *Legends of the Merrimack.* Just how this became transformed into the much more significant *Lays of My Home* is not known. But as author and publishers generally collaborate on title, it is not unreasonable to suppose that the guiding hand of Fields —either by suggestion or the elimination of alternate possi-

ble titles—is revealed in this wonderfully improved alteration.

To consider *Cassandra* first: Whittier had already written
various ballads and near-ballads—anti-slavery and otherwise
—of considerable power but unliterary to a degree. The progress from the best of these to *Cassandra Southwick* is no mere
transitional glide but a startling forward leap. Even if one
feels it is far less perfect than some admiring critics profess
and definitely inferior to his best maturer work in this form,
which so admirably suited the very essence of his genius,
it certainly represents sincere, conscious artistry of high caliber. As compared with Longfellow's *Ballads,* published a
year earlier—a thin little volume including *The Skeleton in
Armor, The Village Blacksmith,* and *Excelsior*—which literally took the reading public by storm, Whittier's *Lays*
scarcely stirred a ripple. But even in *Cassandra,* not only in
method of expression but in choice of theme, one cannot
escape an element of straight-from-the-shoulder to straight-
between-the-eyes earnestness that simply was not part of
Longfellow's endowment, high-minded, courageous, and
gifted gentleman though he was. Wherever one places it
within the category of Whittier ballads, *Cassandra* is a characteristic, major specimen.

The summary of the story of the poem, as printed in the
1888 Collected Edition, is as follows:

In 1658 two young persons, son and daughter of Lawrence
Southwick of Salem, who had himself been imprisoned and
deprived of nearly all his property for having entertained
Quakers at his house, were fined for non-attendance at
church. They being unable to pay the fine, the General Court
issued an order empowering "the Treasurer of the County
to sell the said persons to any of the English nation of Virginia or Barbadoes, to answer said fines." An attempt was
made to carry this order into execution, but no shipmaster
was found willing to carry them to the West Indies.

The complete ballad is in thirty-seven stanzas of four lines
each. The dramatic climax is reached in the four stanzas

below, wherein the rugged sea captain refused to perpetrate
the outrage demanded by the magistrates:

> "Pile my ship with bars of silver—pack with coins of
> Spanish gold,
> From keel-piece up to deck-plank, the roomage of her
> hold,
> By the living God who made me!—I would sooner in
> your bay
> Sink ship and crew and cargo, than bear this child
> away!"
>
> "Well answered, worthy captain, shame on their cruel
> laws!"
> Ran through the crowd in murmurs loud the people's
> just applause.
> "Like the herdsmen of Tekoa, in Israel of old,
> Shall we see the poor and righteous again for silver
> sold?"
>
> I looked on haughty Endicott; with weapon half-way
> drawn,
> Swept round the throng his lion glare of bitter hate
> and scorn;
> Fiercely he drew his bridle rein, and turned in silence
> back,
> And sneering priest and baffled clerk rode murmuring
> in his track.
>
> Hard after them the sheriff looked, in bitterness of
> soul;
> Thrice smote his staff upon the ground, and crushed
> his parchment roll.
> "Good friends," he said, "since both have fled, the
> ruler and the priest,
> Judge ye, if from their further work I be not well
> released."

In his fortunate choice of this subject the poet combined
two of his special interests, one might almost say obsessions
—indignation at the early Quaker persecutions and a deep

affection for all picturesque tales or legends of colonial New England.

There is a certain similarity between *Cassandra,* written when the poet was not yet thirty-six, and *How the Women Went from Dover,* written when the author was just forty years older—possibly the final outburst of the real old Whittier fire though by no means his last noble poem. Here again Quakers are being persecuted—whipped at the cart-tail—but Justice Pike refuses to permit the infliction of such punishment in Salisbury township. One brief stanza is quoted for comparison:

> "Cut loose these poor ones and let them go;
> Come what will of it, all men shall know
> No warrant is good, though backed by the Crown,
> For whipping women in Salisbury town!"

This same year of 1843, about four months after the publication of *Lays,* another Whittier narrative ballad, *The New Wife and the Old,* appeared in the *Democratic Review* and was included in Whittier's first British book publication, *Ballads and Other Poems,* London, 1844. In this instance the subject is an early New England supernatural legend associated with the ill-famed home of General Moulton of Hampton, New Hampshire, whose mansion house, recently much reconstructed, is still standing though somewhat removed from the heath which the Devil blasted after the General outwitted him in their trade for a bootful of gold. Moulton, in his not too lovely old age, had married a beautiful young wife—and the abused first wife came back on the wedding night to snatch her rings off the dainty hand of her successor.

This ghost yarn is genuine Yankee legend all wool and a yard wide, and Whittier knew just what to do with it. As a matter of fact, the writer has always had a sneaking admiration for old Moulton for not being more taken aback than he was by these goings-on. However, if as the town legends say he was really a wrecker and gained fortune by lighting false beacons so as to lure storm-driven ships onto the Rivermouth Rocks, he must have been far too tough to worry about mere phantoms. To digress a bit, Moulton's scheme for beating the Devil (referred to by Whittier in his prose *Supernaturalism of New England* and familiar in the writer's boyhood as native legend) had Daniel Webster's exploit "beat all holler." Moulton sold his soul for a bootful of gold to be poured down the chimney—then cut the toe out of the boot. This made Satan so peevish that he blasted the farm (having looked down the chimney to see just what sort of fool he had been) and, when Moulton died, turned the old sinner into a big black stone, revealed when the pall-bearers couldn't lift the coffin.

Here is the climax of *The New Wife and the Old:*—

> In his arms the strong man folds her,
> Closer to his breast he holds her;
> Trembling limbs his own are meeting,
> And he feels her heart's quick beating;
> "Nay, my dearest, why this fear?"
> "Hush!" she saith, "the dead is here!"
>
> "Nay, a dream,—an idle dream."
> But before the lamp's pale gleam
> Tremblingly her hand she raises,—
> There no more the diamond blazes,
> Clasp of pearl, or ring of gold,—
> "Ah!" she sighs, "her hand was cold!"

Merely starting a fresh line of type seems scarcely an adequate bridge by which to travel from ghostly horrors to the gently reminiscent atmosphere of *Memories*. Nothing is to be found in the poet's earlier work with which this can be seriously compared. In the 1888 *Collected Poems* he classified it exactly by putting it at the head of *Poems Subjective and Reminiscent*—thus incidentally himself fixing the genesis period of his introspective versification.

Memories is clearly in the mood induced by Whittier's retirement to Amesbury after sickness had compelled him

to relinquish control of the *Pennsylvania Freeman*. It might
be described as the first of the bachelor reveries, designed to
include such other poems as *Maud Muller, In School Days,*
and *The Barefoot Boy*. The same inner light which urged
him on to greater accomplishment had already shown him
the solitary nature of his fate and he had accepted it with
Quaker humility—for the motives that unquakerized him
were never personal but always public injustices. This poem
is generally accepted as a tribute to Mary Emerson Smith,
the supposed sweetheart of his youthful days—long since
married and many times a mother—but it is clearly, for all
that, an abstract idealization. There is no reason why the
first two lines, appropriated from *Moll Pitcher*, his first long
published poem, should not have been composed with Mary
Smith very vividly in mind. Rereading those stanzas by some
chance may very well have induced the reminiscent mood
which produced this very gentle and sentimental glimpse
into the inner sanctum of Whittier's soul. The first, fourth,
sixth, and final stanzas express the sentiment:

> A beautiful and happy girl,
>   With step as light as summer air,
> And fresh young lip and brow of pearl,
> Shadowed by many a careless curl
>   Of unconfined and flowing hair;
> A seeming child in everything,
>   Save thoughtful brow, and ripening charms,
> As Nature wears the smile of Spring
>   When sinking into Summer's arms.
>
> I hear again thy low replies,
>   I feel thy arm within my own,
> And timidly again uprise
> The fringed lids of hazel eyes
>   With soft brown tresses overblown.
> Ah! memories of sweet summer eves,
>   Of moonlit wave and willowy way,
> Of stars and flowers and dewy leaves,
>   And smiles and tones more dear than they!

Years have passed on, and left their trace,
    Of graver care and deeper thought;
And unto me the calm, cold face
Of manhood, and to thee the grace
    Of woman's pensive beauty brought.
More wide, perchance, for blame than praise,
    The school-boy's humble name has flown;
Thine, in the green and quiet ways
    Of unobtrusive goodness known.

Thus, while at times before our eye
    The clouds about the present part,
And smiling through them, round us lies
The warm light of our morning sky,—
    The Indian Summer of the heart!
In secret sympathies of mind,
    In founts of feeling which retain
Their pure fresh flow, we yet may find
    Our early dreams not wholly vain!

At this point in his career, Whittier may be said to have tapped all the primary veins and strains of his genius, though the purer gold was yet to be mined. His character and temperament had also assumed permanent mold. Though the money revenue from his writings was pitiably small, he was nevertheless a figure of definite and growing importance as propagandist, politician, editor, and people's poet. He had made the publishing connection which was to endure to the end of his long life. Whittier's trust in Fields and, for that matter, Fields' trust in Whittier, must have been very great. Books which produced only a trifle for the author cannot have been seriously remunerative for the notably honest publisher who gave them to the world. As a matter of record, the association begun in 1843 produced no large profits until exactly twenty-three years later—but then the accumulative harvest was amazing to the publisher and simply dumbfounding to the author.

Apparently Whittier got nothing at all from the original publication of *Lays of My Home* and was even charged for his own copies. In a letter addressed to Fields in 1850 relative to a general money settlement as of that date (seven years after the publication of *Lays*), Whittier wrote:

"Like a lady's P.S. the most important matter of my letter comes last. By the acct. forwarded me I find some $60.56 due me. I am charged in that acct. with $8.20 in books which I had when the 'Lays of My Home' were published. As these books were all I recd from that publication I thought it might be suffered to pass. But I yield to yr judgment entirely. Would it be convenient to send me a check for the balance due?"

Here indeed is a paragraph to make the modern literary grumbler blush with shame.

Or was Whittier just an idiot to keep on writing?

25

WHITTIER REFORMS
HIS PROSE

In 1844 Whittier returned for a few months to the ranks of the regularly employed editors. He did this primarily to support the second presidential candidacy of Birney on the Liberty party ticket. Forsaking his own well-controlled bailiwick of North Essex, he determined to see whether he could not increase the anti-slavery vote in adjoining Middlesex County (Massachusetts) and assumed the editorship of a newly established Lowell paper—the *Middlesex Standard.* Officially he was editor of this paper from July 25, 1844, to March 13, 1845.

Lowell was then the most advertised milltown in the United States, and the months Whittier spent there supplied him with the foundations of the practical information he gradually accumulated concerning free factory workers, their wages, and their living conditions. If readers today are astounded that Whittier did not start an immediate crusade against women's working from twelve to fourteen hours a day for wages that provided little more than the bare necessities, and that he was favorably impressed by the order and cleanliness of factories which would now be rated as unsanitary and badly ventilated, they must remember the slavery endured by the average New England farm wife of those days, who worked just as hard and at the same time managed to bear at least one child every two years. At least the factory girls had all day Sunday to themselves, and they got actual cash money in some proportion to their working-hours—not just the farm wife's perquisites of eggs or other oddments to use for barter at the village store. In those days, nobody expected life to be easy, and the theory that the world owed every loafer a living had not been invented.

When Whittier undertook the editing of the *Standard*, it was probably without the faintest intention or expectation of any very long connection, and his term of intensive activity lasted only until the end of a political campaign in November had resulted in the election of Democratic, pro-slavery Polk, which implied the admission of pro-slavery Texas into the Union and made war with Mexico not a remote contingency but an immediate probability. Even before the election Whittier had persuaded C. L. Knapp of Montpelier, Vermont, to become his assistant editor, a position for which Knapp was well fitted since he had at one time been secretary of the Vermont Anti-Slavery Society and had edited the Montpelier *Voice of Freedom*.

In the November 7, 1844, issue of the *Standard*, Whittier and Knapp signed a joint announcement of Knapp's association with the undertaking, and thereafter Whittier spent comparatively little time actually in Lowell. During the previous four months Whittier had supplied the *Standard* with fifty editorials and articles commenting on public events from the abolitionist viewpoint. How much more of the paper he wrote or rewrote in the period—acting on the time-honored theory that the editor should be the largest contributor—can only be surmised. This much is certain—that in addition to all his political and routine work Whittier composed and published in the *Standard* during his official editorship fifteen of the eighteen highly literary essays and sketches later gathered into book form as *The Stranger in Lowell*. These articles were largely inspired by scenes and personalities he actually encountered in the miniature mill metropolis and the reflections they induced.

About the time that Whittier finally severed all connections with the *Standard* (March 13, 1845), this publication was consolidated with a Worcester paper and thereafter issued in both cities.

Though Whittier retired again to Amesbury, he had either been reinoculated with the editorial virus or else the crowding sensational events culminating in the Mexican War made silence unendurable for him—as they did for many other indignant Northerners who saw in the impending conflict nothing more than a bare-faced political war of aggression to take in new land which would increase the proportion of slave territory in the United States. It was this aspect of the situation, for instance, that led to the writing of Lowell's *Biglow Papers,* which still ranks as the greatest verse political satire since Butler's *Hudibras.*

In order to have at his disposal some vehicle for expressing his views, Whittier persuaded J. M. Pettingill, proprietor of the (Amesbury) *Village Transcript* to rename it the *Essex Transcript* and to make it the Essex County liberty organ. For about two years, Whittier was virtually the unpaid editor of the *Transcript,* and anti-slavery records even name him as assistant editor of that paper in 1846.

Pickard, in his official biography, gives the impression that Whittier's connection with the *Transcript* followed his work on the *Standard.* Currier makes the two connections overlap in 1844—which seems probably correct since both papers were electioneering for the same candidates—but concedes that even the endlessly prolific Whittier cannot have supplied much original copy for the *Transcript* until he called in Knapp to help on the *Standard.*

The unprofitable and worrisome connection with the *Essex Transcript*—which had the sole merit of furnishing him with an uncensored medium for printing his opinions—continued until Whittier became, on January 1, 1847, corresponding editor of the *National Era*—a connection which he maintained for many years, which he developed with consummate ability, and which provided him with a very modest but regular and assured income. After Whittier left, the proprietor of the *Transcript* sold the paper and it again became purely local, returning to the name of the *Village Transcript.*

The improvement in Whittier's versification between *Our*

Fellow Countrymen in Chains and *Massachusetts to Virginia* is no more marked than the development of style between his early prose (even the famous *Justice and Expediency*) and the charming flow of *The Stranger in Lowell*. The literary quality that came to his verse came simultaneously to his prose—but without the same degree of individuality or personality. The prose gained in grace and balance and adroit expression but became to a degree impersonalized. Almost any competent student could identify twenty lines of Whittier's collected verse even if he had never seen the specific poem before or heard of it or had reason to suspect the authorship. The personality of the poet reveals itself in outline treatment, in forms of Yankee speech, in reactions to subject matter, in rhythm and in rhyme. On the other hand, Whittier's literary prose, despite its very genuine appeal, might be almost impossible to identify if unsigned, apart from known themes and opinions. The conscious literary craft that only rounded off the rough edges of his verse, tended to conventionalize his prose. The best qualities of his literary essays, sketches, and criticisms are to be found rather in a certain sagacious combination of Yankee realism with idealist or even spiritualist longings than in word or phrase. At times he seems to be a more didactic Lamb or a less intellectual Emerson. His prose is far better than Longfellow's, but, as with Longfellow, his essential genius was one-sided and poetic—not the dual prose and poetry gifts of Holmes and Lowell.

The Stranger in Lowell, a volume of 156 pages, bound only in brown or light green printed paper wrappers, was published by Waite, Pierce & Co. of Boston in July, 1845. The second edition, so-called—which may or may not have been an actual second printing—carries the words "second edition" on the front cover, but the date remains the same.

The contents of *The Stranger* are eighteen essays, those printed in the *Standard* and three more, *The Yankee Zingali*, *The Farmer Poet*, and *The Training*. The first of these—one of the best character sketches Whittier ever wrote—deals with the exploits of a versatile and shameless Yankee beggar who appealed for alms year after year, always with a new story and a fresh disguise. *The Farmer Poet* extols the dialect verse and personal character of Robert Dinsmoor, "the Rustic Bard," in whose collected *Incidental Poems,* Whittier's own first verses between covers were printed. *The Training* is a reflective essay on the mistake of keeping the spirit of warlike aggression alive through the periodical training periods of the local militia. Fifteen of these eighteen articles were sufficiently esteemed by their author to be reprinted in certain of his various later prose collections.

From cover to cover *The Stranger in Lowell* may be read with pleasure, but it is not a book to stir the average reader. The most significant of the articles is probably *The Lighting* —in which the author alludes to the lighting up of the mills for night work during the period from autumn until spring. It is in this essay that Whittier expresses his feeling that a regular twelve-and-a-half-hour working day is an excessive schedule even though most of the women regard the work as a temporary special effort for high wages; explains the operation of *The Lowell Offering,* a paper entirely conducted by mill girls; and voices his contempt for people so un-American as to be surprised that mill girls have brains. Whittier's *Songs of Labor,* though they were not published in book form until 1850, began appearing periodically in 1845 and undoubtedly reflected his Lowell experiences. But the problem of improving conditions for white laborers was very secondary in Whittier's mind as compared with abolishing actual black slavery. His singleness of purpose, which prevented him from dissipating his force in various humanitarian projects, was an indispensable element in his success secret.

One of the working girls who edited *The Offering* and wrote poetry of unusual merit for its columns was a very smart, good-looking, and determined eighteen-year-old, by the name of Lucy Larcom. Since the death of her father when she was about ten, she had always had a hard row to hoe.

Her mother kept a local millhands' boarding house, and Lucy had gone to work in the mills when still really a child.

Whittier, now thirty-six, recognized the character, ability, courage, and talent in this girl of the people, just half his age. With criticism, advice, and such influence as he had, he helped her on the road to practical success. He took her to Amesbury and introduced her to his mother and his sister Elizabeth, who was charmed with her and quickly accepted her as her most intimate friend.

Miss Larcom was a brilliant woman and natural student. Before long she went West to live with a married sister, taught school there, and then went to school again herself, at a Female Seminary. After a time she returned East and for six years taught in Norton, Massachusetts, while also carrying on varied literary activities.

When *Our Young Folks* (the most important children's magazine of the period) was established in 1865, Lucy Larcom became the assistant editor. The following year she became the editor-in-chief and retained that position until 1874. She established the magazine in its foremost position, and it is to be noted that the most famous serial to appear in its columns, Aldrich's *The Story of a Bad Boy*, was printed during her editorship. In later years she was Whittier's working associate editor on various prose and verse compilations or anthologies which bore his name but for which she did most of the work.

After Elizabeth Whittier's death in 1864, it was Lucy Larcome who procured a fine portrait of her and had it hung in the Amesbury cottage, where it is still to be seen. Apart from his blood relatives, she was beyond doubt Whittier's most trusted and most intimate female friend for the longest term of years. In fact, she was the only person male or female ever taken by Whittier into literary partnership.

When Whittier died, leaving a property in excess of $100,-000, all accumulated after the Civil War, he left Miss Larcom only the royalties of the books they had edited together. This created some comment, and one contemporary remarked that Whittier had left her only the rights to her own books. But Miss Larcom never expressed any dissatisfaction or found any fault. She testified always to her undying gratitude, respect, admiration, and affection. Miss Larcom was not prosperous, but neither was she in any sense destitute.

Gossip about the relationship between Whittier and Lucy Larcom has always persisted, and the writer has heard it from bookdealers and antiquarians of Essex County. The opportunity, the kindred interests, and the mutual affection are all obvious. But there is not one scintilla of fact on which to base even the shadow of scandal. She certainly proved herself worthy of Whittier's confidence and assistance, she positively earned every cent that ever came to her through their joint work, and Whittier's endorsements of her individual writings were merited. The close friendship between Miss Larcom and Greenleaf and Elizabeth Whittier had been cemented for some twenty years at the time of Elizabeth's death, and Lucy had been accepted with open arms by Whittier's mother for more than a decade. That Whittier would have so deceived mother and sister, or that mother and sister could have been so deceived about any woman is preposterous; and when Elizabeth died Whittier was already fifty seven, and firmly entrenched in bachelor habits of life.

The *Poems* of Lucy Larcom, America's first working-girl poet, appeared in 1869 with this dedication: "To the memory of Elizabeth H. Whittier, this book is dedicated by one who owes its best suggestions to the inspiration of her friendship." And the publishers' "blurbs" were written by John G. Whittier.

The romance of Lucy Larcom and John G. Whittier—certainly any consummated romance—is purely a figment of less pure imaginations. The devoted friendship of these two was surely one of the finest things in both their lives.

Miss Larcom never married.

26

THE HAMMER RETURNS
TO THE ANVIL

Massachusetts to Virginia was not only a fresh bugle call
to the abolitionists but a prelude to what may be described
as the second series of anti-slavery poems, published between
1843 and 1850. The total for the seven years is some twenty-
five—three or four a year—most of them direct results of current events. Whittier had become astonishingly adept at
turning news into verse and at making the poems travel
faster and live longer than most of the news. And it may be
noted that there is something veritably uncanny about the
way in which the importance of each poem responds proportionately to the importance of the event which it celebrates. The authentic thrill which the poet felt translated
itself into commensurate expression.

The anti-slavery poems of this second group are far better
average verse than those of the earlier period, but it is difficult to decide whether the propaganda value is greater or
less. Something of the crude force of the earlier appeals is
missing. But these less melodramatic compositions may have
been better attuned to an audience that was steadily improving in intelligence, for the former rabble of anti-slavery adherents was fast becoming a disciplined army, numbering
many of the great names in literature, the pulpit, politics,
and business.

In 1844 Polk was elected president and in 1845 the Independent Republic of Texas, formerly part of Mexico, became
one of these United States. Texas was obviously by nature
destined to be a slave state, and her addition to the Union

as such was over the most violent protests of the champions of freedom. This event engendered two Whittier poems: *Texas* and *To Faneuil Hall,* based on a protest meeting in that historic edifice.

The Sentence of John L. Brown, first printed in 1844 in the *Haverhill Gazette,* and *The Branded Hand,* first published in the *Boston Morning Chronicle,* immortalize events that created profound sensations. John L. Brown (no relative of the Martyr) was condemned to death in South Carolina for helping a Negro woman to escape from slavery and marrying her. In response to appeals from practically the entire civilized world, this sentence was finally commuted to scourging and banishment. Though the modern world still condemns miscegenation, the idea of the death penalty being invoked for such a crime seems almost incredible. *The Branded Hand* belonged to Captain Jonathan Walker of Harwich, Massachusetts, who was imprisoned, heavily fined, and branded for attempting to carry fugitive slaves from Pensacola to the British West Indies. In this instance, the punishment was obviously well within the law, but the indignity of branding a free Northern citizen was considered outrageous. The letters burned into the palm of the Captain's hand were S.S., meaning Slave Stealer.

More strictly political are such poems as *To a Southern Statesman,* and the verses bearing this strange title, *A Letter Supposed to be Written by the Chairman of the Central Clique.* The first is a stinging rebuke to Calhoun for urging the admission into the Union of slave Texas while opposing the admission of free Oregon. *A Letter,* supposedly written by a New Hampshire Democrat, announces the defeat of the Democratic candidate and the election to the Senate of John P. Hale (1846), destined to become in later years the able associate of Charles Sumner in his senatorial abolitionist activities. This poem is odd rather than successful, for its keynote is a type of satire not harmonious with the forthright quality of Whittier's genius.

One of the distinctly better poems of this intermediate

anti-slavery group is *Randolph of Roanoke,* which first reached the public through the *National Era* immediately after Whittier became corresponding editor. The introductory note to this poem in the 1888 collected edition states that various lines indicate that the verses were written as early as 1833 (at the time of Randolph's death and the manumission of his slaves). This is also indicated by Pickard and apparently accepted by Currier. If this is so, then the present writer wishes to suggest that Whittier must have revised it and revised it thoroughly before printing it in the most important medium to which he had ever had access. No earlier text is offered in evidence—and Whittier certainly had no habit of keeping good anti-slavery poems on ice until the events they rehearsed were forgotten. If this was done in 1833 it was surely done over in 1846, for it is most positively in the later manner.

To Delaware (1847) was written while the legislature of Delaware was arguing an abolition bill which it did not enact; *Daniel Neall* and *The Lost Statesman* (Silas Wright) were both eulogies for abolition leaders recently deceased; *A Paean* hailed the revolt of the Van Buren men at the 1848 Democratic Convention which nominated Pierce; and *The Crisis* was penned on learning the terms that concluded the war with Mexico.

The *Lines on the Portrait of a Certain Publisher* did not appear in the *National Era* until April of 1850. But this poem belongs to the intermediate group, preceding *Ichabod* and *A Sabbath Scene,* published the same year and inaugurating the final phase of Whittier's anti-slavery verse campaign. The *Lines* is better sarcasm than *A Letter.* They compliment the anonymous publisher on excluding Grace Greenwood from his list of contributors because of her anti-slavery views and on widely advertising this fact to his Southern readers.

The Mexican War, following quickly on the heels of the annexation of Texas, was fought in 1846-1847, and so disgusted Whittier that for the moment he was disposed to support secession not of the South but of the North. It seemed to him and to many others that the Mexican War proved the intention of the Southerners to go to any wild extreme whatever to increase slave territory and grasp the balance of power. And it is true that triumphant Southern politicians boasted they would eventually make slavery legal throughout the length and breadth of the Union.

The fact that many people today think the vital mistake was not in fighting an unjust war but in failing to take over and pacify the whole of Mexico does not alter the fact that the war was manufactured to order for political reasons. The actual military incidents were highly creditable to the United States, for in all the pitched battles the American troops were greatly outnumbered by the Mexicans. The simple truth is that the old Indian fighters like Generals Taylor and Scott were very able commanders in charge of small forces of hardy frontier troops.

Few things in our history are more quaintly American than the treaty of peace with Mexico by which we paid her $15,000,000 for New Mexico and California, already in our possession by force of arms. The territory officially added to this country in 1848 was greater than the entire territory of the thirteen original states. The question of slavery or freedom for New Mexico and California became at once the overshadowing problem of the hour.

The World War is the only war in American history which definitely failed to produce a military president. The Mexican War produced two—Taylor, a regular army officer, in 1848; and Pierce, a volunteer general, in 1852. For the 1848 campaign the Liberty party and a Western group known as the Free Soilers combined under the second and more specific name. Though Van Buren, as the Free Soil presidential candidate, polled only a small vote, the party began to get practical results all the same by electing both Seward and Chase to the Senate.

General Taylor, destined to live only a few months in office, though a large plantation owner and slaveholder and father-in-law of Jefferson Davis, showed some of the same basic common sense and honesty that Harrison displayed before his equally premature and unfortunate demise. He surprised everybody by giving his unqualified support to the admission of California as a free state. These Indian and Mexican fighters, professional soldiers of the old school, had a certain hard-headedness as well as hard-fistedness. As Harrison was followed by his understudy, the weaker Tyler, so Taylor was succeeded by his vice-president, Millard Fillmore, a self-made prosperous attorney from New York State, who honestly believed with futile sincerity that all North-South difficulties could somehow be compromised and ironed out like conflicting damage claims in litigation.

In 1846, while the Mexican War was in progress, a collection of Whittier abolition verse appeared under the title of *Voices of Freedom*, published by a combination of three firms, including Waite, Pierce & Co., of Boston, who had published *The Stranger in Lowell*. This is a cloth-bound volume about 7½ by 4½ inches in size, and though dated 1846, apparently did not get into circulation until 1847. It contains twelve anti-slavery poems never before between covers, three of which had not previously been printed at all. The more important items have already been discussed. Though Whittier disclaimed responsibility for the publication—as he had done in the case of the 1837 *Poems Written during the Progress of the Abolition Question*—the poems show various corrections and alterations which make it impossible to take his statement too literally. Though published in Philadelphia, Boston, and New York, the volume was printed in Philadelphia and the plates of the 1838 *Poems* used as far as possible. The purpose of the book is manifestly propagandist, and it was doubtless put through the press by one of the old anti-slavery groups in Philadelphia with the private but without the official endorsement of the author.

The most singular feature of the *Voices of Freedom* is that the first printing is announced in the title as "Fourth and Complete Edition." Later there are fifth, sixth, and seventh editions from the same plates and with precisely the same

contents. It has been suggested with a good deal of plausi-
bility that fourth edition does not so much mean fourth edition of this title as fourth edition of the Whittier poems
—1837, 1838, and *Lays of My Home* (announced on the label
merely as *Poems*) being the three earlier ones. The general
appeal of the poems is proved by the successive printings.

In December of the year of the Mexican peace (1848) the
first illustrated and elaborately produced edition of Whittier's *Poems* was published by Benjamin B. Mussey & Co.
under the date of 1849. Whittier had then been installed
for two years as corresponding editor of the *National Era,*
had been enjoying a small but dependable income, had
greatly reinforced the foundations of his reputation, and evidently desired to begin a definitive editing of his poetical
works. Mussey, the publisher, was primarily a Boston book-
seller, but he was a Whittier enthusiast and an ardent Free
Soiler. The book contains eight or nine finely engraved plates
from originals by Hammatt Billings, a distinguished New
England artist and architect of the day, and a portrait engraved by Warren from a painting by Albert Gallatin Hoit
—not a favorite with the author. The volume has gilt edges
and is expensively bound in decorated cloth and leathers of
various colors. In short, it is a genuine old-time de luxe collected edition. It contains 106 poems, of which only the
Proem is first printing, and the beginning of Whittier's selective process is indicated by the omission of various poems
included in earlier volumes. Whittier received from Mussey
$500 outright and a royalty of 2½ per cent, which was ade-
quate according to the standards of the day and apparently
the first liberal treatment he had ever received at the hands
of a publisher. Mussey may well have been influenced by
Whittier's friends, Healy of Philadelphia and Harned of the
Anti-Slavery Reporter, who had both been complaining that
nothing suitable was in existence. In any event, the reprints
of Mussey's edition prove that he guessed right. The Ticknor
company did not specialize in de luxe editions of this character—though, as a matter of fact, Mussey didn't either—and

it is not surprising that another publisher should have sponsored the undertaking.

It seems strange that Whittier should never have commemorated in verse the most dramatic single personal incident of the dramatic year 1848, especially as the person concerned had been for years co-worker and friend—the death of John Quincy Adams. On February 21, present in the House as usual despite a recent paralytic shock, stern old Adams suddenly collapsed and almost expired on the spot. He lingered through Washington's birthday until the twenty-third, and then, unconscious, stepped quietly into the future. He ended his career on the twenty-first day, and during the fight on the Twenty-first Rule—the gag rule—he had struggled so heroically to defeat in his long fight for the right of every citizen to petition Congress and to be heard. Presumably even Whittier's well-trained Pegasus found himself earth-bound when called upon to poetize the Spartan virtues of an acidulous Adams. Such is the penalty of honor and high purpose without human friendliness. To this day, because he was somehow not picturesque even in the heat of solitary conflict against a host of enemies, John Quincy Adams is scarcely more than a name to the average American. A far greater man than his father, he is known mainly as his father's son.

In the *Proem* to the de luxe Mussey edition of his collected *Poems,* Whittier described his long concentration on anti-slavery verse and his conscious limitations, in these words:

> I love the old melodious lays
> Which softly melt the ages through,
>   The songs of Spenser's golden days,
>   Arcadian Sidney's silvery phrase,
> Sprinkling our noon of time with freshest morning dew.
>
>   Yet, vainly in my quiet hours
> To breathe their marvellous notes I try;
>   I feel them, as the leaves and flowers
>   In silence feel the dewy showers,
> And drink with glad still lips the blessing of the sky.

The rigor of a frozen clime,
The harshness of an untaught ear,
    The jarring words of one whose rhyme
    Beat often Labor's hurried time,
Or Duty's rugged march through storm and strife, are
        here.

    Of mystic beauty, dreamy grace,
No rounded art the lack supplies;
    Unskilled the subtle lines to trace,
    Or softer shades of Nature's face,
I view her common forms with unanointed eyes.

    Nor mine the seer-like power to show
The secrets of the heart and mind;
    To drop the plummet-line below
    Our common world of joy and woe,
A more intense despair or brighter hope to find.

    Yet here at least an earnest sense
Of human right and weal is shown;
    A hate of tyranny intense,
    And hearty in its vehemence,
As if my brother's pain and sorrow were my own.

    Oh Freedom! if to me belong
Nor mighty Milton's gift divine,
    Nor Marvel's wit and graceful song,
    Still with a love as deep and strong
As theirs, I lay, like them, my best gifts on thy shrine!

When Whittier wrote this apologia, he had almost attained
his fortieth year. In recent times he had written real poetry,
as has been shown, but the long process of development was
scarcely more than half complete. He had become a celebrity
literally in the process of growth. He had not yet written
a single one of the dozen poems by which he is most widely
known and which are most commonly quoted.

27

THE END OF LITERARY
PROSE EFFORTS

THE *National Era*, already mentioned as Whittier's most important and longest continued periodical connection, was a weekly publication of large newspaper size, established in Washington by the American and Foreign Anti-Slavery Society to combat the threat of augmented slavery influence and enlarged slave territory resulting from the Mexican War. Though the abolition movement had gained enormously in Northern respectability and in organization, it was not keeping pace with the increased pro-slavery power in either the national or the political sense. The paper was formally launched on January 1, 1847, while the Mexican War was in progress. The pro-slavery aquisition of Texas had been offset by the free state addition of Oregon—the huge slice of the Northwest having finally been divided with England to mutual satsifaction—but the problem of continuing this delicate balance of power was hazardous from every viewpoint.

Gamaliel Bailey, Jr., was announced as editor of the *National Era*, Amos A. Phelps and John G. Whittier, as corresponding editors. As a matter of policy, the Society never announced its ownership of the paper, except in its annual financial reports, where this could not be avoided.

Dr. Bailey was a good choice and an entirely obvious one. He had been editor of the Cincinnati *Philanthropist*, founded by Birney, who had been the Liberty party candidate for president in 1840 and 1844. Though the plant had been mobbed on three separate occasions, Dr. Bailey had developed the *Philanthropist* with indomitable courage and much ability. No better man could have been selected to establish an anti-slavery paper in the national capital, where the *National Era* was to be published, perhaps for the very reason that slaveholding was legal there and the slave traders were known to operate in a particularly corrupt manner. The *National Era* of Washington was a blast against slavery from a slaveowning city.

Amos A. Phelps, named as corresponding editor on the same basis as Whittier, was the active secretary of the American and Foreign Anti-Slavery Society and was doubtless appointed as liaison officer between organization and publication. When the paper began publication he was traveling in the West Indies for his health, and never recovered sufficiently to begin the task for which he had been selected. He died on July 29, 1847, and two weeks later his name was removed from the paper, leaving Bailey, in Washington, and Whittier, in Amesbury, as the sole responsible editors.

Bailey carried on the arduous detail of publishing this paper—the most authoritative, dignified, and important of the propaganda journals, well edited and with good literary non-propagandist features—until he was utterly exhausted. In June of 1859 he died while on his way to Europe in search of rest. The Society had transferred the ownership of the paper to Bailey as an individual at the beginning of 1848 (its second year) and he had therefore been the registered proprietor for eleven years. His widow naturally became the owner on his demise and she did her best to carry on; but she had to suspend publication on March 15, 1860.

As a matter of fact, the mission of the paper was ended. Secession was already in full swing and the final political battle had begun. Despite all official denials, the fundamental cause of the war was slavery, and from the outset it was obvious that the North could not compel the maintenance of the old Union without eradicating the root of evil. Thirty years of propaganda had culminated in action, and the fate of that action lay in the lap of the gods.

Even before the death of Bailey, Whittier had begun to

divide his literary contributions between the *National Era* and *The Atlantic Monthly,* founded in 1857 as a vehicle of expression for the great group of New England writers who were recognized masters of their craft but unwelcome in certain quarters because of their unanimous opposition to slavery. The editor—absolute literary head of the publication —was James Russell Lowell, an ardent anti-slavery advocate and the first of the Brahmins to recognize the full stature of the farmer-poet from Amesbury. It thus happened that when the *National Era* ceased to exist, Whittier was already established on a higher plane in *The Atlantic,* without any regular income, to be sure, but with the most appreciative of editors to encourage him in his work, ready to pay prices that seem ridiculously small now but were not too bad in those days.

Says Currier of Whittier's work on the *Era:* "During his connection with the paper Whittier had printed in its columns well over 100 original poems and 275 prose contributions, including editorials, reviews, literary essays and sketches, and the fictional productions, *Margaret Smith's Journal* and *My Summer with Dr. Singletery.*" This is supposed to be an understatement of the actual facts.

After the conclusion of his employment on the *Era,* Whittier discontinued writing literary prose except for an occasional political article, an introduction to a work by some fellow author, or a biographical memoir. As a matter of fact, the last year in which he produced prose in any great quantity was 1854, while the *Era* had still five years of life ahead. During those last five years, Currier lists only eight prose contributions.

No record seems to be available showing the exact compensation which Whittier received from the *Era,* but his wants were as small as the stipend, and the advantage of being able to work at home in his own persistent but intermittent manner was essential. Even at this comparatively early period Whittier had become a bad sleeper and an early riser. If not compelled to write too long at a stretch his output was prodigious without any harmful strain. Numerous friends and fellow workers have testified to his amazing speed and accuracy as a penman. Good, clean copy in purple ink was traced lightly over page after page with untiring, lightning rapidity.

Whatever Whittier's stipulated weekly salary may have been, it seems unlikely that this should have paid for poetry and fiction as well as the more strictly journalistic types of work. It seems reasonable that he should have had some additional compensation for purely literary work, when and if the paper could afford it. Whittier had surely reached a point where such work could have been sold elsewhere for definite amounts—as, indeed, he did sell poems to *The Atlantic*.

The very month that Whittier began his twelve-year engagement on the *Era*, he published a volume of prose as if to clear up unfinished business. This book, entitled *The Supernaturalism of New England*, appeared in paper-covered format very similar to *The Stranger in Lowell*. Wiley and Putnam of New York, a firm no less important than Ticknor in Boston, were the publishers. The articles in this volume, correctly described by the title, were expanded from a series of contributions which appeared an almost identical designation in the three autumn issues of the *United States Magazine and Democratic Review* for 1843. In addition to these sketches, *The New Wife and the Old* was quite properly reprinted and an extract from *The Bridal of Pennacook*, not previously published between covers, was included.

These tales of ancient and modern Yankee haunts and superstitions show Whittier in his very best prose vein, dealing with a subject which always tantalized him but which he always nevertheless subjected to the acid test of New England hard common sense and humor. The legends are genuine indigenous traditions and well worth preserving as folk-lore. Whittier was no such profound and meticulous student of New England witchcraft as either Drake or Upham, the two great contemporary scholarly authorities, but he was at least an ardent amateur and a charming narrator. In these articles,

Whittier is expatiating on his own particular hobby, and when he finds physical explanations for the phenomena one feels he is disappointed at having to confess the mundane truths. Ghosts, the Enemy (he of the cloven hoof), and all the invisible manifestations had a special allure for the mystic part of Whittier's Quaker mind. The little book is more than just good reading and, because of its material, is probably Whittier's most permanently valuable non-political prose.

Whittier's longest and most discussed literary composition in prose—the only sustained effort of short-novel length—was entitled *Leaves from Margaret Smith's Journal in the Province of Massachusetts Bay,* ran serially in the *Era* during 1848, and was published in regular cloth-bound book form by Ticknor, Reed and Fields of Boston in 1849. The first edition was anonymous, with no name of author on title or binding, but any man who could have seriously mistaken it for a genuine journal of the period would have been a blood-brother to that other man who apparently believed *The Song of the Vermonters* to be pre-Revolutionary. The fact that Whittier had no serious expectation of fooling informed readers and that the slight mystification he essayed was only whimsical is indicated by the editorial note with which he prefaced the work, stating that it contained passages indicative of comparatively recent origin. The original editorial note, heading the start of the *Era* serialization, had been less ingenuous —but if Whittier ever contemplated actual deception he thought better of it and merely indulged in a polite effort to create a receptive mood in the reader's mind.

The tragical thread of narrative which extends throughout *Margaret Smith's Journal* has historical foundation in fact. It concerns the deception of Elizabeth Rowson, daughter of the Secretary of the Bay Colony, by an English adventurer whom she finally marries and with whom she goes to London only to discover that he is a worthless bigamist without race or fortune. The narrator of the *Journal* is a young English woman, cousin of Mistress Rowson, on a visit to her relatives in the Bay Colony, whose brother marries a Quaker lass and settles in Rhode Island, where Roger Williams has established a colony enjoying actual religious freedom.

The narrative is graceful, the accounts of persons and places comparatively vivid, and adequate skill is displayed in interweaving the fictitious with the historical elements. But any attempt to dignify this work as a truly notable achievement is unfortunate because it merely tends to force on a pleasing little effort a degree of technical criticism which is unwarranted. This perfectly acceptable picture of early colonial New England had some moderate degree of commercial success—and every Whittier lover or man with an antiquarian brain-slant should peruse it carefully to see just how the poet reconstructed his story of past times so as to include his pet theme of Quaker persecution and to reflect his own philosophy.

In 1850 Ticknor, Reed and Fields issued in book form a little cloth-bound Whittier item entitled *Old Portraits and Modern Sketches,* devoted to essays on the works and personalities of John Bunyan, Thomas Ellwood, James Naylor, Andrew Marvell, John Roberts, Samuel Hopkins, Richard Baxter, William Leggett, Nathaniel Peabody Rogers, and Robert Dinsmoor. With the exception of *James Naylor,* which appeared in the *Democratic Review* for March, 1846, and *Robert Dinsmoor,* republished from *The Stranger in Lowell,* these essays had all appeared previously in the *Era.* They show Whittier at his studious best—and he was a sound natural scholar—as *The Supernaturalism of New England* shows him in his most quaintly human aspect. These essays explain clearly why it was entirely logical for Harvard College to give Whittier a degree and for Harvard University to elect as one of its overseers this Quaker who had never seen the inside of an institution of higher learning.

My Summer with Dr. Singletery first appeared in three January numbers of the *Era* for 1851 and two January issues of 1852. It was reprinted in 1854 as one of the thirty-five component parts of a volume entitled *Literary Recreations and Miscellanies,* issued by Ticknor and Fields. All but three of the articles were reprints either from the *Era* or *The Stranger in Lowell*—and those three were rewritten from articles in *Supernaturalism*. This was rehash, put before the public in new form to meet a moderate but steady and growing demand for anything bearing Whittier's name. The reader who wishes to survey briefly Whittier's literary prose as apart from his editorial, propagandist, and journalistic efforts can do no better than read this one volume, with its wide diversity of subjects, moods, objects, and treatment. The least degree of critical acumen will immediately distinguish both the good qualities—singularly negative for a man who wrote such smashing verse—and the limitations.

Though there were various future collections of Whittier's prose; though he wrote various prefaces, endorsements of other people's works, and occasional articles of many types; though he continued to print new gatherings of verse literally to the day of his death—for *At Sundown,* published two months after his death in 1892 had seven new poems—he never printed another volume of new prose material. In other words, practically all the literary prose written by Whittier which he considered worthy of book publication as such was composed well within the first half of his literary life.

So shrewd a self-critic was Whittier that he knew himself for precisely what he was—an excellent prose journalist and propagandist, a competent writer of literary prose, endowed with highly special talent, genius of its kind, only in composing verse. The proof is in the pudding. The period from 1847 to 1860, which produced so much good but merely good prose—a full two-thirds of it written in the first three years—produced verse about the major merit of which there can be no doubt whatever.

The first new volume of poems to follow the Mussey de luxe collected edition of 1848-1849 was *Songs of Labor and Other Poems,* issued by Ticknor, Reed and Fields in August of 1850, bound in various styles—boards, brown cloth, full gilt gift cloth and full leather. The seven *Songs of Labor* with which the volume begins are neutral—poems neither to make nor to mar an established reputation. *The Shoemakers*, since Whittier wrote from experience, is naturally enough the best of the group, all of them reprinted from the *Democratic Review* or the *Era*, with considerable emendations. The poet wrote a friend that he desired "to invest labor with some degree of beauty," but this purpose was too abstract to provide deep inspiration for Whittier's very concrete mind. Of the twenty-one miscellaneous poems which complete the volume, only five are from earlier volumes and sixteen are from the 1848-1850 issues of the *Era*. One of these, *Ichabod*, belongs in the list of the poet's most important works as being possibly the unchallenged nineteenth-century masterpiece of denunciatory verse, creating an impression so extreme that the author himself felt he had gone too far and tried to make reparation by writing *The Lost Occasion*.

Ichabod is really the opening gun of the third and final series of Whittier's anti-slavery poems and exemplifies the spirit which almost brought on the Civil War in 1850 instead of 1860. It was Whittier's response to Daniel Webster's historic speech of March 7, 1850, in the Senate, in which he bluntly demanded concessions from the North to preserve the Union.

Webster's own constituents, instead of appreciating the high purpose which led him to take the risk of such recommendations, regarded his act as an infamous betrayal of their true sentiments and accused him of helping renegades like the New Hampshire President, Pierce, to force the detested Fugitive Slave Law on the State of Massachusetts lock, stock, and barrel.

In these words, Whittier denounced Webster as turncoat and pariah.

ICHABOD!

So fallen! So lost! the light withdrawn
    Which once he wore!
The glory from his gray hairs gone
    Forevermore!

Revile him not—the Tempter hath
　　A snare for all;
And pitying tears, not scorn and wrath,
　　Befit his fall!

Oh! dumb be passion's stormy rage,
　　When he who might
Have lighted up and led his age,
　　Falls back in night.

Scorn! Would the angels laugh, to mark
　　A bright soul driven,
Fiend-goaded, down the endless dark,
　　From hope and heaven!

Let not the land, once proud of him,
　　Insult him now,
Nor brand with deeper shame his dim,
　　Dishonored brow.

But let its humbled sons, instead,
　　From sea to lake,
A long lament, as for the dead,
　　In sadness make

Of all we loved and honored, nought
　　Save power remains—
A fallen angel's pride of thought,
　　Still strong in chains.

All else is gone; from those great eyes
　　The soul has fled;
When faith is lost, when honor dies,
　　The man is dead!

Then, pay the reverence of old days
　　To his dead fame;
Walk backward, with averted gaze,
　　And hide the shame!

Webster's Seventh of March speech—made in the spirit of
an elder statesman who knows he will not much longer be

among those to steer the Ship of State—was the specific beginning of the crisis culminating on April 12, 1861. The reaction of Whittier—which was the reaction of almost the entire North—should have shown every thinking man, even then, that all hope of compromise had been extinguished.

Webster's death in 1852 brought a popular reaction toward a better understanding of the motives that had led him to urge compromise upon the North, and the ordeal of Civil War in the next decade showed all the horrors he had striven to avoid. Whittier's sense of justice would not let him leave *Ichabod* as his last word on Webster, and impelled him to compose and publish *The Lost Occasion,* which is not an apology for the earlier poem but which mourns the fact that Webster did not survive to prove his patriotism by sounding the trumpet call to arms against open rebellion.

These powerful lines contain the central thought:

> Thou shouldst have lived to feel below
> Thy feet Disunion's fierce upthrow,—
> The late-sprung mine that underlaid
> Thy sad concessions vainly made.
> Thou shouldst have seen from Sumter's wall
> The star-flag of the Union fall,
> And armed Rebellion pressing on
> The broken lines of Washington!
> No stronger voice than thine had then
> Called out the utmost might of men,
> To make the Union's charter free
> And strengthen law by liberty.
> How had that stern arbitrament
> To thy gray age youth's vigor lent,
> Shaming ambition's paltry prize
> Before thy disillusioned eyes;
> Breaking the spell about thee wound
> Like the green withes that Samson bound;
> Redeeming, in one effort grand,
> Thyself and thy imperilled land!

28

THE PULSATING
FIFTIES

THE YEAR 1850, except for compromises that ended by only aggravating basic contentions, might have divided the Republic into halves as it did the century. That year began the third decade of more and more conscious approach to the Civil War—one decade of propaganda, one of organization, and a third of front-line formations.

Despite their rivalries and opposed viewpoints, the three old men who had so long been America's legislative leaders—Calhoun, Clay, and Webster—were all survivals from the eighteenth century, men born at about the time Independent America was being born, and imbued to the bone with such a memory of those great events that even while they wrangled they almost superstitiously hesitated to undo the monumental achievement of their immediate forebears. Even that arch advocate of State Rights, including the right to secede, Calhoun, is now said to have had some curious plan for dividing the United States without really dividing it. The scheme seems to have been to create two countries with two presidents, but to bind the two countries together with an alliance so close that each president should have a veto on the acts of the other.

These mighty old timers, who have somehow become almost superhuman in retrospect, who all sought the presidency and all failed to obtain that highest honor because of the very force of their characters and convictions, had a certain respect for each other. They were not strictly personal enemies. Just as Thomas Jefferson and John Adams—political antagonists for two generations—when Death summoned them on the same Fourth of July, ended their lives asking for each other's welfare, these three giants of yore could joust within the rules of chivalry.

The younger men, soon to take over, had no roots so deeply imbedded in the past; gave full voice to younger and strictly partisan creeds; and made personal hatreds part of legislative procedures.

From 1848 to 1852 the roster of the dead in America's legislative halls was portentous. It has already been noted that John Quincy Adams—mediocre president but ever-glorious representative—died in 1848 almost literally with his boots on, the fatal stroke occurring while he was on the floor of the House. Calhoun, Clay, and Webster lived long enough to sponsor the futile 1850 compromises—Calhoun to help start the movement and the other two to see them enacted. Calhoun died in 1850, at sixty-eight years of age. His last senatorial appearance was made when he was so weak he could barely stand while a colleague read his speech. He was born in 1782, during the last days of the Revolution. Clay died in 1852, seventy-five years of age—born the year after the Declaration. Webster, who had retired from the Senate to join the Cabinet, died in 1852 at the age of seventy—born the same year as Calhoun. With the passing of Adams, Calhoun, Clay, and Webster the Ship of State came completely under the guidance of third-generation pilots.

These changes all directly concerned Whittier in his striving for abolition through political action, and his corresponding editorship of the *National Era* kept him in the closest possible contact with such events. In fact, Whittier's one political master-stroke was to be the designation and election of the successor to Webster's seat in the Senate—the physically and mentally commanding, the politically and ethically uncompromising Charles Sumner.

Millard Fillmore, elected as Taylor's vice-president in 1848, became president in July, 1850, following the death of the old General, and proved to be the first of three Northern chief executives—Fillmore, Pierce, and Buchanan—elected by Southern votes and deliberately used as tools by Southern politicians. By electing a manageable Northern man the Southern leaders could get a percentage of Northern votes that no Southerner could poll and thus, though sectionally a minority, maintain majority control.

Fillmore, self-made successful New York State lawyer, doubtless saw himself as a realist combating the abolition jingoes to maintain national solidarity. Pierce, of New Hampshire—charming but not of large caliber—was already a leading lawyer-politician when he refused a cabinet position under Polk, joined the army for the Mexican War (despite its unpopularity in New England), and rose to be an efficient brigadier general of volunteers, acquiring Southern contacts and viewpoints, including indifference to slavery as a moral issue. Buchanan was a Pennsylvania atttorney and senator, once Ambassador to St. Petersburg and once to London, who had been Polk's Secretary of State during the Mexican War and the acquisition of Texan, Mexican, and Oregon lands—an experienced man but in the hour of trial a weakling dominated by Southern influences.

In 1850 the South was in the saddle but felt the girth was not securely cinched. The pro-slavery advantages flowing from the Mexican War had been less than anticipated. The acquisition of slave Texas had been offset by the inclusion of free Oregon. The pro- or anti-slavery destinies of New Mexico and California remained to be decided, with California surely fated to be free.

The compromise measures, seriously intended to restore some degree of harmony between North and South, were introduced by Clay (border-liner by both birth and politics) as one document in eight sections soon broken down into a series of separate measures. Webster's Seventh of March Speech, urging restraint and moderation on the North, which caused him to be read out of the party in Whittier's furious *Ichabod* (already explained) and denounced by Theodore

Parker as another Benedict Arnold, was the highlight of the debate.

President Taylor, who took a surprisingly impartial and rather Northern view of the situation for a Southern plantation owner, opposed the idea of a new fugitive slave law, which was the essential sop to the South, absolute wormwood to the North. But Taylor died suddenly in July and Lawyer Fillmore was made of far different stuff than the grizzled Indian and Mexican veteran.

The upshot of much legislative jockeying was: the admission of a free California, giving the free states a majority in the Senate; the establishment of New Mexico and Utah as territories with no predetermination of the slavery issue; the abolishing of slavery in the District of Columbia—a decided Northern victory; and the enactment of a more stringent fugitive slave law—a definite Southern victory. Secession was openly discussed in various Southern states; and the North defied the fugitive slave legislation, which did not permit jury trial or allow the alleged slave to testify on his own behalf and which compelled any by-stander to aid the slave-hunter in capturing his prey.

From a strictly practical viewpoint, the North would seem to have won the bigger half of the trade. From an emotional viewpoint, most of the Northern people regarded the new fugitive slave regulations as a direct slap in the face. Imagine John Whittier or any of the thousands that shared his ideals forced to catch an escaping slave! Whittier felt that the wheel of Liberty had turned backward, not forward. All the New England states and some Western states passed personal liberty laws to protect free Negroes, and several specified jury trials for fugitives, in defiance of federal regulations.

Sensational incidents began to happen. A Negro named William Smith was shot dead by his pursuers in Columbia, Pennsylvania. William Parker and another fugitive, in Christiana, Pennsylvania, escaped after the other colored people in the neighborhood had staged a riot in which the master was killed, his son badly wounded and thirty-five people arrested (though none of them was finally convicted) by marines sent from Philadelphia by direct order of Fillmore. Thirty armed men from Kentucky assailed a Michigan community of escaped blacks at night and captured them, only to be captured themselves by an anti-slavery band of two hundred white men the following morning.

Very soon after the new enactment, a colored man by the name of Thomas Sims was apprehended as a fugitive in Boston. He was virtually kidnaped from state custody in the Court House by federal agents aided by city police during the night when the state authorities relaxed their vigilance.

Whittier had been in no position to interfere while Fillmore, Clay, and Webster tried to tinker the rifts in the Union. But even before the legislation was passed, he understood what the result was going to be, and on June 27, 1850, he published in the *National Era* the first and most notable item in his third series of out-and-out anti-slavery poems, entitled *A Sabbath Scene*.

No poem of popular appeal as vivid as this had come from Whittier's pen since *Our Countrymen in Chains*, sixteen years earlier. Of course it is better verse than the earlier exhortation and (perhaps unfortunately) the melodrama ballad of the Negro woman seized by slave-hunters in church during Sunday service is explained as a dream—but it represents Whittier gone back to righteous rabble-rousing just the same —Whittier back in the rôle of God's demagogue.

A Sabbath Scene was printed in broadside form and distributed by thousands; it was reprinted in all the anti-slavery journals and scores of other papers; it was issued in small single-leaflet form. Perhaps no other single Whittier item ever appeared in so many different formats designed to reach so many strata of society. The whole world knew it before it reached book form three years later—and even then it was printed again as a separate pamphlet in paper wrappers.

The end of this same year saw the first publication of

In the Evil Days, an attack on the same fugitive slave outrages, less popular but in more exalted vein:

> O, clear-eyed Faith, and Patience, thou
>   So calm and strong,
> Angels of God! be near to show
> His glorious future shining through
>   This night of wrong!

In May, 1851, appeared in the *Era* Whittier's *Moloch in State Street,* directly aimed at the already mentioned seizure or rendition of Sims. Recalling the shades of Boston's colonial tyrants the poet exclaims:

> Who, dimly beckoning, speed ye on
>   With mocking cheer?
> Lo! Spectral Andros, Hutchinson,
>   And Gage, are here!
>
> Ye make the ancient sacrifice
>   Of Man to Gain,
> Your traffic thrives, where Freedom dies,
>   Beneath the chain.

It will be seen that Whittier shared the popular conviction that the moneyed men of State Street (the Boston Wall Street) were responsible for the aid given federal authorities in recapturing Sims.

Though it is evident that Whittier felt as keenly as ever on the anti-slavery issue, he nevertheless had now become primarily a poet in the broader sense, responding only to special inspiration and no longer a versifying propagandist. This is shown indisputably by the fact that of eighteen poems which he published in the evil days of 1850 and 1851 only four were anti-slavery and only three were so classified by him. He allowed 1852 to pass without a single anti-slavery composition unless one insists on including *Eva,* his little poem about the angel-child of *Uncle Tom's Cabin,* first printed in the Amesbury *Villager* and then published as a song with music by Manuel Emilio.

A *Sabbath Scene* was so important in its day and is so individual in treatment that the gist of this singularly effective first-person vision must be recorded. The twelfth stanza with stanzas 14 to 18 will cover the ground. The pastor, having come down from his pulpit and being engaged in tying knots to secure the female slave for her lord and master who has pursued her into church, explains:

"Although," said he, "on Sabbath Day,
All secular occupations
Are deadly sins, we must fulfill
Our moral obligations":

Shriek rose on shriek,—the Sabbath air
Her wild cries tore asunder;
I listened, with hushed breath, to hear
God answering with his thunder!

All still!—The very altar's cloth
Had smothered down her shrieking,
And, dumb, she turned from face to face,
For human pity seeking!

I saw her dragged along the aisle,
Her shackles harshly clanking;
I heard the parson, over all,
The Lord devoutly thanking!

My brain took fire: "Is this," I cried,
"The end of prayer and preaching?
"Then down with pulpit, down with priest,
And give us Nature's teaching!

"Foul shame and scorn be on ye all
Who turn the good to evil,
And steal the Bible from the Lord,
To give it to the Devil!

29

WHITTIER DRAFTS SUMNER
FOR THE SENATE

ALMOST IMMEDIATELY after Fillmore became president through the death of Taylor in July, 1850, he asked Webster to join his Cabinet. The opprobrium being heaped on Webster at that time because of his Seventh of March Speech in favor of the compromise bills may have influenced him in giving his ready consent and resigning from the Senate. The Governor of Massachusetts appointed Robert C. Winthrop for the brief unexpired portion of Webster's term, but it was evident from the outset that this aristocratic conservative represented neither side of public opinion and that a senatorial election was in order. The gubernatorial election of 1850 for Massachusetts was therefore indirectly a senatorial election also, for the new legislature would choose the new senator.

This was an ideal localized situation for a practical politician—especially for that Amesbury poet-politician who carried tremendous authority with all voters opposed to slavery, who had just damned Webster with his searing *Ichabod*, and who was determined that Massachusetts should be represented in the National Senate by a dyed-in-the-wool-yard-wide-and-unshrinkable abolitionist. Hale of New Hampshire and Seward of New York had shown themselves to be unswerving anti-slavery legislators—in fact, Seward was the brains of Northern senate strategy from 1850 to 1860—but neither of them was the type of inspiring personality to be the Peerless Leader of whom Whittier dreamed.

Charles Sumner seemed to Whittier a man expressly created for this very emergency. He had the overwhelming personal presence, strikingly handsome and six-foot-four in his stockings; he had the most exalted social background, so that his leadership of any cause must make that cause good form among the rich and mighty of New England; he was a graduate of and an instructor in the Harvard Law School; he had all of the ethical theorist's disregard of obstacles or practical considerations; his rhetorical and rather florid style of eloquence was then much in favor; his anti-slavery convictions were boiling hot.

Sumner was four years younger than Whittier. Though they came from extremely unlike social backgrounds they were both old-time Yankee to the marrow; and though they were opposites in almost all characteristics and experiences they shared a ruling passion with mutual respect. Their first meeting, it will be remembered, was in the office of the *American Manufacturer,* when the young poet was working at his first editorial position and Sumner came in with his father, Sheriff Sumner, relative to a printing job. There is nothing to show that they had become special intimates during the intervening years, but it is evident that their acquaintance had reached the stage of very plain-speaking friendship.

For many years after leaving Harvard, despite the advantage of extensive study abroad after being admitted to the Massachusetts bar at only twenty-three, Charles Sumner had failed to attain the success his position and talents seemed to foreshadow. His career as an attorney had not been brilliant and his attention had been largely concentrated on his Harvard Law School lectures. In 1845, however, he delivered a Fourth of July Oration entitled *The True Grandeur of Nations,* a plea for freedom and peace obviously directed against the pending Mexican War, which led to immediate sensational success as a lyceum speaker. Whittier's first recorded letter to Sumner is his note of congratulation on this speech.

In 1846 Sumner had increased his reputation by defending

an anti-slavery resolution rejected in a Faneuil Hall Whig Convention; and this had inspired Whittier's little known but vigorous anti-slavery poem, *The Pine Tree*, the manuscript of which Whittier sent to Sumner with a letter telling him to publish it if he wished. In 1847 Sumner had stirred wide popular enthusiasm by public denunciations of the Mexican War, which Whittier also detested; and in 1848 he had been an unsuccessful congressional candidate for the combined Liberty and Free Soil parties. By 1850 he had become good political timber for any Bay State office.

Before explaining how Whittier and fate elected Sumner to the Senate, one faces the question of how far Whittier was or could have been actually responsible for selecting Sumner as a candidate. Certainly there was no doubt in Whittier's own mind about the part he played in the matter. In his verses addressed to Sumner, published in 1854, he says explicitly:

> Thou knowest my heart, dear friend, and well canst guess
> That, even though silent, I have not the less
> Rejoiced to see thy actual life agree
> With the large future which I shaped for thee,
> When, years ago, beside the summer sea,
> White in the moon, we saw the long waves fall, ...

As Pickard points out, these verses refer specifically to a visit which Whittier paid Sumner at Phillips Beach, Swampscott, in the summer of 1850, when he first persuaded Sumner to become a candidate for the Senate.

No matter how many other people may have recognized the notable qualifications of Sumner for the contested senatorial seat, Whittier was the one who translated the idea into action; who first asked him to run; who overcame his reluctance by persuasion; who was able, through political leadership and management, to insist on his nomination and to overcome the honest prejudice against him, on the part of many people, as too extreme.

When Marshal Joffre was questioned as to his right to claim

responsibility for the success of the Battle of the Marne he replied only that he was perfectly sure who would have been held responsible if the battle had been lost. In the same way, whoever got Sumner into office, Whittier would have been held responsible had he failed of election, as he so nearly did.

Whittier was no idealist in practical political trading. In 1850, as the overshadowing influence of the Free-Soil-Liberty party in Massachusetts, Whittier combined his third party with the Democrats as result of a deal by which, if the Democratic candidate for governor won, the Democrats were to choose Sumner as senator and assign various Free Soilers to other positions. As planned, this combination elected George S. Boutwell governor over the Whig opposition, but, once in office, Boutwell made an inaugural address offensive to the Free Soilers and some of Boutwell's followers repudiated their pledges to vote for Sumner. This was not surprising, for the Democrats were basically far stranger political bedfellows for the Free Soilers than the Whigs would have been.

The Whig senatorial candidate was the ex-speaker of the National House of Representatives, Robert C. Winthrop, now temporary senator, whom they wished to continue in office. The group of Democrats opposed to Sumner were under the leadership of Caleb Cushing, once Whittier's first political protégé and then, because of backsliding on the anti-slavery question, prevented by Whittier, through the printing of old anti-slavery pledges, from becoming Tyler's Secretary of the Treasury—but now, despite Whittier's opposition, a man of high authority in national politics. Thus Sumner had lined up against him the most reputable conservative elements in New England.

When Sumner failed of election on the initial ballot, Whittier's characteristic first impulse was to accept defeat, but as ballot after ballot was taken without any choice his old instinct for hanging on asserted itself. Correspondence shows that by March of 1851 Whittier began to sense that he held a winning hand and was urging Sumner to hold fast. At that time Sumner went to Amesbury to consult Whittier, for Whittier was having a more than usually severe bad spell.

At just this juncture, as if decreed by Divine Providence, came the rendition of the fugitive slave Thomas Sims in Boston—already referred to in connection with Whittier's *Moloch in State Street*—and this created a fresh wave of popular indignation against the new slavery enforcement laws. A vote for Sumner was a vote for abolition and the moderates of the legislature of Massachusetts yielded just enough under pressure of this excitement to save the day for Freedom. On the twenty-sixth ballot, taken on April 24, 1851, Sumner, by a margin of one vote, was elected to the senatorial seat which he filled until his death twenty-three years later.

Sumner's irreconcilable and intransigent anti-slavery attitude was so well understood that there was literally a conspiracy in the Senate to evade any debate that would give him a chance to let loose a flood of oratory tending to swamp all possibilities of compromise for the future. When, after months of delay, he did get his chance, the whole pro-slavery world got an object lesson in the vital truth that no current is as swift as that from a bursting dam. His speech, declaring freedom to be national and slavery sectional, left no more middle ground as an asylum for wary politicians than Whittier's old *Justice and Expediency* had done. It was an 1852 pronunciamento after Whittier's own heart and according to his fondest dreams. The Fugitive Slave had become a dark giant on the skyline of America.

The designation and election of Sumner constitutes the climax of Whittier's achievement in politics. Though he did his formal share in the Republican campaigns of 1856, though he was a Lincoln elector in both 1860 and 1864, he seems gradually to have lost contact with the threads of political alliances and the less obvious trends of professional political opinion. His nearest approach in later years to taking sides actively in favor of an individual was in behalf of John C. Frémont, as against Lincoln for the Republican nomination in 1860. As a matter of fact, Whittier was a Frémont partisan from the time of Frémont's selection as the first Republican candidate in 1856 and, during the Civil War, defended him in stirring verse from Lincoln's entirely just censure, when, as a Union general, he tried prematurely to emancipate the slaves in his department by military order.

It is not too difficult to understand how the romance of Frémont's career as explorer and flag-waver should have appealed to all Whittier's instincts for the picturesque and dramatic in contrast with the somewhat crude and very homespun patience, humor, and tolerance of Abraham Lincoln. Whittier had himself been a sort of silent Lincoln in his carefully astute and persistent manipulating of political problems and trades. But, by those same tokens, Whittier would never have chosen himself or his double for the forefront of the battle at Armageddon.

The political prestige which Whittier enjoyed immediately after the Sumner victory is clearly displayed in a letter which he wrote the new Senator in December, 1851, dealing with the type of address to be made by Kossuth, the Polish hero, then seeking aid in America. Kossuth, not wishing any domestic prejudices to interfere with his own special cause, had explicitly denied any desire to meddle with American conditions, in terms so very definite that he seemed almost to approve of everything, slavery included. This matter being much on Whittier's mind, he wrote Sumner:

"On thy way to Washington, pray see W. C. Bryant, Seward and some other leading men—Greeley, for instance—and caution them to see to it that the 'Union Savers' do not thrust their notions upon Kossuth, and call out from him speeches of the Castle Garden Stamp. Naturally he would deprecate a dissolution of this Union—but he ought to understand that it is not in the slightest jeopardy—that the solicitude of the 'Union Savers' is all for political effect. I wish he could have half an hour's talk with Benton. I do not wish him to be mixed up in any way with our domestic matters."

John G. Whittier would never have written such a letter

of instructions to Charles Sumner on a matter of essential policy, stating his explicit wish as such, unless he felt sure, and Sumner acknowledged, that he had a perfect right to do so.

30

THUNDERHEADS
OF WAR

FROM 1852 to 1860 war clouds gathered North and South and the first actual blood storm burst in Kansas. At the beginning of all this turmoil stand two events—the election of Sumner to the Senate and the publication of Harriet Beecher Stowe's *Uncle Tom's Cabin* in Boston in 1852, after serial publication in the *National Era*. The installation of Sumner was New England's political reply to the compromises of 1850 and Mrs. Stowe's story was a literary onslaught that reëchoed throughout the civilized world. This period was to end with the election of Abraham Lincoln as president of the United States.

Just what influence, if any, Whittier had in arranging the serial publication of *Uncle Tom* in the *Era* is uncertain. At the time, Professor Stowe and his wife were living in Brunswick, Maine. They had moved there from Cincinnati in 1850, when the Professor accepted a position at Bowdoin College. Though born in Connecticut, Mrs. Stowe had moved to Cincinnati when her father, Lyman Beecher, became president of Lane Theological Seminary in that city, having been called West from a pastorate in Boston. She had lived in Cincinnati for eighteen years, and there she had married Calvin Stowe, then a professor at Lane.

By temperament and by family connection an ardent abolitionist, Mrs. Stowe must have been well acquainted with Birney, founder of the Cincinnati anti-slavery *Philanthropist*, and with Bailey, its editor, who later had become chief editor and owner of the *National Era*. Pickard makes no mention of any early acquaintance between Whittier and Mrs. Stowe —though they were fast friends in later years—and thus it seems probable that, even though she was living in New England, her more direct contact was with her old Cincinnati friend, Bailey. At the same time, it seems utterly improbable that a serialization of such importance would have been arranged entirely without Whittier's knowledge and endorsement. As a matter of fact, the novel was largely written during serial publication and there was never a complete advance manuscript for anybody to pass upon.

Though Mrs. Stowe had previously published two volumes of sketches and a school textbook, she had done nothing whatever to indicate her capacity to write this two-volume perfervid melodramatic and sentimental novel. However, it must have been all bottled up inside. She was a mature thirty-nine years of age when she undertook the task, and almost half of those thirty-nine years had been spent in free Cincinnati just across the Ohio River from slave-holding Kentucky, with the problem of Negro serfdom in every form under closest observation. Her *Key to Uncle Tom's Cabin*, published after the book to vindicate her picture of slave conditions, shows what a mass of evidence on the subject she had accumulated.

The year 1852 was an election year—the first time the people had a chance to express by the choice of a president their reaction to the 1850 compromises. On the surface that reaction was surprisingly favorable, taking the country as a whole; for the Northern Democrat, Pierce of New Hampshire, achieved one of the greatest victories in history. He defeated his old Mexican War commander, Whig Winfield Scott, by 254 electoral votes to only 42. John P. Hale, also of New Hampshire, running on the Free Soil ticket, received fewer votes than Van Buren in 1848. Courtly, brave, well-meaning but utterly unfit, Pierce was practically chosen by popular acclaim—to the North he was a favorite son; to the South, a Mexican War general who had no foolishly Northern ideas.

At this point it becomes difficult to summarize as much American history as legitimately concerns Whittier without covering it all. Though Whittier was now playing politics only in an advisory capacity, he was still writing editorials for the *Era* and had become a sort of unofficial poet-laureate for celebrating major events, which somehow always seemed to include the slavery issue.

The first result of the Pierce election was to make it self-evident that the elements opposed to the Democratic party, which was becoming ever more deeply involved in pro-slavery toils, must form a new coalition which should be primarily in favor of emancipation or, at least, opposed to any further spread of slave territory. In 1854 the Whigs, Know-Nothings, Free Soilers, and anti-slavery Democrats finally united to form the Republican party, with Whittier's entire approval.

In January of 1854, Stephen A. Douglas of Illinois introduced into Congress one of the most pernicious bills ever conceived by an upright and able man in good faith. This so-called Kansas-Nebraska bill, on the theory that it was merely extending the idea sponsored by Congress when the territories of New Mexico and Utah were organized with no commitment regarding slavery, undertook to make territories of Kansas and Nebraska while leaving the settlers themselves to decide for or against slavery by local option, thus automatically canceling the last vestiges of the old Missouri Compromise, which had drawn a slavery boundary between North and South across the country. The bill passed readily in the Senate but was enacted by the House only after a prolonged struggle and by a small majority.

In this same year 1854, a fresh fugitive slave incident of the most obnoxious type occurred in Boston and raised Yankee tempers to white heat. One Anthony Burns, a former slave, had escaped to Boston and was earning his livelihood as a waiter in a local hotel. His arrest caused a furore, result-

ing in a Faneuil Hall meeting addressed by both Wendell
Phillips and Theodore Parker. A crowd of determined men
left the meeting to rescue Burns from the Court House where
he was confined, only to find that another rescue band, led by
Thomas Wentworth Higginson, was already battering at
the doors. The Mayor called out troops, who dispersed the
mob after killing one man and making several arrests. There
was no further violence, but when, shortly afterwards, Burns
was led through the streets back to bondage, more than fifty
thousand booing citizens lined the sidewalks. And to cap
the climax, Theodore Parker, one of America's foremost
clergymen, was indicted for his share in the disturbance. The
fact that the abolitionists bought Burns from his owner did
not alter the hatred of Massachusetts for slave-catchers; and
of course this was ideal subject matter for effective Whittier
poems.

But this excitement in Boston was just parlor charades
compared to the situation in Kansas. Pierce's signature had
scarcely dried on Douglas's Kansas-Nebraska monstrosity
when the territory of Kansas became an actual battle-ground
for pro-slavery settlers from Missouri and anti-slavery settlers
from the North. Each side wanted to be the dominant faction
when the time should come to vote on a constitution for the
state, with slavery provisions.

The Southern faction was rough and tough and, for the
most part, consisted rather of marauders than genuine settlers. From the North came real Yankee farmers, encouraged
by abolitionist leaders like Whittier and subsidized by emi-
grant aid societies. Lawrence, Kansas, was named in honor
of the Lawrences of Lawrence, Massachusetts, two millionaire brothers who aided the movement. And in the Northern
ranks there was a belligerent element, ready to fight at the
drop of a hat. John Brown of Ossawatomie—later to be the
insane but haloed martyr of Harpers Ferry—and his brawny
sons stood ready to meet all comers.

This is no place to retell the detailed history of the Kansas
crisis. After two governors had resigned, the Southern fac-

tion, though a clear minority, put through by obvious fraud the pro-slavery Lecompton Constitution, which was most scandalously endorsed by Pierce's successor, Buchanan. Douglas himself, author of the Kansas-Nebraska bill, proved himself to be as honest and fearless a politician as ever lived by defeating the Lecompton Constitution in Congress despite everything Buchanan could do. Kansas ultimately had an honest vote and became a free state not because Stephen A. Douglas was an abolitionist or a friend of abolition but because he would not tolerate fraud in any form.

While the Kansas war—for war it really was—progressed, violence had even invaded the floor of the Senate. In 1856, two days after his vehement speech, *The Crime Against Kansas*, Charles Sumner, while seated in the Senate chamber and unable to defend himself, was brutally and almost fatally beaten on the head by Congressman Preston S. Brooks. The injury was so serious that Sumner was incapacitated for almost four years, and during all this time Massachusetts refused to elect anybody in his place. Sumner's empty seat was a silent speech that could be heard every day and all day long.

The election of 1856 was the first to see a Republican candidate in the field. The new party made the mistake of selecting a widely advertised candidate obviously not suited for the position and with no serious experience in governmental matters—Frémont, the explorer of the Far West. Whittier endorsed Frémont enthusiastically, apparently fascinated by his dramatic career. It is also possible that he was influenced by the fact that Frémont was the son-in-law of Senator Benton of Missouri—the one stalwart unionist and abolitionist from his section of the country.

The Democratic candidate was ex-Secretary of State, ex-Ambassador, Philadelphia lawyer Buchanan. The campaign was carried on along realistic lines. Charges were brought against Frémont of improper use of funds while in charge of Californian affairs, and were never entirely disproved. The electorate as a whole was not unreasonably afraid of the romantic, inexperienced explorer—and Buchanan became president through Southern influence. This Democratic victory was through no fault of Whittier. He had written four election poems and had done his utmost. In fact, Massachusetts went Republican. Whittier was not discouraged by Frémont's defeat and looked forward confidently to the next election ahead.

On March 6, 1857, just two days after Buchanan came into office, Chief Justice Taney announced the Supreme Court decision on all aspects of the first fugitive slave case which had ever reached the ultimate tribunal—the Dred Scott case, which had been in the courts since 1855. Taney——absolutely honest but a deeply prejudiced Southerner—declared: (1) that Scott must return to slavery; (2) that the Missouri Compromise was indeed null and void; (3) that neither Congress nor any territorial legislature could impose restrictions on slavery in any territory; (4) that Congress had no right to grant citizenship to slaves or the descendants of slaves.

The effect of this decision—which exceeded, in every direction, the limits of the case in hand and which was based on manifestly false premises—was absolutely to infuriate the North. Pickard points out that even Whittier came at last to doubt the possibility of peaceful adjustment.

The Whittier current-events poetry of this stirring period is partly anti-slavery and partly campaign. Among the more important items in the anti-slavery category are: *The Kansas Emigrants,* in the *National Era,* July 21, 1854; *The Rendition,* referring directly to the Anthony Burns affair, in the *National Era,* July 29, 1854; *For Righteousness' Sake,* referring to the arrest of Theodore Parker and others for agitating against the recapture of Burns, in the *National Era,* February 8, 1855; *Burial of Barber,* on the death of a Free Soil man shot near Lawrence, Kansas, in the *National Era,* March 20, 1856; and *Le Marais du Cygne,* a tense poem on the massacre of a group of unarmed Northern men by Southerners at this point in Kansas, first published in *The Atlantic Monthly,* September, 1858.

The Frémont campaign poems were: *The Pass of the Sierras*, in the *National Era*, July 17, 1856; *A Song for the Times*, in the *Amesbury Villager*, September 11, 1856; *What of the Day?* in the *National Era*, September 4, 1856; *A Song Inscribed to the Frémont Clubs*, in the *National Era*, November 20, 1856. Also, the long poem entitled *The Panorama*, read by Thomas Starr King at the opening of his 1856 series of Boston anti-slavery lectures, was really a campaign document.

In the definitive 1888 edition, some of the classifications at this point become confusing. *On a Prayer Book*, first printed in the New York *Independent* for September 11, 1859, and *The Summons*, first published in the October, 1860, *Atlantic*, are placed among the anti-slavery poems. *On a Prayer Book* concerns a Southern edition of the prayer book which omitted the figure of a Negro from the picture, Christ the Consoler; and *The Summons* is a poem of self-revelation in which Whittier laments that his age prevents his more active participation in the battles of the Lord. On the other hand, the stirring abolitionist poem *Brown of Ossawatomie* (*Independent*, December 22, 1859) is collected under *Personal Poems;* as is also *To Charles Sumner*, printed in the *National Era* for December 7, 1854.

The final John Brown episode, beginning with Brown's capture of the Arsenal at Harpers Ferry on October 17, 1859, needs no repetition here. Brown's fantastic idea of some hill-protected independent republic as a refuge for slaves was clearly the creation of an unbalanced mind; and the abolition enthusiasts who helped finance his undertakings—like Gerrit Smith of New York and Theodore Parker of Boston—probably never really understood what he planned. Whittier's viewpoint is well expressed in one stanza of *Brown of Ossawatomie,* which reads:

> Perish with him the folly that seeks through evil good!
> Long live the generous purpose unstained with human
>   blood!

Not the raid of midnight terror, but the thought which
        underlies;
Not the borderer's pride of daring, but the Christian's
        sacrifice.

The Rendition and *Le Marais du Cygne* are both powerful
poems, but the most justly famous of this group is *The Kansas
Emigrants*—not written at Whittier's peak of righteous indignation but a fine, simple, marching song actually sung
by thousands of men and women to the tune of *Auld Lang
Syne*. Whittier is said to have sent the song to the first company of Free Soil emigrants bound for Kansas.

> We cross the prairie as of old
>   The pilgrims crossed the sea,
> And make the West, as they the East,
>   The homestead of the free!
>
> We go to rear a wall of men
>   On Freedom's southern line,
> And plant beside the cotton-tree
>   The rugged Northern pine!
>
> We're flowing from our native hills
>   As our free rivers flow;
> The blessing of our Mother-land
>   Is on us as we go.
>
> We go to plant her common schools
>   On distant prairie swells,
> And give the Sabbaths of the wild
>   The music of her bells.
>
> Upbearing, like the Ark of old,
>   The Bible in our van,
> We go to test the truth of God
>   Against the fraud of man.
>
> No pause, nor rest, save where the streams
>   That feed the Kansas run,
> Save where our pilgrim gonfalon
>   Shall flout the setting sun!

We'll tread the prairie as of old
  Our fathers sailed the sea,
And make the West, as they the East,
  The homestead of the free!

The Frémont campaign poem, *What of the Day?* is important because it shows how clearly Whittier recognized the approaching test of strength between "Good and Evil," and that he was not entirely reluctant to have the matter over with:

I fain would thank Thee that my mortal life
  Has reached the hour, (albeit through care and pain)
When Good and Evil, as for final strife,
  Close dim and vast on Armageddon's plain;
And Michael and his angels once again
  Drive howling back the Spirits of the Night.
Oh! for the faith to read the signs aright
And, from the angle of Thy perfect sight
  See Truth's white banner floating on before;
  And the Good Cause, despite of venal friends,
  And base expedients, move to noble ends.

31

WHITTIER EMANCIPATES
HIS OWN INSPIRATION

IN THE YEARS FROM 1852 to 1859, those eventful years of prelude to the Civil War, Whittier's personality and poetical inspiration finally attained long delayed full maturity. It seems almost as if the election to the Senate of Charles Sumner—Whittier's ideal of a knight in shining armor to overthrow slavery—had lifted a certain weight from his own shoulders and given him freedom to envisage the world at large as well as the one burning problem of Negro enslavement.

Whereas in earlier crises, his periodical verse publications had become almost entirely political or ethical anti-slavery productions, such compositions, though the impending climax was obviously closer than ever and more catastrophic in magnitude, were now only a minor part of his literary achievement. No longer devoting hours and days and weeks to the composition of secondary prose, he concentrated his endeavor to write verse that might challenge comparison with the best then being done by his contemporaries and produced surprising results.

It must also be noted that this revision of effort and attitude followed another serious illness in 1850-1851. Less has been said about this sickness than about the collapses of the early thirties and forties because he was not forced actually to surrender any active editorial position, to move from one city to another, or to change his mode of life. But his correspondence with personal friends shows definitely that at

244

one time he almost despaired of recovery—and there is now no means of ascertaining how far this apprehension was justified and how far it was purely neurotic. On the one hand, he continued his writing for the *National Era,* which, however, was done under the most flexible home conditions; on the other hand, he made Sumner come to see him in Amesbury at a time when he would naturally have liked to visit the center of activities in Boston. That each successive specific illness made Whittier more cautious in the matter of subjecting himself to strenuous excitement and over-exertion is not to be denied.

The year of the Dred Scott decision Whittier's life reached the half-century mark and *The Summons* shows clearly that he already regarded himself as an old man. In his peculiar case, that mental attitude, tending to induce moods of reminiscence, was a poetical advantage in fostering a type of inspiration ideally suited to his somewhat quaint and uncomplex habits of speech, rhyme, and meter. He began to see the earlier days of his own life in something of the same glowing retrospect which glorified for him the legends and stories of early New England.

Whittier's periodical publications between 1850 and 1859 —collected into various first-edition volumes—include many of his most characteristic and celebrated poems. According to the wonderfully accurate Currier, the total number for this period, by actual count, is 102. Even embracing borderline poems like the very good *Kossuth,* only twenty-two of these —scarcely more than one-fifth—can honestly be rated as either anti-slavery or political, despite the poet's enthusiasm for Frémont, which, in previous periods of his work, would have produced a veritable flood of tributes in one form or another. And of these only two—as already shown—*Le Marais du Cygne* and *The Kansas Emigrants,* represent the best of the species.

From being, over the space of many years, first propagandist and then poet, Whittier had unconsciously become first poet and then propagandist only when roused by events of deep significance. In a word, Whittier had finally emancipated his poetical inspiration from the slavery of antislavery.

During this period five major collections of verse appeared in book form: *Songs of Labor* (1850), already discussed and secondary; *The Chapel of the Hermits* (1853), of some distinction; *The Panorama* (1856), which contains three of the Whittier masterpieces; The Blue and Gold edition of the *Poetical Works* (1857), adding thirteen items of little consequence; and *Home Ballads* (1860), which really belongs to this period because it contains only four poems that were not first printed before the end of 1859 and which, it has always seemed to this writer, contains more fine, brief verse than any other one Whittier first edition, though only one of the thirty-six items is frequently quoted. In range, maturity, variety, and high average excellence *Home Ballads* stands apart—the achievement of a full-fledged poet who has arrived at breadth of vision as well as simplicity, intensity, sympathy, and a wealth of local color.

Interspersed among these five volumes are various leaflets and pamphlets and broadsides, most of them mere curios for exhaustive Whittier connoisseur collections. Among the few essentials are the four-page leaflet, *Lays of the Emigrants* (1854), which is the first other than periodical printing of the *Kanzas [sic] Emigrants*, to be sung to the music of *Auld Lang Syne; The Campaign* (1856), two Frémont songs set to music; and *The Sycamores*, a charming personal and historical poem privately printed in Hartford in 1857 (only nine pages in blue wrappers), which is almost fabulously rare.

The Chapel of the Hermits, as so often seems to be the case with Whittier volumes, takes its title from the longest and least interesting item in the group. It consists of 118 pages of text, is bound in chocolate cloth, and was published by Ticknor, Reed and Fields of Boston in February of 1853. It contains twenty-six poems, of which Whittier retained twenty-five in all future gatherings. *A Sabbath Scene* (already quoted); *Kossuth,* a personal poem with anti-slavery trimmings; and *To My Old Schoolmaster*, a reminiscent poem, are clearly the best it has to offer.

To My Old Schoolmaster is in honor of Joshua Coffin, who taught Whittier in district school, who gave him that first fateful volume of Burns, who was one of the twelve founders of New England's first anti-slavery society, who became a noted historian-antiquarian, and who was one of the poet's lifelong friends. Too long, it yet has the real stone-wall Yankee Whittier flavor, as this brief excerpt indicates:—

> I, the urchin, unto whom,
> In that smoked and dingy room,
> Where the district gave thee rule
> O'er its ragged winter school,
> Thou didst teach the mysteries
> Of those weary A, B, C's—
> Where, to fill the every pause
> Of thy wise and learned saws,
> Through the cracked and crazy wall
> Came the cradle-rock and squall,
> And the goodman's voice, at strife
> With his shrill and tipsy wife,—
> Luring us by stories old,
> With a comic unction told,
> More than by the eloquence
> Of terse birchen arguments
> (Doubtful gain, I fear), to look
> With complacence on a book!—

The Panorama—likewise named from the lengthiest and most tedious item in the collection—was published by Ticknor and Fields in March of 1856—141 pages of text, chocolate cloth binding. The minute collectors' points of lettering at the base of the spine and details of advertisements are interesting but indefinite. It is entirely probably that the very first copies released had no advertisements at all. The fact that these small differences should be so carefully noted in a book so widely circulated and so comparatively common in first editions as to be purchasable for only a few dollars is a tribute to its literary importance.

The twenty-seven poems of *The Panorama* include two of America's most important, profoundly indigenous classics— two ballads, *The Barefoot Boy* and *Maud Muller*—one a poem of specific recollection of the author's own boyhood and the other imaginatively retrospective. Also, *The Kansas Emigrants* appears here for the first time in book form as does the anti-slavery *The Rendition.* Throughout the collection there is a definite upward trend in the average of achievement. *Burns, Rantoul, Official Piety, Mary Garvin,* all have something real to convey.

After much hesitation, the conviction that *The Barefoot Boy* and *Maud Muller* should be printed complete—the first in this chapter and the second in the following one—has become irresistible. The Whittier enthusiast who knows and respects them can merely skip. The casual reader—who may have only sour grammar school recollections of them or who, by some chance, may have never known them—may be surprised to discover that they are no mere jingles but poetical engravings of rare charm executed with cameo-carving skill of artistic simplicity. The informed but censorious member of the younger generation—who has hypnotized himself into believing that one essence of poetry is that it shall not scan or rhyme—if perchance he has read this book with the hope of proving the very things it seeks to disprove, may have the courtesy to heed the writer's serious plea to read these verses ALOUD, trying for the moment to forget that all twentieth-century prejudices are omnisciently superior to everything that has gone before and honestly striving to hear the less sophisticated old fogy heart-beat of eighty-five years ago. After all, it is provable that the men and women of those days who found inspiration and beauty in Whittier were not morons but had the valiant minds of empire builders. Be it remembered that Thomas Wentworth Higginson— astute literary critic, writer, and heroic colonel of a Negro regiment in the Civil War—almost worshiped the ground

Writtier walked on and yet was broad enough to discover the genuine more modern note in Emily Dickinson and give it to the world. Why is it not right to appreciate poems, like painting, in the proper relation to period?

THE BAREFOOT BOY

Blessings on thee, little man,
Barefoot boy, with cheek of tan!
With thy turned-up pantaloons,
And thy merry whistled tunes;
With thy red lip, redder still
Kissed by strawberries on the hill;
With the sunshine on thy face,
Through thy torn brim's jaunty grace:
From my heart I give thee joy—
·I was once a barefoot boy!
Prince thou art—the grown-up man
Only is republican.
Let the million-dollared ride!
Barefoot, trudging at his side,
Thou hast more than he can buy,
In the reach of ear and eye—
Outward sunshine, inward joy:
Blessings on thee, barefoot boy!

O, for boyhood's painless play,
Sleep that wakes in laughing day,
Health that mocks the doctor's rules,
Knowledge never learned of schools,
Of the wild bee's morning chase,
Of the wild-flower's time and place,
Flight of fowl and habitude
Of the tenants of the wood;
How the tortoise bears his shell,
How the woodchuck digs his cell,
And the ground-mole sinks his well;
How the robin feeds her young,
How the oriole's nest is hung;

Where the whitest lilies blow,
Where the freshest berries grow,
Where the ground-nut trails its vine,
Where the wood-grape's clusters shine;
Of the black wasp's cunning way,
Mason of his walls of clay,
And the architectural plans
Of gray, hornet artisans!—
For, eschewing books and tasks,
Nature answers all he asks;
Hand in hand with her he walks,
Face to face with her he talks,
Part and parcel of her joy,—
Blessings on the barefoot boy!

O, for boyhood's time of June,
Crowding years in one brief moon,
When all things I heard or saw
Me, their master, waited for.
I was rich in flowers and trees,
Humming-birds and honey-bees;
For my sport the squirrel played,
Plied the snouted mole his spade;
For my taste the blackberry cone
Purpled over hedge and stone;
Laughed the brook for my delight
Through the day and through the night,
Whispering at the garden wall,
Talked with me from fall to fall;
Mine the sand-rimmed pickerel pond,
Mine the walnut slopes beyond,
Mine, on bending orchard trees,
Apples of Hesperides!
Still, as my horizon grew,
Larger grew my riches too;
All the world I saw or knew
Seemed a complex Chinese toy,
Fashioned for a barefoot boy!

O, for festal dainties spread,
Like my bowl of milk and bread,—

Pewter spoon and bowl of wood,
On the door-stone, gray and rude!
O'er me, like a regal tent,
Cloudy-ribbed, the sunset bent,
Purple-curtained, fringed with gold,
Looped in many a wind-swung fold;
While for music came the play
Of the pied frogs' orchestra;
And, to light the noisy choir,
Lit the fly his lamp of fire.
I was monarch: pomp and joy
Waited on the barefoot boy!

Cheerily, then, my little man,
Live and laugh, as boyhood can!
Though the flinty slopes be hard,
Stubble-speared the new-mown sward,
Every morn shall lead thee through
Fresh baptisms of the dew;
Every evening from thy feet
Shall the cool wind kiss the heat:
All too soon these feet must hide
In the prison cells of pride,
Lose the freedom of the sod,
Like a colt's for work be shod,
Made to tread the mills of toil,
Up and down in ceaseless moil:
Happy if their track be found
Never on forbidden ground;
Happy if they sink not in
Quick and treacherous sands of sin.
Ah! that thou couldst know thy joy,
Ere it passes, barefoot boy!

Here is indeed a complete poem, progressive to the finish
from the very first line—a long poem in miniature divided
into four cantos. Here indeed is accomplished artistic simplicity without banality—complete, impersonating recollection, minute observation of nature, sincerity of sentiment,

ending with a moral too brief and too visual in its metaphor to be trite.

The art of the poem is no more important than the spontaneous and independent spirit of the Barefoot Boy as an individual. In this Barefoot Boy is no kernel of defeatist youth, regimented youth, or communistic youth. He could never grow into faking surrealist painter, nonsense-jabbering pretended poet, radio crooner, treasury-raiding politician, new thought religionist, Wolf of Wall Street. He could never have resolved the mystery of how to hold a private job and receive government charity at the same time. In real life his ideas of sanitation were rather rudimentary; his feet were not always as clean as they should have been at bedtime; he knew all about the propagation of animal life; and in many ways he was not quite the ideal of this poem—but he was courageous and independent and American in three dimensions. The Barefoot Boy grown to manhood was a congenital abolitionist—seeking, for himself and for all the world, freedom of action as God's great blessing and man's absolute right.

It was two years after the publication of *The Barefoot Boy* and *Maud Muller* that the Massachusetts legislature, which still exercised a certain control over Harvard, elected Whittier an overseer of the University. An extant letter from Whittier to Lowell jokingly threatens Lowell that he will be jeopardizing his Harvard professorship if, as editor of *The Atlantic*, he fails to show proper appreciation of Whittier's contributions. Two years later, in 1860, the University itself confirmed the legislature's opinion of Whittier's intellectual stature by conferring on him the degree of honorary Master of Arts.

The Quaker barefoot boy had traveled a long road—from the farm to the Academy; thence to propagandist, editorial and political power that culminated in the virtual appointment of a United States senator; thence to a commanding literary position that brought formal scholastic recognition to the man whose only school of higher learning had been self-education and self-discipline.

# 3²

MAUD MULLER AND
SKIPPER IRESON

IT IS A CURIOUS THING that *The Barefoot Boy* and *Maud Muller*—two of the four most widely known Whittier short poems—appeared within one week of each other, the first in the January, 1855, number of a juvenile monthly and the second in the January 28, 1855, issue of the *National Era*. This does not prove that they were actually conceived or written one right after the other, but it does establish that these two poems—both a million miles removed from current events—came into existence during days of tense political excitement that would have entirely absorbed the poet's attention in earlier life. Just after the Anthony Burns excitement, and while the Republican party was in the process of organization, Whittier the poet and Whittier the poet-politician-propagandist had begun to function entirely separately, not as one confused or dual personality with the propagandist element dominant or rampant.

Maud Muller is not so good a poem as *The Barefoot Boy*. It is one of the few major Whittier ballads which suffer from the Longfellow tendency to be just a bit too pat. It is the nearest that Amesbury ever got to Brattle Street, Cambridge. Like *The Barefoot Boy* it is reminiscent, but with a difference. *The Barefoot Boy* is specifically Whittier at forty-seven recalling the Whittier of nearly two score years earlier. The two people in *Maud Muller* are both imaginary—a country woman and a rich man from the city. *Maud Muller* has a main trunk of narrative supporting two branches of reminiscence; the incident proper is followed first by her recollection

253

of it and then by his, these two being bound together with a moral tag. It should be particularly noted that *Maud Muller* has precisely the same verse form as the later and incomparable *Barbara Frietchie*—perhaps the greatest modern short ballad in the English language. It is in the same staccato two-line stanzas; and it has the same lilt, so simple that it is almost subconscious.

Man has not invented and cannot invent (because it doesn't exist) any verse form simpler to memorize. Wherein, from the very rudimentary nature of the composition, written almost as if each couplet were a rosary bead to be counted, lies much of its power. Each two lines say a definite something, visual or sentimental, which registers by brevity, directness, rhyme, and rhythm. The most famous couplet from *Maud Muller,* and one of the most quoted in modern literature, is these two lines:

> For of all sad words of tongue or pen,
> The saddest are these: "It might have been!"

Commonplace this may be, for the fact it states is no psychological novelty, but it rings true to the most intellectual as well as to the most elemental mind, and, once heard, is almost if not entirely impossible to forget.

Maud Muller has 110 lines—precisely eight more than *The Barefoot Boy. Barbara Frietchie* has only sixty lines, being scarcely more than half as long. The entire poem of *Maud Muller* is worth reading if only in a spirit of inquiry to determine how an innocuous summer idyl, with no dramatic clash beyond the exchange of a few words and glances between a man and a maid in a hay field, could become household verse for the United States.

It may be naïve. Indeed, it is undeniably very naïve; but it has an honesty of sentiment and a verity of detail—such as the description of Maud's children playing under their mother's feet to be within reach of weary glance and querulous voice—which raise it above all banality.

MAUD MULLER

Maud Muller on a summer's day,
Raked the meadow sweet with hay.

Beneath her torn hat glowed the wealth
Of simple beauty and rustic health.

Singing, she wrought, and her merry glee
The mock-bird echoed from his tree.

But, when she glanced to the far-off town,
White from its hill-slope looking down,

The sweet song died, and a vague unrest
And a nameless longing filled her breast—

A wish, that she hardly dared to own,
For something better than she had known.

The Judge rode slowly down the lane,
Smoothing his horse's chestnut mane.

He drew his bridle in the shade
Of the apple-trees, to greet the maid,

And ask a draught from the spring that flowed
Through the meadow, across the road.

She stooped where the cool spring bubbled up,
And filled for him her small tin cup,

And blushed as she gave it, looking down
On her feet so bare, and her tattered gown.

"Thanks!" said the Judge; "a sweeter draught
From a fairer hand was never quaffed."

He spoke of the grass and flowers and trees,
Of the singing birds and the humming bees;

Then talked of the haying, and wondered whether
The cloud in the west would bring foul weather.

And Maud forgot her brier-torn gown,
And her graceful ankles bare and brown;

And listened, while a pleased surprise
Looked from her long-lashed hazel eyes.

At last, like one who for delay
Seeks a vain excuse, he rode away.

Maud Muller looked and sighed: "Ah me!
That I the Judge's bride might be!

"He would dress me up in silks so fine,
And praise and toast me at his wine.

"My father should wear a broadcloth coat;
My brother should sail a painted boat.

"I'd dress my mother so grand and gay,
And the baby should have a new toy each day.

"And I'd feed the hungry and clothe the poor,
And all should bless me who left our door."

The Judge looked back as he climbed the hill,
And saw Maul Muller standing still.

"A form more fair, a face more sweet,
Ne'er hath it been my lot to meet.

"And her modest answer and graceful air
Show her wise and good as she is fair.

"Would she were mine, and I to-day,
Like her, a harvester of hay:

"No doubtful balance of rights and wrongs,
Nor weary lawyers with endless tongues,

"But low of cattle and song of birds,
And health and quiet and loving words."

But he thought of his sisters proud and cold,
And his mother, vain of her rank and gold.

So, closing his heart, the Judge rode on,
And Maud was left in the field alone.

But the lawyers smiled that afternoon,
When he hummed in court an old love-tune;

And the young girl mused beside the well,
Till the rain on the unraked clover fell.

He wedded a wife of richest dower,
Who lived for fashion, as he for power.

Yet oft, in his marble hearth's bright glow,
He watched a picture come and go;

And sweet Maud Muller's hazel eyes
Looked out in their innocent surprise.

Oft, when the wine in his glass was red,
He longed for the wayside well instead;

And closed his eyes on his garnished rooms,
To dream of meadows and clover-blooms.

And the proud man sighed, with a secret pain,
"Ah, that I were free again!

"Free as when I rode that day,
Where the barefoot maiden raked her hay."

She wedded a man unlearned and poor,
And many children played round her door.

But care and sorrow, and child-birth pain,
Left their traces on heart and brain.

And oft, when the summer sun shone hot
On the new-mown hay in the meadow lot,

And she heard the little spring brook fall
Over the roadside, through the wall,

In the shade of the apple-tree again
She saw a rider draw his rein.

And, gazing down with timid grace,
She felt his pleased eyes read her face.

Sometimes her narrow kitchen walls
Stretched away into stately halls;

The weary wheel to a spinnet turned,
The tallow candle an astral burned,

And for him who sat by the chimney-lug,
Dozing and grumbling o'er pipe and mug,

A manly form at her side she saw,
And joy was duty and love was law.

Then she took up her burden of life again,
Saying only, "It might have been."

Alas for maiden, alas for Judge,
For rich repiner and household drudge!

God pity them both! and pity us all,
Who vainly the dreams of youth recall.

For of all sad words of tongue or pen,
The saddest are these: "It might have been!"

Ah, well! for us all some sweet hope lies
Deeply buried from human eyes;

And, in the hereafter, angels may
Roll the stone from its grave away!

Admittedly, this is the genius of the commonplace expressed with the most uncanny knack of provoking from Mrs. Grundy a sympathetic "How True!" Whittier never professed to follow strange emotional gods. He was the epitome of the most reputable middle class convictions of his era. He defied established society on one ground only—that of Negro slavery; but for that issue he would fight to the last ditch.

The superior average excellence of Whittier's *Home Ballads* and *Poems,* has already been emphasized. In addition to *Skipper Ireson's Ride,* the following poems are notable: *Telling the Bees, The Swan Song of Parson Avery, Le Marais du Cygne,* and *Brown of Ossawatomie*—the last two already treated among the anti-slavery poems. Not to be passed over casually are these others: *The Garrison of Cape Ann, The Double-Headed Snake of Newbury, The Sycamores,* and *The Pipes at Lucknow.*

The Sycamores is a charming tribute to the one lone pioneer Irishman of colonial Haverhill:

> Pioneer of Erin's outcasts,
> With his fiddle and his pack;
> Little dreamed the village Saxons
> Of the myriads at his back.

The Pipes of Lucknow tells how the Scots rescued the besieged English of Lucknow in the Sepoy Mutiny, and is one of those outbursts of martial ardor which Whittier never entirely understood in himself and could never entirely suppress.

The Garrison of Cape Ann narrates the quaint legend of how the Garrison in the old Fort on the Cape was beset by demon specters of Evil who only mocked at gunpowder and lead but who could not face the power of prayer.

The Double-Headed Snake of Newbury tells how the whole countryside came to gape at this wonder and is remarkable if only for this graphic description of Whittier's pet ecclesiastic hate, Cotton Mather:

> Cotton Mather came galloping down
> All the way to Newbury town,
> With his eyes agog and his ears set wide,
> And his marvellous inkhorn at his side;
> Stirring the while in the shallow pool
> Of his brains for the lore he learned at school,
> To garnish the story, with here a streak
> Of Latin and there another of Greek:
> And the tales he heard and the notes he took,
> Behold! Are they not in his Wonder-Book?

It is only natural that any man rereading an author for an extended survey of this nature should end by playing favorites. This writer's two special selections are *The Swan Song of Parson Avery* and *Telling the Bees*. Eliminating *Snow-Bound* as the admitted masterpiece and excluding all anti-slavery material as of a special category, the writer's favorite shorter poems would rank in about this order: *Barbara Frietchie* (60 lines); *The Barefoot Boy* (102 lines); *Telling the Bees* (56 lines); *Abraham Davenport* (65 lines); *Skipper*

Ireson's Ride (102 lines); *The Swan Song of Parson Avery* (58 lines); *Eternal Goodness* (88 lines); *In School Days* (44 lines); *Maud Muller* (110 lines).

Telling the Bees is the very simple tale of the returning lover who finds the chore-girl performing that old Yankee ritual of "telling the bees" (literally, by chanting to them) of his sweetheart's death. Incidentally, it is an exact word-etching of the approach to the Whittier homestead. Here we have an example of vivid action and emotion—complete dramatic narrative with atmosphere and background—in the amazingly condensed space of the fifty-six lines. For once, the climax is faultless and moral-less. Only in the last four lines does the youth discover that Death has come not for the old grandsire but for his darling, the maiden of the household.

> And the song she was singing ever since
> In my ear sounds on:—
> "Stay at home, pretty bees, fly not hence!
> Mistress Mary is dead and gone!"

Parson Avery is veritable New England chronicle in verse —a shipwreck and a miracle in just fifty-eight lines. Let the student of American verse compare this with Longfellow's *Wreck of the Hesperus* to see the vast difference between the two men when both performing at their best.

Father Avery, his whole family drowned, is cast upon the surf-beaten rocks, and asks God for death:

> The ear of God was open to His servant's last request;
> As the strong wave swept him downward the sweet
>   hymn upward pressed,
> And the soul of Father Avery went, singing, to its rest.

Now as to the ride of Skipper Ireson—"tarred and feathered and carried in a cart by the women of Marblehead"; first published in *The Atlantic Monthly*, December, 1857. It is in nine stanzas—a total of ninety-nine lines, twenty-seven of which are repeated choral refrain.

This poem reveals peculiarly little of Whittier's own soul but is beyond all argument a really splendid narrative ballad, and for purposes of recitation—one fine and fair test of balladry as being its original purpose—his very top success. The fact that Ireson's crew rather than Ireson himself should have been blamed for refusing aid to the sinking sister ship is meaningless today and Whittier was not intentionally unjust. Of course it is the individual guilt of the captain (in which Whittier believed when he wrote the poem) that gives point and focus to the story.

Each stanza of *Skipper Ireson's Ride* consists of four rhymed couplets followed by a three-line refrain, sometimes given in pure English and sometimes in Cape Ann dialect—

> Old Floyd Ireson, for his hard heart,
> Tarred and feathered and carried in a cart,
> By the women of Marblehead!

Putting the refrain, when actually quoted, in Marblehead dialect was suggested by Lowell, then editor of *The Atlantic* and an enthusiast for Yankee peculiarities of speech. He wrote out the dialect refrain for Whittier, who after considerable hesitation accepted the suggestion. Ireson finally protests:

> "Hear me, neighbors!" at last he cried,—
> "What to me is this noisy ride?
> What is the shame that clothes the skin
> To the nameless horror that lives within?
> Waking or sleeping, I see a wreck,
> And hear a cry from a reeling deck!
> Hate me and curse me,—I only dread
> The hand of God and the face of the dead!"
> Said old Floyd Ireson, for his hard heart,
> Tarred and feathered and carried in a cart
> By the women of Marblehead!

The total number of lines in the nine favorite Whittier short poems listed in this chapter, including the four later poems still to be analyzed, is only six hundred and eighty-five.

If verse-conscious Americans of today could be persuaded to reread *Snow-Bound* and these six hundred and eighty-five lines—even eliminating all the stirring anti-slavery items—Whittier would be re-appraised at his full stature—not as an intellectual giant or emotional colossus among world-poets, nor as among the greatest poetical technicians, nor even among the few most gifted with instinctive expression—but as an entirely indigenous, earnest, unlifting voice, sincere and vivid, with a rare gift of simplicity and quotability, doing his utmost to make America honorably conscious of her own traditions, ideals, and destiny.

33

THE YEAR 1860

REPUBLICAN CONVENTION TIME in 1860 was crucial time for the cause of emancipation, recognized as such by Whittier with all his natural acumen but with an extraordinarily false estimate as to the respective powers of prospective standard bearers. Despite the defeat of 1856, Whittier was still loyal to Benton's picturesque son-in-law, Frémont. Whittier seemed blind to the unanswered charges of corruption in California and also to Frémont's temperamental disqualifications for the high executive office to which he aspired.

In the last analysis it is not too difficult to understand how the lawyer-legislator-story-teller, ex-rail-splitting Lincoln of Illinois, unwilling to make absolute commitments or to lay all his cards face up on the table, failed to seem an ideal candidate to a rock-ribbed New England abolitionist. How was Whittier to know that the long and lanky Kentuckian had adamantine purposes even while playing practical politics—much as Whittier did—and would play politics with the Devil himself to gain those ends?

However, when Lincoln had once been nominated, Whittier stood by the Republican party and its candidate 100 per cent. He put his whole heart into the work as he had not done since the excitement caused by the Douglas Kansas-Nebraska bill. Despite the manner in which Douglas himself thwarted Buchanan and the politicians who tried to make corrupt use of the legislation he had fathered, Lincoln's best recommendation to Whittier must have been his rivalry with Stephen Douglas.

In the momentous election of 1860, there were four presidential candidates: Lincoln for the Republicans, who were now generally regarded as favoring emancipation; Douglas for the loyal Democrats, largely Northern men; John C. Breckinridge, for the State Rights Democrats, who demanded that slavery should not only be tolerated in the territories but should be safeguarded by the federal government; and John Bell, of Tennessee (with Edward Everett of Massachusetts as vice-presidential candidate), representing the mushroom Constitutional Union party, a refuge for disillusioned old-line Whigs and others who wanted to stay on the fence.

The main issue of the campaign was a flat challenge to abolitionists the world over. The Republicans attacked slavery as an evil that must spread no further and must be rigidly prohibited in new territories. The Breckinridge Democrats claimed that as slaves were constitutional property, their safe possession in territories must be guaranteed by Congress. The Douglas Democrats still stood for local option, with congressional interference on either side absolutely barred. From the outset, the division of the Democratic party into two great wings, gave Lincoln and the new Republican organization an advantage. Moreover, the threats of Southern leaders to secede if Lincoln should be elected, which might have influenced many wavering votes, were not taken seriously in the North.

It is curious that the fate of Douglas—a very able and honest man whom Lincoln knew to be such and did not hesitate to use on confidential missions during the few months Douglas lived after his defeat in this 1860 election—should have been to advance the fortunes of his opponent. Even though Douglas won and Lincoln lost the senatorial seat for which they were both campaigning at the time of their world-famous debates, those debates first brought Lincoln before the country as a possible major political force; if, earlier, Douglas with his Kansas-Nebraska bill had not attempted to establish local option for slavery, half of the cause for the debates would have been non-existent; if, later, Douglas had not split the Democratic party, Lincoln might never have been president.

Before the election of 1860, it was predicted that Lincoln could be elected if Pennsylvania went Republican in its gubernatorial election preceding the national election; and that Pennsylvania could be brought into the Republican ranks if the Quakers could be aroused to active participation in the struggle. The results of this state election were awaited with anxiety, and were entirely satisfactory.

On October 11, 1860, a Republican mass meeting was scheduled for Newburyport. For this occasion, Whittier wrote a poem to be sung by the audience—much his best endeavor at that sort of thing since *The Kansas Emigrants*. This sixteen-line four-stanza poem was printed on a leaflet headed, *A Voice from John G. Whittier*. The title of the poem itself was

THE QUAKERS ARE OUT

Not vainly we waited and counted the hours,—
The buds of our hope have burst out into flowers.
No room for misgiving—no loop-hole of doubt,—
We've heard from the Keystone! The Quakers are out!

The plot has exploded—we've found out the trick;
The bribe goes abegging; the fusion won't stick.
When the Wide-Awake lanterns are shining about,
The rogues stay at home, and the true men come out!

The good State has broken the cords for her spun;
Her oil-springs and water won't fuse into one;
The Dutchman has seasoned with Freedom his krout,
And slow, late, but certain, the Quakers are out.

Give the flags to the winds!—set the hills all aflame!
Make way for the man with the Patriarch's name!
Away with misgiving—away with all doubt,
For Lincoln goes in when the Quakers come out!

During that nerve-wracking period of suspense between Lincoln's election, his inauguration and the firing on Fort Sumter, Whittier still hoped against hope that war might be averted. He even wrote Sumner that the old scheme for purchasing the slaves might be revived. With actual conflict unmistakably imminent, all his Quaker qualms about bloodshed were reawakened. He, who had so largely contributed to creating a situation with only one possible solution, was among the very last to accept that solution as inevitable. Though he had written that "the great body of our people can no more hunt slaves than commit cannibalism," he could not seem to understand that this very truism closed the door to compromise.

In his own mind, Whittier had been and always was absolutely positive that slavery was intolerable. But he does not seem to have been equally sure that the Southern states had not a right to secede peacefully. In a letter to F. H. Underwood, who first conceived the idea of *The Atlantic Monthly*, Whittier said frankly:

"For myself I would like to maintain the Union if it could be *the* Union of our fathers. But if it is to be in name only; if the sacrifices and concessions on which it lives must all be made by the Free States to the Slave; if the peaceful victories of the ballot-box are to be turned into defeats by threats of secession; if rebellion and treason are to be encouraged into a standing menace, a power above law and Constitution, demanding perpetual sacrifice, I, for one, shall not lift a hand against its dissolution. As to fighting, in any event, to force back the seceders, I see no sense in it!"

However, once actual firing on Fort Sumter disposed of all arguments as to what might or might not be done by way of compromise, Lincoln had no more faithful supporter than Whittier, even though he always insisted with much basic truth that slavery and not disunion was the actual cause of conflict. He did his best to reconcile his Quaker faith with the fact that many a noble Quaker youth was enlisting for active service in the ranks—and would allow nothing to be said against them for doing so. Whittier felt that the Quakers, if their participation in actual fighting was a minimum, should at least contribute all possible help other than slaying their fellow men. A circular, printed in Amesbury on June 18, 1861, entitled *To Members of the Society of Friends,* explains Quaker war obligations in these very blunt terms:

"We have no right to ask or expect an exemption from the chastisement which Divine Providence is inflicting upon the nation. Steadily and faithfully maintaining our testimony against war, we owe it to the cause of truth, to show that exalted heroism and generous self-sacrifice are not incompatible with our pacific principles. Our mission is, at this time, to mitigate the sufferings of our countrymen, to visit and aid the sick and the wounded, to relieve the necessities of the widow and the orphan, and to practice economy for the sake of charity. Let the Quaker bonnet be seen by the side of the black hood of the Catholic Sister of Charity in the hospital ward. Let the same heroic devotion to duty which our brethren in Great Britain manifested in the Irish famine and pestilence be reproduced on this side of the water, in mitigating the horrors of war and its attendant calamities. What hinders us from holding up the hands of Dorothea Dix in her holy work of mercy at Washington? Our society is rich, and of those to whom much is given much will be required in this hour of proving and trial."

Let the reader peruse this paragraph twice—once for substance and once as an example of the forceful prose this man could write when determined to speak his mind. No finer example of Whittier's editorial prose (for that is what this is, though published as a printed slip) exists anywhere.

During the early days of the Civil War, Whittier, having no further regular income from the *National Era,* was reduced to serious financial straits. His mother had died in December of 1857, and his sister was now becoming a permanent invalid. His expenses were considerable and his income from his books and from *The Atlantic* and the *Independent* and other publications that occasionally bought his poems was still very small although beginning to increase steadily.

Joseph Sturge, the wealthy British Quaker, whose help Whittier had once declined in earlier days, acting through the New York merchant, Lewis Tappan, had provided gladly all the help Whittier could be prevailed upon to accept. He could not refuse for his sister's comfort what he probably would have never accepted for himself.

The outbreak of the war, uniting all opposed Northern political factions in one common purpose, naturally ended Whittier's value as an adept controversialist. The men of the moment were generals and executives able to ride the whirlwind and compel some degree of order in a world of chaos rather than the poets and propagandists who had released the gory spirit of war. The political leaders of *The Atlantic* were not written by Whittier as might have been expected, but by Lowell, with much rare good judgment and solid common sense. The same powers of sane analysis that made Lowell— whatever else he may or may not have been in the field of literature—the keenest of all American literary critics, proved serviceable in the political arena. Lowell, not Whittier, was the first of the Yankee prophets to understand Lincoln fully, and, despite his birth at the opposite pole of society, to value him as the world at large valued him only after the curtain had rung down abruptly on his ultimate tragedy.

This does not insinuate that Whittier was passing out of the picture. He was merely passing further into perspective and higher above the horizon. The poems he wrote, whether of war or peace, were listened to as never before. He was beginning to inspire not only interest and affection but some of that reverence which followed him throughout all the later years of life. Like the patriarchs of old, he had walked with God all his days and the truth had been revealed to him.

34

WHITTIER IN
WAR TIME

Not as we hoped; but what are we?
Above our broken dreams and plans
God lays, with wiser hand than man's,
The corner-stones of liberty.

I cavil not with Him: the voice
That freedom's blessed gospel tells
Is sweet to me as silver bells,
Rejoicing!—yea, I will rejoice!

THESE TWO STANZAS from *Astræa at the Capitol*, first published in *The Atlantic* for June, 1862, and later in *In War Time,* summarize Whittier's attitude toward the Civil War. The poem was written to celebrate the abolition of slavery in the District of Columbia—and emancipation was the masterpiece of God whether he revealed it on the wings of the dove or on a pediment of human sacrifice, not conceivably too great for the blessing conferred.

Throughout the entire active period of the Civil War, Whittier published only one small volume in book form, *In War Time and Other Poems,* issued by Ticknor and Fields in November of 1863, after the turn of the tide at Gettysburg. *National Lyrics,* a little volume of Whittier patriotic verse, was issued cheaply, with paper wrapper covers, in August of 1865, about four months after Lee's surrender. Only two poems in *National Lyrics* were first collected, but one of these, *Laus Deo,* has definite importance as being in celebration of the ratification of the Constitutional amendment abolishing slavery and therefore a past-due final anti-slavery poem. Many good critics rank it high among the Whittier major compositions. Its force is undeniable, but it does not seem characteristic or particularly spontaneous—an entirely personal reaction to the poem, however.

Undeniably, the inhibitions of Quakerism prevented Whittier from responding as might have been expected to certain of the tremendous emotions of the period. Walt Whitman, who actually nursed the wounded in Washington hospitals, came much closer to the heart of the struggle and left a far more impressive eye-witness record than any of the New England brotherhood. He, also, was the only poet to give adequate expression to the national grief at the shock of Lincoln's assassination.

However, Whittier caught the fire of one incident and imprisoned it for all eternity as living flame in unforgettable verse. *Barbara Frietchie* first appeared in *The Atlantic* for October, 1863. It was immediately reprinted as a leaflet, and, within six weeks, collected in the volume entitled *In War Time*. Its overwhelming success probably led to the publication of *In War Time* at just that moment when poetry books, as a whole, must surely have been far from the thoughts of the multitude.

Seeking for a comparison, the mind naturally turns to Tennyson's *Charge of the Light Brigade,* immortalizing an episode of battle conflict far more heroic in the literal and physical sense but less psychologically significant. As between these two extraordinary compositions, both undoubtedly inspired in the most actual sense, it is not national prejudice that gives the palm to Whittier. *Barbara Frietchie* is the less artificial, more moving, and more completely rounded out of the two poems.

The story on which *Barbara Frietchie* is founded was supplied by Mrs. E. D. E. N. Southworth, the then most popular American sentimental novelist, who narrated it as fact and wrote the details to Whittier in Amesbury. Either the Southworth imagination had been at work or she got two stories confused. However, there appears to have been a Mrs. Quan-trell (not Mrs. Frietchie) who displayed a Union flag in the presence of Confederate troops and if Mrs. Frietchie was only an onlooker—as is now said to be the case—at least she had an ideal name for versification. It is true that Whittier had rather a penchant for scrambling his stories but he also had too much common sense to let this trouble him unduly—so Heaven only knows why it should concern anybody else. He didn't pretend to be Jared Sparks or George Bancroft. The only important fact is that he believed the Barbara Frietchie story to the point of being completely thrilled when he wrote it, and always held it to have had sufficient foundation in truth.

Whittier sent the poem, with more confidence than usual, to his publisher, Fields, who had become editor of *The Atlantic*. Fields recognized its value immediately and wrote the author:

"Barbara is most welcome and I will find room for it in the October number, most certainly.... You were right in thinking I should like it, for so I do, as I like few things in this world.... Inclosed is a check for fifty dollars but Barbara's weight should be in gold."

The most remarkable feature about the thirty couplets which pound out Barbara's immortal story with a beat like old-time heavy army boots tramping on rough granite paving, is not only the vignette visual sharpness of the picture but the extraordinary combination of brevity and completeness. It is a finished drama, consisting of Prologue, for atmosphere; first, second, third, and fourth acts; epilogue of benediction. It is the perfect rounded dramatic ballad—a miniature that took thirty practice years—a year for each couplet—to produce spontaneously in white heat at the forge of inspiration. There is no manuscript to tell us whether Barbara came into existence laboriously or in a flash—but the poem sounds as if the sixty lines might well have been put down in sixty minutes. Certainly, the customary long period of Whittier revising must have been omitted, for Whittier acknowledged Mrs. Southworth's memorandum on September 8, stating that he has "just written out a little ballad of Barbara Frietchie" and, to make the October *Atlantic*, it must have been mailed almost on the instant.

In connection with this ballad it must be remembered that Stonewall Jackson was a praying soldier and had a Covenanter quality about him that had made him more than half a hero even to the hostile Northern troops. This bravest and most religious enemy's respect for the old woman's loyalty and the symbol she displays is the very apotheosis of patriotic appeal. One feels the mystic permanence of the Union flag exemplified in the sentiment which it still inspires in the breast of its most noble repudiator. One suspects that even Stonewall has his regrets—that, in his heart, the fraternity of North and South is not entirely sundered.

As realistic side-commentary, it may be remembered that at the time the poem was written Jackson had been dead for several months—and that heroic enemies dead are always better poetic subject matter than heroic enemies alive, spreading ruin and disaster.

BARBARA FRIETCHIE

[Prelude] *

Up from the meadows rich with corn,
Clear in the cool September morn,

The clustered spires of Frederick stand
Green-walled by the hills of Maryland.

Round about them orchards sweep,
Apple and peach tree fruited deep,

Fair as the garden of the Lord
To the eyes of the famished rebel horde,

On that pleasant morn of the early fall
When Lee marched over the mountain wall,—

---

* The indications of prelude, four acts, and epilogue are, of course, interpolations.

[Act I]

Over the mountains winding down,
Horse and foot, into Frederick town.

Forty flags with their silver stars,
Forty flags with their crimson bars,

Flapped in the morning wind: the sun
Of noon looked down, and saw not one.

[Act II]

Up rose old Barbara Frietchie then,
Bowed with her fourscore years and ten;

Bravest of all in Frederick town,
She took up the flag the men hauled down

In her attic window the staff she set,
To show that one heart was loyal yet.

[Act III]

Up the street came the rebel tread,
Stonewall Jackson riding ahead.

Under his slouched hat, left and right
He glanced: the old flag met his sight.

"Halt!" the dust-brown ranks stood fast.
"Fire!"—out blazed the rifle-blast.

It shivered the window, pane and sash;
It rent the banner with seam and gash.

Quick, as it fell, from the broken staff
Dame Barbara snatched the silken scarf;

She leaned far out on the window-sill,
And shook it forth with a royal will.

"Shoot, if you must, this old gray head,
But spare your country's flag," she said.

A shade of sadness, a blush of shame,
Over the face of the leader came;

The nobler nature within him stirred
To life at that woman's deed and word:

"Who touches a hair of yon gray head
Dies like a dog! March on!" he said.

[Act IV]

All day long through Frederick street
Sounded the tread of marching feet:

All day long that free flag tost
Over the heads of the rebel host.

Ever its torn folds rose and fell
On the loyal winds that loved it well;

And through the hill-gaps sunset light
Shone over it with a warm good-night.

[Epilogue]

Barbara Frietchie's work is o'er,
And the Rebel rides on his raids no more.

Honor to her! and let a tear
Fall, for her sake, on Stonewall's bier.

Over Barbara Frietchie's grave,
Flag of Freedom and Union, wave!

Peace and order and beauty draw
Round thy symbol of light and law;

And ever the stars above look down
On thy stars below in Frederick town!

The poems included in the volume entitled *In War Time*
are uniformly the production of developed genius but are
naturally overshadowed by the flag of Frederick Town.

Second in interest is a poem of comparatively small literary
value but of consequence because of the event it celebrates

and Whittier's reaction to the event. The name is simply
To John C. Frémont, and the twenty-six lines endeavor to
uphold Frémont's premature attempt in 1861 to emancipate
the slaves of Missouri by military proclamation—an act which
Lincoln, in order not to antagonize the border states at that
juncture, necessarily had to countermand when Frémont refused to rescind it himself. Frémont was still Whittier's romantic idol of manhood, and, from the poet's viewpoint, the
manner of slavery's going mattered little so long as it went at
once. The poem begins:

> Thy error, Fremont, simply was to act
> A brave man's part, without the statesman's tact,
> And, taking counsel but of common sense,
> To strike at cause as well as consequence.

This mistake of Frémont's, tantamount to a seizure of civil
authority with which he was not vested, provoked an investigation of the Western department which revealed gross
extravagance in administration. Frémont's military achievements added up to virtually a cipher and he resigned in 1862
rather than serve under Pope, whom he outranked. Nevertheless, in the spring of 1864, he was nominated by a radical
wing of the Republicans to oppose Lincoln for reëlection. In
September, he withdrew; and Pickard traces this uncharac-
teristically discreet act to advice given by Whittier during a
visit to the Frémont family at Nahant, establishing the connection by a long-subsequent but explicit letter of Mrs. Frémont to the poet. Mrs. Frémont states unequivocally that
Whittier's advice to her husband to stand aside was the de-
ciding word.

Frémont hadn't a ghost of a chance against Lincoln or
even Lincoln's chief opponent, General McClellan, who accepted the nomination even though he explicitly repudiated
the platform, declaring the war a failure. But Frémont's candidacy would have somewhat confused the basic issues, and
Whittier's advice was right advice. John Greenleaf Whittier

was never misled for long. By 1864 he had seen both Frémont
and Lincoln in action.

Among the war poems in this volume some mention must
be made of Whittier's song to the music of Luther's *Ein' Feste
Burg*, which was separately issued in various sheet music
editions and widely used throughout the North and in the
armies. The poet dwells on the fact that victory without
emancipation would be futile. The words fit the music admirably and are more impressive when sung than when spoken.
Says the poet:

> In vain the bells of war shall ring
>   Of triumphs and revenges,
> While still is spared the evil thing
>   That severs and estranges.
> But bless the ear
> That yet shall hear
> The jubilant bell
>   That rings the knell
> Of Slavery forever!

This song was generally known as *The Furnace Blast,* from
the first two lines, reading

> We wait beneath the furnace-blast
> The pangs of transformation;

Its popularity was certainly increased by a military political
incident of most picturesque character.

The Hutchinson family (one of the most famous entertain-
ment troupes of the period) used this song as a leading feature of their repertory in the Union camps across the Potomac
after the first battle of Bull Run. Because of the anti-slavery
sentiments so openly expressed, General Kearny ordered
Hutchinson to do no more singing in the camps and his permit to entertain the soldiers was formally revoked by General
McClellan. But Hutchinson was as much a fighter as either of
the generals. He went to Washington and appealed to Secretary Chase, who asked for a copy of the published song and
submitted it at the next cabinet meeting. Lincoln, with that

illuminating common sense that never bothered about small inconsistencies, declared roundly that *The Furnace Blast* was just the sort of thing he wanted his soldiers to hear and sent Hutchinson, singing Whittier to the tune of old Luther, back to the boys across the Potomac. Lincoln could not tolerate Frémont's unauthorized military emancipation order as a political act, but he knew in what direction he and Whittier had long been marching together just the same.

Bound in with the militant poems of *In War Time* are eleven occasional poems of secondary caliber and three new home ballads—*Cobbler Keezar's Vision, Amy Wentworth,* and *The Countess*—the first a bit above the level and the others just good Whittier. *Keezar's Vision* is of a future when good folk of all creeds shall live and mingle in complete accord. The point of special interest is that Keezar sees his vision in a magic lapstone such as Whittier must have used when cobbling to earn those few dollars which paid for his first term at the Haverhill Academy.

Elizabeth Whittier, long ill, died on September 3, 1864. Though Whittier never sold the Amesbury cottage but, indeed, returned to spend many of his last days within its narrow but memory-laden walls, this was the final breaking up of his home. It was indeed the irony of fate that financial success, in what seemed to him inexhaustible bounty, should have come to him only two years later, but too late for him to share it with the one human being on whom he would have most loved to lavish small luxuries.

The first person to whom Whittier wrote the news of Elizabeth's death, on the day it occurred, was Lucy Larcom.

The solitude in which the poet now found himself induced more strongly than ever the mood of reminiscence which had been shaping in his mind for years and finding not infrequent nor inadequate expression. It cannot have been long after Elizabeth's death before Whittier began work on American literature's most famous monument to a family circle, for the complete manuscript of *Snow-Bound* was sent to Fields just thirteen months later.

35

SNOW-BOUND

Once freedom for all men had become a part of our Constitution, Whittier knew that the main purpose of his life in so far as it influenced the welfare of his fellow citizens had been achieved. He understood that serious problems of reconstruction lay ahead and had his opinions on the matter, but he also understood that they were the particular concern of the younger generation which had fought the war rather than of the survivors dating from his crisis-building era. Within less than ten years he had lost the three definite activating elements of his life—his mother, his sister, and his Cause. Yet within that same period instinctively persistent self-improvement, combined with less immediate concern for the objectivities of existence, had made him more and more essentially a poet.

Whittier had no trace of Whitman's jubilation in living and feeling—no approach to the spiritual or the pantheistic through emotional responses in his own body. For many years his sense of the poetic, apart from verse allied to current events, had been retrospective, whether dealing with history, legend, or introspection. This independence of physical reactions may be the reason why time did not quench his inspiration but mellowed it as successive years gave patina to the memories of earlier days.

Snow-Bound—Whittier's longest poem and his obvious indubitable claim to rank among major writers of pure literature—contains a little more than 750 lines. The clear intention of tribute to the family group in which he was born and raised is stated in the dedication: "To the Memory of the

Household which it Describes, this poem is Dedicated by the Author."

Though sub-titled *A Winter Idyl,* it is a mistake to consider *Snow-Bound* as essentially celebrating New England farm life. Had Whittier been born fifteen miles from Haverhill, at Boar's Head, Hampton, with fishermen and sailors for family familiars, the poem would have undergone an entire sea change. Had he been born in Vermont's Green Mountains, the atmosphere and personalities would have been very different. Had he been city born and city bred, he very probably wouldn't have been at all the Whittier we know—but the country background is mere accident of place, mere frame for the family portrait.

Snow-Bound is a memorial poem, the only characters alive at the time of writing being the poet's younger brother and Harriet Livermore, "the Vixen and the devotee." Winter is used as the background because it was the period when leisure and harshly inclement weather drew the family circle most closely together in its most responsive mood. It is a composite of Yankee vignettes all mounted on one mat. The only portrait missing is that of the author.

To say that any one composition is the greatest American serious poem of the nineteenth century would be mere arbitrary assertion. Many other poems would have to be considered. But one can say definitely that *Snow-Bound* is the greatest nineteenth-century American poem of its type. Indeed, one can go further and, in simple truth, proclaim it unique for America, because there is nothing with which to make reasonable comparison.

Some years ago this writer—already a *Snow-Bound* addict —was expatiating on the subject rather to the amusement of the late Temple Scott, justly famous editor, critic, and rare-book authority. Scott, born abroad, could see merit in virtually every school of literature except that of nineteenth-century New England. He had a tendency to believe that everything good and beautiful about lowly country life (always excepting the *Elegy*) had been said by Burns, especially in *The*

Cotter's Saturday Night—a poem about one-quarter the length of *Snow-Bound* and, beyond all dispute, a masterpiece of masterpieces. But he made the mistake of admitting that he had read *Snow-Bound* only once many years previous to the discussion, and he finally agreed to read it again.

A fortnight later Mr. Scott handed back the *Snow-Bound* which had been sent him to peruse with the remark that he still preferred *The Cotter* but that, admittedly, there was nothing in between. Temple Scott never loved and revered Burns more than Whittier did, and Whittier would himself surely have agreed with Scott, insisting that the chair next below the Scotch Bard was far too exalted for a graduate maker of political jingles.

Anybody reading *The Cotter* must see that there is a similarity of sentiment between it and *Snow-Bound,* and even a similarity of treatment, but that the descriptions concern types instead of actual individuals with specific histories. It is not in the least improbable that Whittier found some suggestion for *Snow-Bound* in *The Cotter,* but this writer conscientiously believes that Whittier wrote far the greater poem. However, he has no quarrel with any man who will agree that these two poems—neither of them literally by Englishmen—occupy a special niche in English literature.

Snow-Bound was published in February, 1866, by Ticknor and Fields; it consists of fifty-two pages and has a frontispiece portrait; it is bound either in blue, plum, terra cotta, or green cloth, with some few copies in white, supposed to have been for the poet's own use as gifts. The first issue ONLY has the last page numbered. The present value is from $75 to $200 per copy, depending on the condition of the volume, for the correct first issue printing. Earlier Whittier rarities have greater monetary value today. None of them has anything approaching the same potentialities for the future.

To a man for whom almost every line of *Snow-Bound* has special significance, an effort at condensation seems little short of sacrilege. And yet there is no other practical means of letting Whittier speak for Whittier.

SNOW-BOUND.

A WINTER IDYL.

BY

JOHN GREENLEAF WHITTIER.

BOSTON:
TICKNOR AND FIELDS.
1866.

TITLE-PAGE OF THE FIRST EDITION OF
SNOW-BOUND

Photo John Blacklo

THE FIREPLACE OF *SNOW-BOUND*

The furniture belonged to Whittier's mother. The boots on t
hearth were his.

> *"And ever, when a louder blast*
> *Shook beam and rafter as it passed,*
> *The merrier up its roaring draught*
> *The great throat of the chimney laughed."*
> —Snow-Bound

The reader must be warned that this digest of the poem is only an outline, and that the major charm lies in the detail which it necessarily omits and in contemplative passages unrelated to the story. If he is at all a wise reader he will presently go to his copy of Whittier's *Poems* and read *Snow-Bound* complete. The purpose of reproducing what is printed here is not to obviate the need of reading the complete text but to inspire such reading. The first sixty-five lines are given in full, for they defy abbreviation.

SNOW-BOUND

The sun that brief December day
Rose cheerless over hills of gray,
And, darkly circled, gave at noon
A sadder light than waning moon.
Slow tracing down the thickening sky
Its mute and ominous prophecy,
A portent seeming less than threat,
It sank from sight before it set.
A chill no coat, however stout,
Of homespun stuff could quite shut out,
A hard, dull bitterness of cold,
 That checked, mid-vein, the circling race
 Of life-blood in the sharpened face,
The coming of the snow-storm told.
The wind blew east; we heard the roar
Of Ocean on his wintry shore,
And felt the strong pulse throbbing there
Beat with low rhythm our inland air.

Meanwhile we did our nightly chores,—
Brought in the wood from out of doors,
Littered the stalls, and from the mows
Raked down the herd's-grass for the cows:
Heard the horse whinnying for his corn;
And, sharply clashing horn on horn,
Impatient down the stanchion rows
The cattle shake their walnut bows;

While, peering from his early perch
Upon the scaffold's pole of birch,
The cock his crested helmet bent
And down his querulous challenge sent.

Unwarmed by any sunset light
The gray day darkened into night,
A night made hoary with the swarm
And whirl-dance of the blinding storm,
As zigzag wavering to and fro
Crossed and recrossed the wingéd snow:
And ere the early bed-time came
The white drift piled the window-frame,
And through the glass the clothes-line posts
Looked in like tall and sheeted ghosts.

So all night long the storm roared on:
The morning broke without a sun;
In tiny spherule traced with lines
Of Nature's geometric signs,
In starry flake, and pellicle,
All day the hoary meteor fell;
And, when the second morning shone,
We looked upon a world unknown,
On nothing we could call our own.
Around the glistening wonder bent
The blue walls of the firament,
No cloud above, no earth below,—
A universe of sky and snow!
The old familiar sights of ours
Took marvellous shapes; strange domes and towers
Rose up where sty or corn-crib stood,
Or garden wall, or belt of wood;
A smooth white mound the brush-pile showed,
A fenceless drift what once was road;
The bridle-post an old man sat
With loose-flung coat and high cocked hat;
The well-curb had a Chinese roof;
And even the long sweep, high aloof,
In its slant splendor, seemed to tell
Of Pisa's leaning miracle.

.   .   .   .   .

All day the gusty north-wind bore
The loosening drift its breath before;
Low circling round its southern zone,
The sun through dazzling snow-mist shone.

. . . . .

As night drew on, and, from the crest
Of wooded knolls that ridged the west,
The sun, a snow-blown traveller, sank
From sight beneath the smothering bank,
We piled, with care, our nightly stack
Of wood against the chimney-back;—
The oaken log, green, huge, and thick,
And on its top the stout back-stick;

. . . . .

We watched the first red blaze appear,
Heard the sharp crackle, caught the gleam
On whitewashed wall and sagging beam,
Until the old, rude-furnished room
Burst, flower-like, into rosy bloom;
While radiant with a mimic flame
Outside the sparkling drift became,
And through the bare-boughed lilac-tree
Our own warm hearth seemed blazing free.

. . . . .

What matter how the night behaved?
What matter how the north-wind raved?
Blow high, blow low, not all its snow
Could quench our hearth-fire's ruddy glow.
O Time and Change!—with hair as gray
As was my sire's that winter day,
How strange it seems, with so much gone
O life and love, to still live on!
Ah, brother! only I and thou
Are left of all that circle now,—

. . . . .

We sped the time with stories old,
Wrought puzzles out, and riddles told,

. . . . .

Our father rode again his ride
On Memphremagog's wooded side;
Sat down again to moose and samp
In trapper's hut and Indian camp;

.   .   .   .   .

Or, nearer home, our steps he led
Where Salisbury's level marshes spread
  Mile-wide as flies the laden bee;
Where merry mowers, hale and strong,
Swept, scythe on scythe, their swaths along
  The low green prairies of the sea.

.   .   .   .   .

We heard the tales of witchcraft old,
And dream and sign and marvel told
To sleepy listeners as they lay
Stretched idly on the salted hay,
Adrift along the winding shores,
When favoring breezes deigned to blow
The square sail of the gundalow
And idle lay the useless oars.
Our mother, while she turned her wheel
Or run the new-knit stocking-heel,
Told how the Indian hordes came down
At midnight on Cochecho town,
And how her own great-uncle bore
His cruel scalp-mark to fourscore.

.   .   .   .   .

Our uncle, innocent of books,
Was rich in lore of fields and brooks,

.   .   .   .   .

A simple, guileless, childlike man,
Content to live where life began;
Strong only on his native grounds,
The little world of sights and sounds
Whose girdle was the parish bounds,

.   .   .   .   .

He told how teal and loon he shot,
And how the eagle's eggs he got,

The feats on pond and river done,
The prodigies of rod and gun;

. . . . .

Next, the dear aunt, whose smile of cheer
And voice in dreams I see and hear,—
The sweetest woman ever Fate
Perverse denied a household mate,

. . . . .

There, too, our elder sister plied
Her evening task the stand beside;
A full, rich nature, free to trust,
Truthful and almost sternly just,
Impulsive, earnest, prompt to act,
And make her generous thought a fact,
Keeping with many a light disguise
The secret of self-sacrifice.

. . . . .

As one who held herself a part
Of all she saw, and let her heart
   Against the household bosom lean,
Upon the motley-braided mat
Our youngest and our dearest sat,
Lifting her large, sweet, asking eyes,
   Now bathed within the fadeless green
And holy peace of Paradise.

. . . . .

And yet, dear heart! remembering thee,
   Am I not richer than of old?
Safe in thy immortality,
   What change can reach the wealth I hold?
   What chance can mar the pearl and gold
Thy love hath left in trust with me?

. . . . .

And while in life's late afternoon,
   Where cool and long the shadows grow,
I walk to meet the night that soon
   Shall shape and shadow overflow,
I cannot feel that thou art far,
Since near at need the angels are;

. . . . .

Brisk wielder, of the birch and rule,
The master of the district school
Held at the fire his favored place,
Its warm glow lit a laughing face
Fresh-hued and fair, where scarce appeared
The uncertain prophecy of beard.

. . . . .

Another guest that winter night
·Flashed back from lustrous eyes the light.

. . . . .

A woman tropical, intense
In thought and act, in soul and sense,
She blended in a like degree
The vixen and the devotee,
Revealing with each freak or feint
    The temper of Petruchio's Kate,
The raptures of Siena's saint.

. . . . .

At last the great logs, crumbling low,
Sent out a dull and duller glow,
The bull's-eye watch that hung in view,
Ticking its weary circuit through,
Pointed with mutely warning sign
Its black hand to the hour of nine.

. . . . .

Within our beds awhile we heard
The wind that round the gables roared,
With now and then a ruder shock,
Which made our very bedsteads rock.
We heard the loosened clapboards tost,
The board-nails snapping in the frost;
And on us, through the unplastered wall,
Felt the light sifted snow-flakes fall.

. . . . .

Next morn we wakened with the shout
Of merry voices high and clear;
And saw the teamsters drawing near
To break the drifted highways out.

Down the long hillside treading slow
We saw the half-buried oxen go,
Shaking the snow from heads uptost,
Their straining nostrils white with frost.

.   .   .   .   .

So days went on: a week had passed
Since the great world was heard from last.
The Almanac we studied o'er
Read and reread our little store
Of books and pamphlets, scarce a score;

.   .   .   .   .

At last the floundering carrier bore
The village paper to our door.
Lo! broadening outward as we read,
To warmer zones the horizon spread;

.   .   .   .   .

Welcome to us its week-old news,
Its corner for the rustic Muse,

.   .   .   .   .

The chill embargo of the snow
Was melted in the genial glow;
Wide swung again our ice-locked door,
And all the world was ours once more!

.   .   .   .   .

Clasp, Angel of the backward look
  And folded wings of ashen gray
  And voice of echoes far away,
The brazen covers of thy book;

.   .   .   .   .

Even while I look, I can but heed
  The restless sands' incessant fall,
Importunate hours that hours succeed,
Each clamorous with its own sharp need,
  And duty keeping pace with all.

.   .   .   .   .

Yet, haply, in some lull of life,
Some Truce of God which breaks its strife,

> The worldling's eyes shall gather dew,
>   Dreaming in throngful city ways
> Of winter joys his boyhood knew;
> And dear and early friends—the few
> Who yet remain—shall pause to view
>   These Flemish pictures of old days;
>
> .   .   .   .   .
>
> The traveller owns the grateful sense
> Of sweetness near, he knows not whence,
> And, pausing, takes with forehead bare
> The benediction of the air.

The success of *Snow-Bound* was truly phenomenal. The poet's first royalty cheque came to some $10,000 and he could scarcely believe in such wealth. Almost forty years of meagerly remunerated labor suddenly began turning into substantial financial fortune.

Though *Snow-Bound,* which had no previous magazine publication that might have taken off the edge of its success, was immediately recognized at its full value as an American classic, the sale was too tremendous to be attributed entirely to the merit of the work or to that merit plus the judicious promotional activities of Ticknor and Fields. The explanation seems to be that Whittier, as a personality, had become, before his sixtieth year, almost legendary. The thousands who knew *Maud Muller* and *The Barefoot Boy* at least partly by heart; the tens of thousands who had read his propaganda anti-slavery verses; the hundreds of thousands to whom *Barbara Frietchie* had brought a thrill, all wanted to know about the man as well as his latest and greatest work. The autobiographic quality of the poem added greatly to its interest. The complete Yankeeism of it made a tremendous appeal to the deep pride of Massachusetts in the very act of celebrating the victory to which she had contributed the largest proportionate share of troops of all the Northern states—115,000 men, of whom more than 100,000 were volunteers.

The circumstance that *Snow-Bound* was long enough to

make a separate little volume, yet short enough to be easily read, made it the ideal gift book. Its graphic simplicity made it comprehensible to the untrained mind just as its utter integrity of thought and emotion made it acceptable to the most cultivated taste. Harvard professor, Haverhill farmer, Lowell girl mill-hand and State Street banker could all read it and understand its appeal. Despite the fact that *Snow-Bound* is a regional poem, there is only one localism in it not surmountable by the average imagination of almost any country or race. This exception is the reference to a "gunda-low"—that large, old-fashioned, flat-bottomed type of scow, built to float over the salt water marshes on the high autumn tides, onto which the giant stacks of salt marsh hay (held above tidal water by bottoms of four-foot stakes driven into the soggy soil) were pitched for conveyance to firm land and hay-rick. The writer has ridden in a gundalow, propelled by long and very heavy sweeps—but never one with a sail such as apparently existed in Whittier's early days.

The paramount sentiment of *Snow-Bound,* that of family solidarity, is as universal as the background is local. This universality of basic appeal, against a background etched with infinite detail of local comprehension, makes world poetry. *The Elegy, The Cotter,* and *Snow-Bound* all have it.

Whittier was fifty-eight when *Snow-Bound* was published. No other poet, American or English, ever wrote his masterpiece so late in life, with the possible exception of Milton. He was fifty-nine when *Paradise Lost* was published in 1667, but the manuscript had been finished two or three years earlier.

Naturally there is no intention here of comparing the simple art of Whittier with the divine gift and imagery of Milton. However, it is surely apposite to note that these men were both engaged as active publicists for years in propaganda which they believed to be in direct service of the Lord their God; that they both experienced conflict and turmoil; that they both attained their poetic destinies in life's late harbour following grievous storms—the plain Yankee knowing his work had been successful, the towering Englishman tragic in blindness and temporal, not spiritual, defeat. Quaker and Puritan—one devoid of mythology, the other's imagination seething with a pantheon of religious creations thronging a literal heaven and hell—both great doers of deeds and devout believers; in both of them, genius found fullest expression in ripened years of sorrow and experience, not in the beautifully instinctive babblings of youth.

Twenty-one years after the publication of *Snow-Bound,* Archdeacon Frederick W. Farrar of London, in 1887, wrote to George W. Childs of Philadelphia, who was defraying the cost of a Milton Memorial Window in St. Margaret's Church (London), these words: "I can think of no one so suitable as Mr. J. G. Whittier to write four lines for the Milton window. Mr. Whittier would feel the fullest sympathy for the great Puritan poet, whose spirit was so completely that of the Pilgrim Fathers. I have always loved and admired Mr. Whittier's poems. Could you ask him as a kindness to yourself and to me, and as a tribute to Milton's memory, if he would be so good as to write this brief inscription, which I would then have carved in marble or otherwise under the window."

Whittier wrote this simple quatrain:

> The new world honors him whose lofty plea
>   For England's freedom made her own more sure,
> Whose song, immortal as its theme, shall be
>   Their common freehold while both worlds endure.

Whittier's instinctive reaction to Milton was as a fellow worker for Freedom.

Three years after the publication of *Snow-Bound,* in 1869, Whittier was elected a trustee of Brown University. In 1886, at the 250th anniversary of the founding of Harvard, John Greenleaf Whittier—farmer-boy, propagandist, author of *Snow-Bound,* received the honorary degree of Doctor of Laws from the University which had made him Master of Arts in 1860. The two-term star pupil of the Haverhill Academy, honor graduate of no schools of higher education except those of Experience, Self-Reliance, and Self-Improvement, was accepted by and enrolled among the intellectual leaders of the Western World. One prophet, at least, was not finally without ample honor among his own people.

36

THE TENT ON
THE BEACH

The Tent on the Beach and Other Poems, by John Greenleaf Whittier, was published by Ticknor and Fields in February, 1867, just a year after *Snow-Bound.* There were several successive rapid printings with no change on the title-page. The first issue is identified by the beginning of the second stanza on page 46, which reads "With quick heart-glow," etc. The passage dissatisfied Whittier and he changed it twice after the first copies were off the press.

The commercial success of *The Tent on the Beach* not only equalled but eclipsed that of *Snow-Bound.* Though it contains much excellent verse and some of definite importance, none of it reaches the caliber of his autobiographical masterpiece, and the extent of its sale, which reached a thousand copies a day, is a bit staggering.

The Tent on the Beach proper, exclusive of the thirteen other incidental poems appearing in the same volume, is not strictly a single work but a regrouping of nine poems all previously printed in *The Atlantic,* interspersed with three songs, either new or much revised. These twelve separate entities are connected by a slight thread of poetical narrative, concerning a publisher and two friends to whom he reads various manuscripts while they are all camping together on Hampton Beach. It is obvious that these three characters are three actual persons. The publisher is James T. Fields. The friends are Whittier himself and Bayard Taylor, both exclusive clients of the Ticknor and Fields publishing concern, and special cronies. Whittier used to say that he didn't need to run around the world himself because Taylor (most famous travel writer of his time and a minor poet) did all that sort of thing for him.

The contour of Hampton Beach, finest sand beach on the short New Hampshire shore extending from the Merrimack on the south to the Piscataqua on the north—has in recent years been defaced and radically altered by the construction of a long wooden bridge across the mouth of the Hampton River, separating Hampton from Seabrook on the south. In this writer's boyhood it was precisely as described by Whittier. The tent was pitched near the southern end of the beach, not far from the actual mouth of the Hampton River, from which point the famous Rivermouth Rocks—a main channel barrier between river and open sea—would always be clearly in view.

In boyhood the writer learned every foot of those sands while bent on slaying yellow-legs with an old-time twelve-gauge double-barrel shotgun which he could scarcely hoist to shooting position; he caught perch from the Rivermouth Rocks at low tide; and, once, almost within a stone's throw of the rocks, came uncomfortably near being swamped and drowned in an old flat-bottomed rowboat, trying to make a short cut to the open sea by crossing the sandbar at a place where the waves seemed not to be breaking, instead of following the winding channel close to the shore. At high tide, the river, at its mouth, used to be about half a mile across, and when the salt marsh, extending some five to ten miles inland and down toward Massachusetts, was flooded, the appearance was of a wide expanse of water, more a bay than a harbor. According to tradition, early eighteenth-century local wreckers, whose descendants are still alive, lured vessels to destruction in this false harbor on stormy winter nights by lighting false beacons on Rivermouth Rocks, thus leading skippers to imagine they were steering for safe anchorage at Portsmouth or Newburyport.

No wonder that Whittier, who knew this shore almost as

well as he knew every rock on the Isles of Shoals, chose this beautiful out-of-the-world spot as a setting for his poem.

Hampton, New Hampshire, is second only to Salem, Massachusetts, in its store of colonial folk-lore and Whittier used many of its local legends. In fact, two of the nine poems in *The Tent* concern the Hampton witch, Goody Cole, who died a natural death but who, as a precautionary measure, was buried with a stake through her body to keep her down, and whom the townspeople formally restored to good standing by special ceremony only two or three years ago. The two poems of *The Tent* group in which she appears are *The Wreck at the Rivermouth*, in which she predicts the disaster and is suspected of having brought it about by her curse, though she had no such intention; and *The Changeling*, in which she is saved from jail and possible execution by the timely recovery of a demented mother.

Of the nine major elements of *The Tent*, seven are narrative poems of Yankee-land. The most important are *The Wreck* and *Abraham Davenport*, this latter being Whittier's one notable experiment in blank verse.

Of the thirteen unrelated short poems included in the volume after the conclusion of *The Tent on the Beach*, five, under the collective heading of *National Lyrics* (title of the booklet of Whittier patriotic poems published in 1865) have to do with the victorious end of the war and reëstablishment of peace. Of the other eight, one alone is noteworthy, *The Eternal Goodness*. Most famous and most thoughtful—if not most familiar—of Whittier's devotional poems, this will be considered at length in the special chapter devoted to Whittier's religious verse.

Abraham Davenport, one of the few Whittier items included by Bliss Carman in his anthology of American verse, is very effective in both theme and treatment. It tells the story of one of those mysterious dark days which so terrified our colonial ancestors as evidences of God's implacable wrath or the imminent and most Presbyterian crack of Doom, now thought possibly to have been caused by distant inland forest fires and merely worse instances of the more recent yellow days—an enveloping darkness not caused by storm and not accompanied by high winds. Whittier shows a meeting of the colonial Connecticut Council on such a day—all the members but one too terrified with their conviction that the Day of Doom according to the horrific details of old Wigglesworth's poem had indeed arrived, to concentrate on any business save that of prayer—prayer that each one might turn out to be a predestined sheep and not a predestined goat.

Abraham Davenport, delegate from Stamford, alone objects to adjournment of the meeting, and his argument, for which there is historical authority, runs in this wise:

> "It is the Lord's Great Day! Let us adjourn,"
> Some said; and then, as if with one accord,
> All eyes were turned to Abraham Davenport.
> He rose, slow cleaving with his steady voice
> The intolerable hush. "This well may be
> The Day of Judgment which the world awaits;
> But be it so or not, I only know
> My present duty, and My Lord's command
> To occupy till he come. So at the post
> Where he hath set me in his providence,
> I choose, for one, to meet him face to face,—
> No faithless servant frightened from my task,
> But ready when the Lord of the harvest calls;
> And therefore, with all reverence, I would say,
> Let God do his work, we will see to ours.
> Bring in the candles." And they brought them in.
>
> Then by the flaring lights the Speaker read,
> Albeit with husky voice and shaking hands,
> An act to amend an act to regulate
> The shad and alewive fisheries. Whereupon
> Wisely and well spake Abraham Davenport,
> Straight to the question, with no figures of speech
> Save the ten Arab signs, yet not without
> The shrewd dry humor natural to the man:
> His awe-struck colleagues listening all the while,
> Between the pauses of his argument,

To hear the thunder of the wrath of God
Break from the hollow trumpet of the cloud.

And there he stands in memory to this day,
Erect, self-poised, a rugged face, half seen
Against the background of unnatural dark,
A witness to the ages as they pass,
That simple duty hath no place for fear.

This is a grand poem, and if only a Yankee can appreciate it, so much the worse for the rest of the world!

Though Whittier was to write many poems in the succeeding twenty-five years before his death, including several of considerable length but not especially important, half a dozen short poems of more than casual merit, and one miniature masterpiece, *The Tent on the Beach* was the crest of the wave. This, therefore, seems an appropriate time to interpolate some consideration of a phase of his work that most people have entirely forgotten—the publication of various poems and songs, set to music, in sheet music form.

The all-searching and all-recording Currier lists thirty-eight Whittier poems, some originally intended as songs and some with no such first intention, set to music—some with music by one composer only, and others with variant music by half a dozen different composers. Thirteen of the thirty-eight are distinctly religious. The compositions range from short vocal scores with accompaniments to formal cantatas.

Of the secular songs, those most in actual use were undoubtedly *The Kansas Emigrants*, *The Furnace Blast*, the Frémont Campaign Songs, and *The Song of the Negro Boatmen*—Whittier's one attempt to write Negro dialect, more popular than its commonplace character indicates that it should have been. Directly or indirectly these all had to do with the anti-slavery movement. *Maud Muller*, *Skipper Ireson*, and *Barbara Frietchie* were also set to music, but they were certainly used more as recitations than as songs. *Laus Deo*, written to celebrate the end of the war and final emancipation, was more effective sung than spoken. True to the eternal contradiction of theory and instinct that governed so much of his life, Whittier, who consistently opposed singing at Quaker meetings, could not stifle the instinct to break into song. The total number of the known Whittier sheet-music first editions, counting each different musical setting as a first, is seventy-eight, and more of them may be lurking in collections or forgotten corners of old bookstores and music shops or in dusty attics. This is no flood of music publishing, but it is sufficient to indicate one of the many ways in which the name and fame and favorite writings of the poet became taken-for-granted component parts of late nineteenth-century American word consciousness.

Though many good things were still to come, by the time he was sixty Whittier had composed the bulk of those poems which were to be standard recitations not only in hundreds but literally in thousands of American public schools. As indicated at the very beginning, this stupendous popularizing force made the entire first generation after the Civil War respectfully and impressively Whittier-ized, but for the following generation, the very familiarity of the verses acted as a sort of boomerang.

As the great majority of the Grand Army of the Republic passed over to the even more vast majority of the dead, there passed also the patriotic thrill which had been the overtone of Whittier's reputation before blue ranks had been thinned by the silent gunnery of time. For a while he drifted into the shadow-land of worn-out poets. His rhymes and rhythms seemed too simple for the modern ear; his concepts of life too unsophisticated for the complex modern soul. The recent enormous revival of interest in American history and American nineteenth-century literature has inevitably included a renewed acknowledgment of Whittier's political and literary achievement. But he is regarded with respect, as traditionally important, rather than with real sympathy or understanding or enthusiasm.

The sole purpose of this book is to transform this vague respect into concrete appreciation.

37

TWILIGHT INSPIRATION

IN ALL FIELDS EXCEPT that of reverential verse, Whittier's writings after 1867 are less important, though with surprising after-glow. He continued to write poetry—and good poetry—almost to the day of his death at eighty-four. These later works are a long twilight of inspiration, shot through with occasional gleams of vivid sunlight and never darkening into night or void. They cover an entire quarter century, from 1867 to 1892.

In all this long period of placid and prosperous living and writing, only two religious poems and one short reminiscent poem added materially to his popular reputation. The one youth-recalling poem, *In School Days,* has already been listed among the inescapable favorites, but the idea expressed by at least one great English critic that it is the culminating expression of Whittier's genius is entirely unjustified. It is no more to be compared with the best of Whittier in mature vein than the juvenile stories of Hawthorne are to be grouped with *The Scarlet Letter.* Written for children, it was first published in *Our Young Folks* for January, 1870. Within the limits of the poet's intention, it is a notable moral miniature in verse.

IN SCHOOL DAYS

Still sits the school-house by the road,
    A ragged beggar sunning;
Around it still the sumachs grow,
    And blackberry-vines are running.

Within, the master's desk is seen,
    Deep scarred by raps official;

The warping floor, the battered seats,
  The jack-knife's carved initial;

The charcoal frescos on its wall;
  Its door's worn sill, betraying
The feet that, creeping slow to school,
  Went storming out to playing!

Long years ago a winter sun
  Shone over it at setting;
Lit up its western window-panes,
  And low eaves' icy fretting.

It touched the tangled golden curls,
  And brown eyes full of grieving,
Of one who still her steps delayed
  When all the school were leaving.

For near her stood the little boy
  Her childish favor singled;
His cap pulled low upon a face
  Where pride and shame were mingled.

Pushing with restless feet the snow
  To right and left, he lingered;—
As restlessly her tiny hands
  The blue-checked apron fingered.

He saw her lift her eyes; he felt
  The soft hand's light caressing,
And heard the tremble of her voice,
  As if a fault confessing.

"I'm sorry that I spelt the word:
  I hate to go above you,
Because,"—the brown eyes lower fell,—
  "Because, you see, I love you!"

Still memory to a gray-haired man
  That sweet child-face is showing.
Dear girl! the grasses on her grave
  Have forty years been growing!

He lives to learn, in life's hard school,
How few who pass above him
Lament their triumph and his loss,
Like her,—because they love him.

However, if Whittier in his last quarter century did little to enhance his fame he did much to consolidate it and nothing to injure it. Conscious that he now had a standard to maintain, he composed with meticulous care and his penchant for revision became almost a minor obsession. In late life he got the habit of working over proofs which were supplied gratis by a local printer named Fred Brown in return for being permitted to retain the original drafts! Sometimes Brown would run off a few extra copies of an item in its final revised form for Whittier to give to personal friends. Such printings—especially the early proofs—are among the rare desiderata of collectors.

Whittier's later works, including several poems of considerable length, form a body of commendable if conventional verse in the forms with which he had become most familiar. They show the inevitable slackening of intensity but, at times, surprisingly defined visualization and keen understanding of humanity. His viewpoint is consistently that of looking back on his mundane life and forward only when writing of the life to come. The bulk of his subjects are legends, historical episodes, reflections on the past, personal poems of reminiscence, and religious poems.

The last Whittier ballad to have an unmistakable spark of the old fire was published in *The Atlantic* for June, 1883, in the poet's seventy-fifth year. It was entitled *How the Women Went from Dover* and was first collected in *The Bay of Seven Islands*, 1883. When *Cassandra Southwick*, Whittier's first important ballad, was under discussion in connection with the publication of *Lays of My Home*, this poem, written just forty years later, was cited for comparison. And it is undeniable that the later poem is better than the earlier one, the general similarity of character and theme being such as to make the comparison entirely just.

A still later poem that must have specific mention (collected in *At Sundown,* Whittier's last volume of verse) is *The Captain's Well,* first printed by the *New York Ledger,* with illustrations by Howard Pyle, as a special supplement for its issue of January 11, 1890, when the poet was eighty-two. For the first publication of these ninety-six lines he received $1000, an extreme price for those days, showing in what Whittier himself called the Arabic symbols how great his fame had become. The poem is a simple and charming ballad in two-line stanzas founded on a quaint bit of local history already used once, less completely, for poetizing, by Harriet Prescott Spofford. It recounts the tale of an Amesbury-born sea captain who, nearly dying of thirst in the Arabian desert, vowed to dig a well of pure water for all passers-by if he should ever reach home and who did precisely that even though the townspeople, in Yankee phrase, suspected he was not quite all there. True to a fatality which Whittier could never seem to escape when writing a particularly successful ballad, there was an essential error of fact which had to be corrected in later printings. The captain, pictured by Whittier as returning to his wife and family, had, at that time, been a bachelor! But the well itself was so very real that it is still in use in front of the Amesbury High School, marked with a proper inscription, though the actual water supply is now from the city main.

The very last poem written by Whittier was entitled merely *Dr. Holmes,* and was first printed in the *Boston Morning Journal* for August 27, 1892—two days before Dr. Holmes's eighty-third birthday and eleven days before Whittier's own death. The September number of *The Atlantic,* published almost the same day, had a more formal birthday poem from Whittier to Holmes which must necessarily have been written some time earlier. This last charming little poem to his old friend, described as the "beloved physician," shows how remarkably Whittier retained all his faculties to the end.

When Whittier died he had over $100,000 invested in gilt-edged securities, all accumulated after the publication of

Snow-Bound. This was due less to the sale of the various small volumes of new poems issued after *The Tent on the Beach* than to the skill with which the publishers kept the whole body of his work alive and continually issued new collected editions augmented by the latest new material.

The chronological table of Whittier's works in the Cambridge Edition lists 177 poems between 1866 and 1892. These titles—including half a dozen really long ones and another half dozen of more than usual length—appeared in a series of eleven books or booklets. During this same twenty-six-year period no less than sixteen complete collections of or extensive selections from Whittier's works were issued in a wide variety of formats, sustaining public interest. And these numerous publications were supplemented with four special issues of *Snow-Bound,* three of them illustrated, and various other individual items in gift form. In addition to all this original Whittier work, three anthologies appeared over his name though most of the work was done by Lucy Larcom: *Child Life,* 1872; *Child Life in Prose,* 1874; and *Songs of Three Centuries,* 1876.

When Charles Sumner died in 1874, a poem by Whittier was read as a main feature of the memorial exercises held in Music Hall. It was manifestly fitting that Whittier, who had contrived Sumner's election to the Senate, should say a last farewell. The official version of this poem, which Whittier later expanded by the addition of several stanzas, was published by the State of Massachusetts. Whittier poems had become vital features of many public occasions, from celebrations as important as that of the One Hundredth Anniversary of the Battle of Lexington to such intimate affairs as school reunions.

The list of Whittier's new publications in book form after *The Tent on the Beach* is as follows:

Among the Hills and Other Poems. 1869. Actually issued in December, 1868. The long title poem is a romantic idyl telling how a woman summer visitor, seeking health, marries a rugged farmer of the hills. The ten short poems are not particularly distinguished.

Miriam and Other Poems. 1871. Published in November, 1870. The title poem narrates the story of an Oriental Shah who is persuaded to show mercy by his Christian Slave. Among the thirteen short poems are *In School Days* and the very good *Howard at Atlanta.*

The Pennsylvania Pilgrim and Other Poems. 1872 (September). The poem which gives its name to the volume is Whittier's tribute to the colonial Quakers of Philadelphia and, in particular, to Francis Daniel Pastorius, first Quaker opponent of slavery. One of the twelve shorter poems, *The Brewing of Soma,* contains the lines which constitute Whittier's most familiar hymn.

Hazel Blossoms. 1875. Published in October of 1874. This collection includes sixteen short poems by Whittier and nine by his sister Elizabeth, who never succeeded in transferring her personality to the printed page. The Whittier items include the *Sumner* poem and also the widely known *The Prayer of Agassiz.*

Mabel Martin. 1876. Actually published in October of 1875, contains only the one long poem, being the sole Whittier item, with the exception of *Snow-Bound,* to enjoy original individual book publication. It is far better than *Among the Hills, Miriam,* or *The Pennsylvania Pilgrim*—less prolix (the others are obviously built up to size), more characteristic, with much more narrative and dramatic value. The publishers must have been conscious of this in bringing it out as a separate book. The tale is of a prosperous colonial farmer who takes pity on the outcast daughter of the local witch (Susanna Martin, the only woman actually hanged for witchcraft north of the Merrimack) and defies the community by making her his wife.

The Vision of Echard and Other Poems. 1878 (September). The comparatively short name poem details the vision of a Benedictine Monk. *The Centennial Hymn* and many of the other twenty-three items are very readable.

The King's Missive and Other Poems. 1881 (February). The title poem is not over-long and is a very good ballad of Boston colonial life in 1661. It has an infusion of the genuine Whittier spirit, which never got too old to be roused at the thought of a persecuted Quaker. This ballad narrates the historical story of the manner in which Governor Endicott was compelled by

royal decree, borne from London to Boston by a Quaker, to release all his Quaker prisoners. The other twenty-eight items in
the volume are not particularly notable.

The Bay of Seven Islands and Other Poems. 1883 (October).
The name poem is a good Yankee sea-faring ballad—the yarn of
a skipper who sailed down East to the edge of Canada, where he
fell in love with one of two French Canadian twin sisters but had
the misfortune to be loved by both. Because of the duplicity of
the mother, he sailed away with the wrong twin and when he
returned to claim his sweetheart found her dead. The twenty-one
short items include *How the Women Went from Dover* and the
famous religious poem, *At Last.*

St. Gregory's Guest and Recent Poems. 1886 (April). This is a
pamphlet, with paper wrappers, containing eighteen short poems,
the title poem being a comparatively short recounting of the
famous tale of St. Gregory and the Christ-beggar. Whittier's beautiful paraphrases of two Buddhist hymns are included in this
booklet.

At Sundown. 1890 (December). A privately printed but publicly sold edition of 250 copies, which includes twelve short
poems, among them the first book printing of *The Captain's Well*
and the first of Whittier's three poems to Holmes.

At Sundown. 1892 (November). Issued in two forms—a large
paper limited edition of 250 copies and an unlimited trade printing. The seven short poems in this volume are new compositions
not in the earlier volume of the same name. Though posthumously published, Whittier had prepared it for the press. It includes the birthday poem to Holmes, published in the September
Atlantic of the same year.

It would appear that from 1867 to 1876 Whittier over-
reached in his longer poetical efforts, by choosing unfamiliar
topics and by over-writing; that he recaptured something of
his old vein in *Mabel Martin, The King's Missive* and *The
Bay of Seven Islands,* and enjoyed an amazing poetical Indian
summer from the age of sixty-nine to seventy-five. This
mental fecundity in late life is without a parallel among
American poets.

38

DEVOTIONAL WRITINGS

NOTHING IS MORE TYPICAL of the very logical development of Whittier's talents than that he wrote his best devotional poetry after he had reached an age when the contemplation of death becomes unavoidable. On the mystery of life's revolutions he produced no youthful confession of faith such as *Thanatopsis* by Bryant, no glamorous creed of pantheism like Millay's *Renascence*. His religious convictions—rather less orthodox as he grew older but no less profound—and his ability to voice them developed as time brought the mystery closer and closer. The invisibility of the far shore never led him to doubt its existence.

Merely a glance at the *Religious Poems* as arranged in sequence for the Cambridge Edition of Whittier, shows the progress of his philosophy from the conventionally concrete to the abstract and abstruse—from legend and tradition to Christianized mysticism.

Poem Number 1, *The Star of Bethlehem,* is a tale or legend of a Christian Pilgrim in Moslem Palestine. Number 2, *The Cities of the Plain,* is Sodom and Gomorrah in the same rhyme and rhythm Byron used to picture how the Assyrian came down like a wolf on the fold. Number 3, *The Call of the Christian,* celebrates the early martyrs. Number 4 is *The Crucifixion,* and Number 5 is *Palestine. The Familist's Hymn* is still concrete, the first poem on the early New England persecution, as one might say, of the non-Matherites; the next is on a text from Ezekiel. Following is the first of the more abstract poems with a flavor of the real Whittier religious touch. It is entitled *What the Voice Said*—a good Whittier

305

idea at any time—and it is a vigorous warning that even
Duty must be tempered with Love.

What the Voice Said appeared first in the *Poems,* 1849.
Though Christian tradition reappears thereafter now and
then, the progression toward ethical thought in the abstract
is continuous. In *The Wish of To-day (Songs of Labor,* 1850)
Whittier definitely states his theory of complete unquestion-
ing dependence on the Father. And yet the mystery of the
Trinity—to which he never refers in his much later work—
still troubles him and he tries to solve it in *Trinitas (Home
Ballads,* 1860). He writes—

> The equal Father in rain and sun,
> His Christ is the good to evil done,
> His Voice is thy soul;—and the Three are One!

Home Ballads contains four major religious poems, and it
will be noted that they show the same unmistakable advance
in average excellence commented upon in relation to the lay
poems when the volume was cited for analysis of *Skipper
Ireson.*

Consensus of opinion would certainly identify Whittier's
three foremost religious poems as *The Eternal Goodness,
Dear Lord and Father of Mankind* (an excerpt from *The
Brewing of Soma*) and *At Last. The Eternal Goodness* will be
found first in *The Tent on the Beach,* 1867; *Dear Lord and
Father of Mankind (The Brewing of Soma)* appeared in *The
Pennsylvania Pilgrim,* 1872; and *At Last* was first collected in
The Bay of Seven Islands, 1883.

In all these poems the thought tends to be mystic and is
basically and emotionally Quaker. The poet's dependence is
entirely on the goodness of God; and he attempts no literal
or allegorical specific concept either of Jehovah or His realm.
No literal Hell appears to his imagination, which demands
trust so complete in the Spirit of Goodness that specific inquiry as to the exact fate of the human soul is not only vain
but unworthy. Eternal Goodness becomes his name for the
Supreme Spirit.

The Eternal Goodness seems probably to have been written while Whittier was working on the manuscript of *Snow-Bound*, certainly while under the emotional reactions to Elizabeth's recent death. The fundamental preachment is complete belief and absolute submission; the warning is against all sectarian righteousness. If one is to understand the atmosphere of sanctity which truly surrounded Whittier in old age, study of this poem is vital. Stanzas one to five inclusive; followed by stanzas sixteen to twenty-three, omitting eighteen and nineteen, will cover the ground.

THE ETERNAL GOODNESS

O FRIENDS! with whom my feet have trod
    The quiet aisles of prayer,
Glad witness to your zeal for God
    And love of man I bear.

I trace your lines of argument;
    Your logic linked and strong
I weigh as one who dreads dissent,
    And fears a doubt as wrong.

But still my human hands are weak
    To hold your iron creeds;
Against the words ye bid me speak
    My heart within me pleads.

Who fathoms the Eternal Thought?
    Who talks of scheme and plan?
The Lord is God! He needeth not
    The poor device of man.

I walk with bare, hushed feet the ground
    Ye tread with boldness shod;
I dare not fix with mete and bound
    The love and power of God.

I long for household voices gone,
    For vanished smiles I long,
But God hath led my dear ones on,
    And He can do no wrong.

I know not what the future hath
  Of marvel or surprise,
Assured alone that life and death
  His mercy underlies.

And so beside the Silent Sea
  I wait the muffled oar;
No harm from Him can come to me
  On ocean or on shore.

I know not where His islands lift
  Their fronded palms in air;
I only know I cannot drift
  Beyond His love and care.

O brothers! if my faith is vain,
  If hopes like these betray,
Pray for me that my feet may gain
  The sure and safer way.

And Thou, O Lord! by whom are seen
  Thy creatures as they be,
Forgive me if too close I lean
  My human heart on Thee!

It would be very difficult indeed to find in devotional
literature a finer statement of essential faith for the man who
is neither atheist nor complete agnostic but who feels that a
pantheon of Christian deities, with their accompanying
legends, are unworthy of mature belief.

The Brewing of Soma (1872) begins as a beautiful poem
of Oriental legend showing how a specially brewed religious
potion was part of early worship; proceeds to the reflection
that much modern worship still has its madness; and then,
rather unexpectedly, at the twelfth stanza breaks into inspired devotional lyric. The last six stanzas, which constitute
virtually a separate poem—Whittier's most widely sung hymn
—are almost universally known by the first-line title of *Dear
Lord and Father of Mankind*. The first two stanzas read:

Dear Lord and Father of mankind,
  Forgive our foolish ways!

Reclothe us in our rightful mind,
In purer lives thy service find,
In deeper reverence, praise.

In simple trust like theirs who heard
Beside the Syrian sea
The gracious calling of the Lord,
Let us, like them, without a word,
Rise up and follow thee.

Since this volume will appropriately end with the twenty-eight lines of the poem *At Last*—the finest devotional poem by an American and one of the finest ever written outside the Book of Psalms, an astounding *tour de force* to have been achieved by a man in his seventy-fifth year—it need not be quoted now. It summarizes and distills his religious thought rather than amending or amplifying it.

Whittier's closer and closer approach in old age to pure idealism, impersonal except for the completeness of his faith in a supremely understanding and utterly inscrutable God, is shown by his growing interest in Buddhistic thought. During later life he made a total of five translations of Oriental religious poems, the best being the versions of two Brahminical hymns printed in *St. Gregory's Guest*, 1886.

In the Cambridge Edition of the collected poems, the final item under the heading of religious poems is entitled *Revelation*, and is preceded by a prose quotation from George Fox, founder of Quakerism. Stanza nine shows how completely God and Eternal Goodness have merged in the poet's mind:

No picture to my aid I call,
I shape no image in my prayer;
I only know in Him is all
Of life, light, beauty, everywhere,
Eternal Goodness here and there!

The final stanza of *The Mystic's Christmas* is also revealing, this being one of the short poems in *The Bay of Seven Islands*. It reads:

"Keep while you need it, brothers mine,
With honest zeal your Christmas sign,
But judge not him who every morn
Feels in his heart the Lord Christ born!"

The man who seriously wishes to understand Whittier's philosophic attachment to Quakerism should read, line by line, *The Meeting* (*Among the Hills*, 1869) and get the information at the source.

Many devout readers have great admiration for Whittier's *A Christmas Carmen,* which is substantially a carol and which was included in *Hazel Blossoms,* 1875. Since Whittier's death it has been set to music by four different composers, the first in 1896 and the last in 1933.

Though the poet's faith was so impersonal, it was by no means passive. He was most anxious that the world should share his belief in Eternal Life and Eternal Goodness. In a sense he became a propagandist for Faith, and so versed was he in skill as a publicist that he could not allow a striking current event to go unnoticed. In 1873, Professor Agassiz, then the most important American scientist, opened his new School of Natural History by unpremeditatedly asking the audience to join him in silent prayer and then making an address that was really a fervent sermon. Instantly, Whittier saw the value of this incident as an argument against growing scientific agnosticism and wrote *The Prayer of Agassiz,* which was first published in *The Christian Union* for January 14, 1874. Agassiz died suddenly a few months later and the poem was reprinted in the *Agassiz Memorial* before appearing in *Hazel Blossoms,* 1875, its first publication in a Whittier collection.

Whittier's persistent adherence to Quakerism, and to its most conservative branch and customs, seems to have been in later life more a matter of sentiment and custom than of theological conviction. His objection to singing in Quaker meetings, though humorously expressed as based on the lack of Quaker practice in the musical arts, was an instinctive reaction to all innovations among the Friends. The silent worship, interspersed with extemporaneous inspired addresses by members of both sexes, satisfied him, not only because it aided the religious reverie natural to his temperament, but because it had satisfied his forebears.

In old age, one of Whittier's ardent admirers was the Bishop of the Protestant Episcopal Church in Massachusetts, Phillips Brooks. He and Whittier both felt the very different dogmas of their respective sects to be unessential as compared to the serious work of leading godly lives and doing godly deeds.

It has been said of New England's foremost anti-slavery preacher, Theodore Parker, that he had to build a special church for himself (and his overflowing congregation) because none existed broad enough to hold him. Ralph Waldo Emerson left the Unitarian Church because even its vague restrictions galled him. But John Greenleaf Whittier stuck to his Meeting—and did his own thinking against its background of peaceful introspection.

As a rule, Whittier discussed religion with diffidence. In any group of arguing friends he was generally chief listener. Yet there is an eye-witness account of his speaking earnestly and at length on religious topics one Sunday morning when he was a guest at the home of Celia Thaxter on the Isles of Shoals. In the midst of a casual ethical discussion among the other guests, all of them friends, Whittier picked up a volume of Emerson's Essays, read a few paragraphs and, using them as a text, launched into an exposition of his devotional ideas which they all regarded as an unforgettable sermon.

There is one other religious poem, first collected with Barbara Frietchie in In War Time, which happens to be the personal favorite of this writer. The last portion of this poem, unmistakably a religious ballad—a fact in itself curious and interesting—has been separately printed as an illuminated Christmas booklet under the title My Prayer. The official name of the full poem is Andrew Rykman's Prayer. The

stanzas at the end are obviously Whittier himself addressing
Eternal Goodness:

> Scarcely Hope hath shaped for me
> What the future life may be.
> Other lips may well be bold;
> Like the publican of old,
> I can only urge the plea,
> "Lord, be merciful to me!"
> Nothing of desert I claim,
> Unto me belongeth shame.
> Not for me the crowns of gold,
> Palms, and harpings manifold;
> Not for erring eye and feet
> Jasper wall and golden street.
> What Thou wilt, O Father, give!
> All is gain that I receive.
> If my voice I may not raise
> In the elders' song of praise,
> If I may not, sin-defiled,
> Claim my birthright as a child,
> Suffer it that I to Thee
> As an hired servant be;
> Let the lowliest task be mine,
> Grateful, so the work be Thine;
> Let me find the humblest place
> In the shadow of Thy grace:
> Blest to me were any spot
> Where temptation whispers not.
> If there be some weaker one,
> Give me strength to help him on;
> If a blinder soul there be,
> Let me guide him nearer Thee.
> Make my mortal dreams come true
> With the work I fain would do;
> Clothe with life the weak intent,
> Let me be the thing I meant;
> Let me find in Thy employ
> Peace that dearer is than joy;
> Out of self to love be led

> And to heaven acclimated,
> Until all things sweet and good
> Seem my natural habitude.

If all Christian ministers would repeat this to their congregations once every Sunday, it might be good for the congregations—and especially good for the ministers themselves.

39

THE CELIBATE
PATRIARCH

WHITTIER'S CHARACTER during the early years of his life and even up to the beginning of the Civil War must be interpreted essentially in terms of action with the well known periods of introspective revaluation. His final and almost complete separation from worldly concerns really began during the war itself, clearly of too great magnitude to be directly influenced by what little he could do. The approach to the *Snow-Bound* mood began well before Elizabeth's death.

Whittier of the period after *Snow-Bound* is more elusive. More by the fame of an hallowed personality than by what he continued to write, he exerted an almost incredible private and public influence, but upon national thought rather than upon practical affairs. His rare and brief appearances at the public functions he so dreaded, were occasions to be chronicled. A celibate in life, he had become an intellectual patriarch on the grand scale. He had become a popular symbol for nobility of purpose and purity of heart.

Beyond all doubt, he must have been a most lovable old man—but one who very decidedly knew his own mind and was never lost in the clouds. He was too discerning not to sense his own position, but he never acquired the conscious graciousness of Longfellow or the self-importance of Lowell. Without any of Holmes's sparkling wit (which he thoroughly appreciated) Whittier retained throughout his long life a sense of dry humor which kept him down to earth in the business of earthly living. In his own way, Holmes—humorist and professor of anatomy—was almost as deeply religious as Whittier, and in old age the two men were drawn more and more closely together, wrote poems to each other on their birthdays, and craved each other's company.

In considering Whittier's social contacts it must be remembered that though he spoke the Quaker speech and hated public occasions, there was nothing countrified about his manners or his dress. Even throughout his years of poverty his personal appearance was always scrupulously neat. Various of his intimates have recorded his well brushed and well fitting overcoat with a fine fur collar, and have suggested that he knew it became him well. As a matter of fact, during the early years, at least one opposition paper spoke of him as a dandy and mentioned his yellow gloves. He was not only careful of his own dress but noticed details in the dress of others, particularly women. At times he would jokingly insist that Lydia Child—for whom he had a very particular regard —had made some alteration in her old "bunnit" and on one formal occasion he made no secret of his exasperation at having to take in to dinner a woman he considered overdressed.

Though portraits of Whittier in old age, showing him with a considerable expanse of white beard, are so common that it is difficult to imagine him clean shaven, the fact is, as shown by the frontispiece of *Snow-Bound*, that his face was innocent of either beard or mustache until he was over sixty. And the penetrating vigor of his glance is said to have been as alert at eighty as when he wrote *Justice and Expediency*.

Whittier never lost his interest in youth. He got much pleasure from associating with young people whom he liked, and he could be very natural and charming with them. As the poet's income grew until it far exceeded his simple needs, he spent a bit more freely, but long habit had made him incurably frugal. He gave graciously but modestly to worthy individuals and causes, but with no public gestures and in no major sums. His investments were canny. He was in favor of woman suffrage and of all reasonable and enlightened social betterment legislation, readily sympathetic in such problems as educating the Negroes, the blind, and the feeble-minded. Most emphatically he was an individualist and no radical. He favored the Quaker speech because it came most readily to his tongue, but he could lay it aside instantly at will. He was a sectarian in name only, for all good men and women of all creeds and races were to him one brotherhood or sisterhood.

His friends all agree that Whittier enjoyed the singing of simple songs, especially Scotch ballads, but since singing was doubtful orthodox Quakerism, he always spoke of music evasively though he must have known that many of his own verses had been set to music and certainly wrote some of them to fit definite tunes of the day. On the same theory, it is recorded that he always spoke of any statue, large or small, as a "graven image." But such idiosyncrasies as these were so much a part of his personality that they never seemed out of place.

The two best collections of Whittier anecdotes are by two smart women, who had spacious homes he liked to visit and who had a gift for putting him completely at ease and making him talk. Annie Fields, wife of Whittier's publisher, was one of them, and the other was Mary Claflin, wife of a noted Massachusetts governor, who contrived to make Whittier so entirely at home that he used his standing invitation freely and wrote her frankly how disappointed he was to come to the city and find the family away.

As an example of the manner in which Whittier shied off at anything savoring of flattery or overstatement, Mrs. Claflin relates his reply to her entirely sincere remark that she was happier to know he was in the house even when he was secluded in his own room. "Thee is a sensible woman," said the old poet, "Don't thee talk so. . . . I cannot believe thee." And when she indulged in some feminine extravagance of language, he would say, in gentle reproof, "Thee is a little Oriental in thy speech."

One of Mrs. Claflin's most vivid stories is of an attempt, during one of Whittier's visits, to arrange a tea for a number of his old friends without his knowledge, fearing that otherwise he might slip away as he sometimes did if a social event was in the offing. The old man sensed that something was in the air and when she tried to avoid questioning he insisted quaintly, "Oh, I know thee is going to have some kind of Fandango." The sequel is that he stayed, received the guests cordially, and said to his hostess afterwards, rather sheepishly, "I think thee managed that very well!"

Mrs. Claflin tells another anecdote of a Whittier party she gave, at which all the guests were very old people once active in the anti-slavery cause. In this instance, Whittier's final word was "Don't thee think we are pretty cheerful martyrs?"

After the Civil War, Whittier, Elizabeth Stuart Phelps, and Mrs. Stowe were all fast friends. Mrs. Phelps, whose spiritualistic *Gates Ajar* was the supreme consolation volume for women who had suffered war bereavement, had implicit faith in visual manifestations of life after death and spoken communications from beyond the grave. Mrs. Stowe wouldn't go the whole distance with her but was very strong for spirit rappings. Whittier was the gentle sceptic, though he did his best to keep pace with Mrs. Stowe. His report was: "Much as I have wooed them [the spirits] they never appear to me. Mrs. Stowe is more fortunate—the spirits sometimes come at her bidding, but never at mine—and what wonder? It would be a foolish spirit that did not prefer her company to that of an old man like me."

A characteristic retort that cannot be omitted was given to a woman who complained that she feared she would not have money enough to pay for her burial. "My friend," said Whittier, "did thee ever know of anyone to stick by the way for lack of funds?"

The most widely repeated anecdote of the old poet on a public occasion refers to a memorial service for Charles Sumner at which he found himself absolutely obliged to break his rule against public speeches. To make an extemporaneous oration on his love for Sumner—one of the subjects dearest to his heart and on which he had already composed a notable poem—was beyond his strength, capacity, or control. He dodged the question in true Lincoln manner by telling a story which seems rather out of place in the retelling but which apparently created no such impression on anybody present. According to this little tale, the final salute at the burial of a certain Scotch Colonel was fired by a detail from the one regiment the deceased most specifically and positively detested, which caused a friend to exclaim, "If the Colonel could have known this he wouldn't have died!" "So I feel," concluded Whittier, "if my friend Sumner could have known that I would speak at his Memorial Services, he would not have died."

After the services were over, one of the poet's friends mentioned to him the hush that had fallen over the assembly during his brief address, and drew this retort: "Don't thee think they would have listened just as attentively if Balaam's animal had spoken?"

The remembrances of Mrs. Fields naturally overlap those of Mrs. Claflin, and her two or three best anecdotes have already been woven into this narrative. She indicates that Whittier was interested not only in spiritualism but in the social experiments of Robert Dale Owen. She and Pickard both quote this singular and yet pertinent reference to Thoreau's *Walden* in one of his letters: "Thoreau's 'Walden' is capital reading but very wicked and heathenish. The practical moral of it seems to be that if a man is willing to sink himself into a woodchuck he can live as cheaply as that quadruped."

Whittier's somewhat belated appreciation of Lincoln ripened with the years. On being shown Marshall's engraving of the martyr president, he said, "It is the face of the speaker at Gettysburg and the writer of the second inaugural."

Almost invariably Whittier judged the literary work of other people more favorably than his own—and he had a way of being right when he selected anything as especially fine.

He spotted Holmes's *Chambered Nautilus* as a permanent masterpiece the moment he clapped eyes on it.

No example of Whittier's cautious attitude toward his own work is better than his letter to Lowell about his very famous little poem, *Telling the Bees.* He wrote: "I send thee a bit of rhyme which pleases me, and yet I am not quite sure about it. What I call simplicity may be only silliness, and my poor bantling only fit to be handed over to Dr. Howe's school for feeble-minded children. But I like it and hope better things of it. Look it over and let me hear from thee, if but a line."

Whittier was always fond of animals and they apparently trusted him even though sometimes he teased them a bit amusingly. The Amesbury household pets included a long line of dogs and cats, but the most famous was a gray parrot named Charlie. When Charlie died in 1866, Whittier sent Lucy Larcom a little poem about him for *Our Young Folks* with this comment in his letter: "I have met a real loss—poor Charlie is dead. He has gone where the good parrots go. He has been ailing and silent for some time and he finally died. Don't laugh at me—but I am sorry enough to cry if it would do any good. He was an old friend; dear Lizzie liked him. And he was the heartiest, jolliest, pleasantest old fellow I ever saw."

Charlie's coat of sedate gray did not entirely suit the colorful vocabulary which he had acquired before joining the Quaker household and which would occasionally recur to him. One Sunday morning he climbed onto the lightning rod of the cottage at church-going time and shocked the towns-folk by there dancing, singing, and pouring out varied profanity. At meals he was well-behaved and sat on the back of the poet's chair. His favorite roost was the chimney top from which he would shout "Whoa!" to the horses in the street. At last he fell down the chimney, was A.W.O.L. for two days before he could be traced, and when finally fished up in the middle of the night could only whisper, "Poor Charlie wants water." And he then went into a real New England decline with the fatal results noted.

Charlie was succeeded by a gaudy little bantam rooster, who liked riding on Whittier's shoulder or being buttoned into the front of his coat. When it was time for his niece "Lizzie"—then his young housekeeper—to get up in the morning, Whittier would put the bantam atop the half-open door of her room where he would perch and crow until the objective was attained.

Of course, Pickard has a host of stories buried among an endless array of facts and correspondence. Perhaps this is the best of all:

Joshua Coffin, Whittier's old schoolmaster, friend, and fellow abolitionist, got to taking his Calvinism very literally in his old age and was obsessed by the idea that he had been predestined to suffer for eternity in Hell. This distressed his friends very much, but only Whittier was able to talk him out of it by a little colloquy almost worthy of Socrates.

John began by asking Joshua whether he didn't hate God for condemning him to Eternal Torment.

"No," responded Joshua, "it is for the good of all that some are punished."

John was stumped for a moment, but then he continued:

"Joshua, thee has spent thy life doing good, and now thee is of course getting ready to do all the hurt thee can to thy fellow men?"

"No, indeed, my thoughts have not changed in the least in this regard."

Then Whittier smiled and broke the evil spell at one thrust.

"Now, Joshua," said he "thee is going to Hell with a heart full of love for everybody,—what can the Devil find for such a one as thee to do?"

John G. Whittier

THE MORE FAMILIAR WHITTIER

"The penetrating vigor of his glance is said to have been as alert at eighty as when he wrote *Justice and Expediency*."

Photo John Blacklock

WHITTIER'S BEDROOM IN THE AMESBURY HOME

This room is just as it was when Whittier occupied it. The engraving above the mantel is "Zenobia," and on the mantel are pictures of Whittier's mother and sister. "The little bedroom, with narrow bed . . . speaks a volume of Spartan philosophy."

40

ETERNAL GOODNESS

THIS STUDY OF WHITTIER is not intended to include non-essentials of his later domestic life or of routine events that in no way further illuminate his character or the outlines of his career. Details of all his occasional reluctant appearances at public literary or charitable or memorial functions, or his absence from them—as when he remained away from the Dickens dinner but met Dickens later, privately—are readily obtainable from the Pickard *Life* for those who seek them. His few public utterances, consisting almost entirely of acknowledging, in the simplest manner, tributes to himself or paying tributes to others are without material significance. The celebrations of all his later birthdays, with meetings of friends and the publication of congratulatory poems, merely emphasize the universal admiration and affection with which he was surrounded. That Dom Pedro of Brazil, top social lion of the period, should have concentrated his attention, at a notable function, on Whittier, one of whose poems he had himself translated, shows that this appreciation of the old poet was not local or, indeed, confined to the English-speaking world.

For the last twenty-five years of his life, Whittier was free to do precisely whatever he wished. Not strong, he was far from being a helpless invalid and was physically better, on the whole, than might have been expected. He took every precaution to preserve his health, and the very simplicity of his tastes undoubtedly tended to prolong his life. He was content to write verse, visit friends, keep abreast of public affairs, and move almost entirely within the circle of long established connections. No record exists of any journey further from home than one carefully planned trip to New York.

After his eightieth birthday Whittier began to fail gradually and without inconveniences other than those inevitable at such an advanced age. As in earlier years, he sedulously avoided concentration for exhausting periods. The insomnia, of which he had complained for many years, naturally increased. However, many aged people sleep lightly and for only a few hours at night, refreshing themselves by dozing for a few minutes now and then during the daytime.

After the death of his beloved sister, Elizabeth, just before the close of the Civil War, another Elizabeth, the daughter of his brother Matthew, then just growing to womanhood, came from her home in Portland to the Amesbury cottage and was installed as her uncle's housekeeper. Whittier was devoted to her and absorbed in all the details of her life and education; and she seems to have reciprocated his affection and to have made his home very pleasant. The fact that the arrangement continued for more than ten years, until her marriage to Samuel T. Pickard, is proof that it worked very well indeed. Elizabeth's decision to marry Pickard, the Portland journalist who was to become his official biographer, was entirely acceptable to the poet, who seems to have regarded him as almost a son-in-law.

The marriage of this second Elizabeth in April of 1876 altered Whittier's whole plan of life. During the winter before the marriage, his cousins and old friends, Joseph and Gertrude Whittier Cartland, who had given up their home in Providence, lived with him in Amesbury, but it was understood that this was a temporary thing only. The Cartlands presently bought a house in Newburyport—the mansion which had once been the home of Harriet Livermore, the eccentric of *Snow-Bound*—and Whittier had to make entirely new plans for his personal living. The result of this was finally that the old poet had not one home but three: the old cottage in Amesbury; the Cartland house in Newburyport, where he frequently passed the more severe winter months; and Oak Knoll, Danvers, once the home of the Reverend George Burroughs, hanged as a wizard at Salem—a fine old estate of more than sixty acres, with ancient trees, lovely gardens, and a fine orchard—where he arranged to spend part of every year with three female cousins, the Misses Johnson and Mrs. Woodman, all granddaughters of his uncle Obadiah Whittier. Mrs. Woodman had an adopted daughter whose enthusiasms amused him and in whom he found a refreshing youthful companion.

Whittier seems to have spent most of his springs and autumns, and some of his winters, at Oak Knoll, which was for a time his established main residence. During the summer he would generally go with the Cartlands to inconspicuous White Mountain resorts—apparently changing residence from time to time in order to avoid the curiosity seekers who pursued him and whom he always called "the pilgrims"—and, a little later, to Centre Harbor, on Lake Winnepesaukee. As he grew older he spent less time at Oak Knoll, which he had himself christened with this charming name; rather more time with the Cartlands; and returned more frequently to the Amesbury cottage, where the crowded memories of many years beckoned him, and where he felt, with the local Quaker Meeting, closest to Eternal Goodness.

Other homes were open to him at all times—not only the Boston home of Governor Claflin, which he so frankly preferred to the alternative of the Hotel Marlboro, but also the Celia Thaxter home at the Isles of Shoals, and Elmfield, the home of an old friend, Miss Sarah Gove, in the village of Hampton Falls. Elmfield was dear to him because he had often been there with his mother. Also, it was only a short drive from Amesbury, and from his favorite bedchamber there he could overlook the ever-changing great salt marsh extending to the sea.

Though Whittier approached death as a profound believer in personal survival—not a shadow of doubt on that subject apparently ever having crossed his mind—he counted his long life in comfort and with full command of his faculties as a particular blessing. The strength of his own belief in individual immortality made him sorrow over the comparative agnosticism of his good friend Emerson. He is quoted as having declared that Emerson never cared to discuss the subject. Pickard quotes him as saying: "Near the close of his life when our conversation had turned upon it and I saw him for the last time, he said, 'Come to Concord and see me, and we will let the bucket deep down into the well and see what we can draw up.'"

John Greenleaf Whittier was eighty-four years old on December 17, 1891. His very precise handwriting now wavered feebly and he was clearly, in the good old Yankee phrase, not long for this world. He passed a quiet birthday in the Cartland home but shortly afterwards had an attack of grippe which was nearly fatal. His condition improved so much in the spring that he planned an expedition to Centre Harbor but abandoned it in favor of an invitation to visit at the near-by Gove house, in Hampton Falls, where he felt completely at home and where, because it was not one of his known residences, he could escape uninvited visitors.

He went to Hampton Falls and established himself at Elmfield in June and seemed to grow stronger. He would walk to the village post office, stroll down the river path to the little falls, and take short drives. There he wrote his last poem to Oliver Wendell Holmes; and there he corrected the proofs of the posthumously published *At Sundown*. He occupied his favorite chamber and left the curtains up every night so that he could see dawn break over the wide expanse of shaded browns and greens, veined with the winding river and with the fine tracery of the marsh ditches. The door of this room opened directly onto a wide balcony where he often sat on clear days, gazing across the marsh and beyond to the horizon-like blue ocean and the perfectly visible white sails of coastwise vessels. The peace of the scene must have been well attuned to his mood and must have soothed the aged soul waiting for its summons to renewed youth. Indeed—as anyone may see, for the marsh and the house and the sea are still there—no more beautiful place can be imagined for a human soul to take off in its mystic flight to infinity.

On the morning of September 3, 1892, Whittier suffered a paralytic shock affecting his entire right side. He knew it was the end, and, though he had always expressed the hope that he might die in the Amesbury cottage, seemed entirely resigned to greet Eternal Goodness in the house of his old friend. Speech was difficult, but he retained full consciousness. Early on the morning of September 6 he seemed drowsy and his nurse started to draw the curtains. He exclaimed "No! No!" and gestured with his left hand to indicate that he wanted them raised. And so he once more saw the sunrise— on his last day of consciousness, the day before his death.

Whittier thanked both physician and friends for their care, saying gently that he was worn out and nothing more could be done. He repeatedly murmured—"Love—love to all the world." His last audible words, spoken on the afternoon of the sixth in response to a question from his niece Elizabeth, were "I have known thee all the time."

The last night passed in what seemed to be quiet sleep. Death, when it came early on the morning of the seventh, was a severing of soul and body without visible struggle of any kind. While the soul of this good old man was gently releasing itself from the flesh in a passing as beautiful as that shown in Blake's immortal drawing, one of the group about the bedside recited his poem:

AT LAST

When on my day of life the night is falling,
　　And, in the winds from unsunned spaces blown,
I hear far voices out of darkness calling
　　My feet to paths unknown,

Thou who hast made my home of life so pleasant,
　　Leave not its tenant when its walls decay;
O Love Divine, O Helper ever present,
　　Be Thou my strength and stay!

Be near me when all else is from me drifting;
  Earth, sky, home's pictures, days of shade and shine,
And kindly faces to my own uplifting
  The love which answers mine.

I have but Thee, my Father! let Thy spirit
  Be with me then to comfort and uphold;
No gate of pearl, no branch of palm I merit
  No street of shining gold.

Suffice it if—my good and ill unreckoned,
  And both forgiven through Thy abounding grace—
I find myself by hands familiar beckoned
  Unto my fitting place.

Some humble door among Thy many mansions,
  Some sheltering shade where sin and striving cease,
And flows forever through heaven's green expansions
  The river of Thy peace.

There, from the music round about me stealing,
  I fain would learn the new and holy song,
And find at last, beneath Thy trees of healing,
  The life for which I long.

Whittier's funeral, which was held in the garden behind
the Amesbury cottage because the hundreds of friends and
admirers who attended could not possibly have found room
in the little house, was on a beautiful early autumn cloudless
day. Edmund Clarence Stedman, last of the several lay and
religious speakers to make brief addresses, eulogized Whittier
as poet and as human being. The only music was singing by
the Hutchinsons—members of the same family which, by
Lincoln's direct permission, had sung *The Furnace Blast*
almost countless times to the Boys in Blue.

Whittier lies buried in the Quaker section of the local
Amesbury cemetery. With him are all the members of the
family described in *Snow-Bound*.

Episcopal Bishop Phillips Brooks of Massachusetts wrote

to Quaker John Greenleaf Whittier, on the occasion of his eighty-fourth and last birthday:

"I have no right save that which love and gratitude and reverence may give, to say how devoutly I thank God that you have lived, that you are living, and that you will always live."

APPENDIX

THE FOLLOWING original source material, now the property of Mr. P. D. Howe, has just been discovered. It is a "Round Robin" of four pages, 4to, from Harriet Minot, Sarah Parker, and John Greenleaf Whittier of Haverhill, Mass., addressed to a cousin of the two young women, Eliza Page, of Poughkeepsie, N. Y. It is evident that Miss Page has visited her cousins in Haverhill and has met Whittier, who, in this round robin, sends her a copy of "Moll Pitcher," of which he denies authorship. Whittier's letter is the last, occupying about half of the last page, the other half being devoted to the address of the recipient, for this letter was written in 1832, before the use of envelopes and adhesive stamps.

The two girls comment frankly on Whittier's appearance and his poetry and discuss all sorts of village matters in lively vein, supplying a fascinating contemporary viewpoint of the young poet and also showing a spirit of companionship entirely and utterly normal between themselves and Whittier. In its background as well as in Whittier's specific references to his work and prospects this is a most remarkable document.

THE ROUND ROBIN

Haverhill, May 12, 1832

I could not begin a letter better, dear Miss Page, than by quoting a few of the lines with which you commenced your last for I have felt as deeply as any can, the advantages of answering a letter as soon as it is received and I resolved to answer yours of March the day after I received it. As you were pleased to give "one of the likeliest poets which broad brims ever overshadowed" so large a share of the credit of my writing last fall (as if I had no love for you, and no desire to hear from you, to induce me to write) he must bear all the blame of my not carrying my resolve into effect and writing six weeks ago. I saw J. G. Whittier a few days after you wrote & told him I had heard from you, but not the fine compliments you paid him, lest he should become vain. I told him that I meditated writing in a short time, & he wished to send a message, so I agreed to wait until I saw him again. The next day, however, he left the village for the East Parish, thence he went to Hartford, concluded to take the stage from that place to Middlebury, thinking you were there, but was disappointed in some way and did not go. About a week since he returned to Haverhill, called, asked for your direction, & said he was about to send you a small pamphlet, but would not tell me what it was. Was it Moll Pitcher?—He is carrying on a farm here, at present, will remain the principal part of the summer, I believe.—So much for one who should not have had so large a share here, did he not speak of you so often and in such high terms that he seems to be connected with thoughts of you.

May 18. I was sadly vexed the afternoon I commenced this by the entrance of company who remained all the afternoon, & until to-day have had no opportunity to write. [The next long paragraph is devoted to the change of ministers in the church, local sicknesses, engagements, messages from friends, etc.] Mr. Mirick has published his History of Haverhill [Whittier gathered the material] and is now editing a paper in Lowell, the Middlesex Telegraph.—Sarah Parker and myself are having a great dispute about William Lloyd Garrison, and I wish your opinion upon the man for I sincerely respect your judgment. Sarah considers him one of the worst and I think him one of the best men in the world. I talk of his

... "bearing up his lofty brow
In the steadfast strength of truth"

and the naughty girl says, lofty, I should think it was, so
lofty that it reaches the top of his head and turns down again
he is so bald. I think him perfectly handsome, she says he is a
fright, but no wonder for she calls J. G. Whittier, a "horrid
monster" and a "frightful beast" and he is nearly, but not
quite, as good looking as Garrison.—Now, dear Eliza, am I
not right in thinking well of the noble hearted Garrison? etc.
etc.

[To this point the letter is all by Harriet Minot. Here Sarah
Parker begins, without any date line, introduced by Harriet's
remark, "I am going to let Sarah spout a while." This first
contribution by Miss Parker is devoted almost entirely to an
account of her terrible experience with scarlet fever in the
family during the past winter, making mention of Dr. Bige-
low as the physician called in consultation. It must have been
a fearful ordeal. Under the date of May 22, this is followed
by Miss Minot—a long paragraph decribing the efforts of
Dr. Peter Osgood, a man of seventy, to marry Mary Marsh,
aged about twenty. Then comes a mention of Whittier—and
further mention by both girls.]

May 22.... Mr. Parker and Ann and Mr. J. G. Whittier
have been in since I commenced. The Gentlemen wished to
help me write to you, but we could not agree upon terms, for I
insisted upon seeing theirs and that they should see nothing
of mine; so Mr. Parker says Give love and tell Miss P. I wish
very much to see her in Haverhill. Mr. Whittier may speak
for himself.

Wednesday afternoon. Whittier has been in, written, and
told me most abominable fibs to say the least. Says he did
not write Moll Pitcher. I am certain of one thing, that I
received the poem upon which was written "from the author"
in his hand writing. That he did write the direction he does
not deny.... After writing the first part rather poorly [evi-
dently referring to Whittier's letter on the back of the same

sheet] he has written his name handsomely, so Sarah pro-
poses to cut out the name and trace it for you, so Miss Page
we will just tell you our trick. I have been writing and talking
the whole time so that may be a partial excuse for this letter.
I want, dear Miss Page, to have you write very soon, so that
Sarah and myself and perhaps Whittier may again write
to you, if possible before you leave Ithaca. Were I not con-
fident that you know me well, I would take pains to refute
the slander Whittier has written of me (see his letter), that I
am *provokingly obstinate*. I suppose he glanced at the mirror
as he wrote those words, saw his own image, and thought himself the subject, and tried to describe his own character. [Miss
Minot says then that she and Sarah are going horseback riding
and that her father has given up his law office, etc., etc.]

[signed] Yours truly, Harriet.

[Miss Parker now takes her pen in hand.]

My dear Eliza:—I have taken the pen used by the poet
while writing to you hoping that some measure of his poetical
fire and fancy may have been imparted to his pen and flow
thence for your edification, but I cannot write with it as he
does and find another proof of the superiority of his capacity
over my own inasmuch as he writes so beautifully with a pen
which in my hand is [?] unmanageable like a high spirited
and noble horse which tho it prances and paws the ground
is yet perfectly submissable to its master, and its spirited
movements impart only added grace to the rider, while the
same horse, if mounted by an inexperienced horseman spurns
all control and concludes by running away with the booby
who pretended to govern it. There, Cousin Eliza, don't you
think Whittier's pen has by this time run away with poor
me? Do write me soon—as a little bit of a bribe I must tell
you that I admire Whittier's personal appearance very much.
I have one thing which is very much against him—he has
written so beautifully that my best writing is thrown into
the shade—quite in the background—but I will console myself that I have the distinguished honor to be allowed to
sit at the same desk where he has been and to write on the

same paper. Hattie [Harriet] says, tell her that we have altered our minds and think too bad to take from your letter anything so valuable as John G. Whittier's autograph. Ever yrs., dear cousin, Sah. Parker.

[Now Whittier has his say. Obviously he wrote on the back leaf and the girls both read his letter before writing their final remarks. They believe Whittier was a good bit impressed by Miss Page, and, as we would say, they have been "kidding" her about it. Whittier writes to Miss Page without any "thees and thous." Perhaps he felt that he was affording Misses Minot and Parker fun enough without giving them that extra "handle." Of course he wrote English in either the Quaker or normal form at will. He says:—]

By permission of my friend Miss Minot I would say a few words to Miss Page. Having but little room for this purpose as Harriet has most ungenerously monopolized three pages, I shall divide what I have to say into three heads: 1st Yourself. Allow me then to say that I have always regretted that our acquaintance did not commence earlier while you were in the village. I know we should have been the best friends in the world. I have ordered the publisher of a poem having the sentimental cognomination of "Moll Pitcher" to send you a copy. Some people say I am guilty of it. The Lord forgive them for lying. I agree with Falstaffe that the world is dreadfully given to it. Will you accept of it, however, as the gift of a friend? 2nd Harriet. She accuses me for aught I know in this very letter of the authorship of "Moll Pitcher." Don't believe her. There is too much of love and sentiment in it for me: and I wish when you write her in reply you would give her your opinion on the subject, which I am quite certain will agree with me. Now Harriet is a good girl but she has a most provoking obstinacy in her opinions. 3rd Myself. A most wretched subject, but n'importe—better than none. I have done with poetry. I abjure and renounce it. I would that all my odes, songs, similes and sonnets were hung upon the horns of the moon. I have this consolation, however. They will soon be gathered to that "common receptacle of things lost upon earth" ...

> "the wallet
> Which envious Time hath ever on his back,
> Wherein he puts alms to oblivion. ."

I am now a politician and a farmer—both the very antipodes of poetry. I have only room to wish you a thousand blessings and to assure you of my warm friendship and esteem.

[signed] John G. Whittier.

Excuse Harriet's pen.

A NOTE ON SOURCES
AND METHOD

As a post-graduate newspaper reporter—and one who earned his first extra money years ago by compiling personal records for a famous reporting agency—I naturally regard honest biography as just an assignment to investigate a man's life and work. The primary requisite, if possible, is to imagine "the subject under inquiry" as living rather than dead, and this may be done by becoming so familiar with the period in which he lived that it seems entirely normal and natural. The second basic tenet, from this point of view, is a resolve to study all of the subject's own work and the provable details of his life as minutely as if searching for a crime and its motive; and to disregard previous commentaries except as they suggest angles of approach. The easy error is to read too much *about* the subject while failing to rearrange, analyze, and revalue the established truths.

This book, composed on the theory stated above, is the result of an interest extending back to Whittier's funeral in 1892, vividly described to me by my mother and my aunt, who had both been present; and of more concentrated professional study during the past twelve years. It is positively not the product of a research crowded into a brief period of high-pressure effort.

My immediate motive in undertaking the work was provided by a chance reading of Albert Mordell's *Quaker Militant: John Greenleaf Whittier* (Boston and New York, Houghton Mifflin Company, 1933)—a picture of Whittier which left me bitterly indignant and which I felt must not go on record as the last word. Appreciating that some variant treatment would be necessary to obtain a hearing, I determined to emphasize Whittier's early activities as an anti-slavery politician and propagandist in verse and prose—for these reasons: (1) This would give me the best basis on which to controvert Mordell's misinterpretation of Whittier's early life; (2) This part of the poet's life had obviously been chronicled imperfectly to date; (3) The anti-slavery agitation as a whole was a subject with which I was already very familiar through my dealings in rare Americana; (4) I felt a certain confidence in my personal ability to explain the anti-slavery campaign because so much of my own early life had been devoted to large-scale publicity work both as writer and as executive.

My second determination was to treat the history of Whittier's life not in phases but in strictly chronological order, the desire to present all pictures in strictly panoramic sequence being my pet obsession, acquired, I believe, from Dr. Wilberforce Eames during the last ten years of his life, when he had the habit of visiting my book-bindery several times a year to give instructions and to examine the unusual items which I customarily laid aside for him. His appalling mass of knowledge (these words are not too strong) was, so to speak, riveted into place by his memory of "when." On three memorable occasions he invited me to spend long evenings with him alone in the stacks of the New York Public Library reserve book department and explained to me, while calling my attention to individual books, the importance of the "whenness" of things, as nobody had ever done before.

My first actual step in the work was to read the 1888 Whittier *Poetical Works* from cover to cover. My second step was to read all the prose in the nine-volume set of Whittier's *Works* that seemed at all significant. My third move was to reread Samuel T. Pickard's authorized *Life and Letters of John Greenleaf Whittier* (2 vols. Boston and New York, Houghton, Mifflin and Company, 1894), written with the poet's approval by his niece's husband, from beginning to end of its eight hundred pages. And my next undertaking was to make a chronological skeleton outline of the events which Pickard records very honestly but very confusingly. When this was done, I felt that I had rechecked the poet's character from his own writings and the outline of his life as he himself understood it.

At this point I must explain that almost from the day when, a refugee from other business misfortune, I established my hand book-bindery and rare book business in New York City (about March of 1926), I have specialized in the handling of American first editions. The original modern selective bibliography of such books, *High Spots of American Literature*, was written by Merle Johnson and published by me in 1929. My own *Practical Guide to American Book Collecting* was issued in February of this current year. Between 1928 and 1940 my records show that, as a business venture, I have bought and sold not hundreds but thousands of dollars worth of Whittier first edition books, booklets, pamphlets, leaflets, broadsides, magazines, and newspaper files. And, in addition to this mass of Whittier material, I have examined many times more Whittier items sent to me by bindery clients for repairs or for protective cases, the sum total of this experience being really very great, especially if one adds to it some hundreds of items examined in collections and at auctions for purely bibliographical reasons.

With the initial steps in rechecking Whittier's life accomplished, I next verified by anti-slavery information, mainly from Albert's Bushnell Hart's *Slavery and Abolition, 1831-1841* (American Nation Series, Vol. XVI, New York, Harper and Brothers, 1906) and from the same author's *American History Told by Contemporaries* (New York, The Macmillan Company, 1897-1938), and made a brief chronological skeleton of the salient events.

It now seemed time for collateral reading. I found much to fill in my picture of Whittier as an individual from three little books—Mary B. Claflin's *Personal Recollections of John G. Whittier* (New York, Thomas Y. Crowell and Company,

1893); Mrs. James T. [Annie] Fields's *Whittier: Notes of His Life and of His Friendships* (New York, Harper and Brothers, 1893); and Thomas Wentworth Higginson's *John Greenleaf Whittier* (New York, The Macmillan Company, 1902). Higginson, member of an important old Boston family of note, was Whittier's personal disciple, who proved the sincerity of his convictions during the Civil War by accepting the command of a Negro regiment.

I also felt bound to reread the old lives by William Sloane Kennedy (*John Greenleaf Whittier, His Life, Genius, and Writings,* Boston, S. E. Cassino, 1882; rev. and enl. ed., D. Lothrop and Company, 1892. Also by the same author, *John G. Whittier, The Poet of Freedom,* American Reformers Series, New York, Funk and Wagnalls Company, 1892); Francis H. Underwood (*John Greenleaf Whittier. A Biography,* Boston, Houghton, Mifflin and Company, 1884); W. J. Linton (*Life of John Greenleaf Whittier,* London, W. Scott, 1893); B. O. Flower (*Whittier, Prophet, Seer and Man,* Boston, The Arena Publishing Company, 1896); and George Rice Carpenter (*John Greenleaf Whittier,* Boston and New York, Houghton, Mifflin and Company, 1903)—but found very little in them that was new or interesting.

It seemed proper that I should check the Mordell references to magazine articles, etc., and I did so to some considerable extent—until I had convinced myself that his records of bare facts were complete and trustworthy, his errors being the result of his own psychosis. To be perfectly frank, I felt that most of the writers had seen far less Whittier work than I, and had handled very few Whittier letters as compared to my own experience in the mere routine of book dealing and book clinic.

During all this process I had been coördinating the personal activities of Whittier with the exhaustive record of his publications as detailed in Thomas Franklin Currier's colossal seven-hundred-page bibliography (*A Bibliography of John Greenleaf Whittier,* Cambridge, Harvard University

Press, 1937)—and the story was beginning to take cohesive form.

The final preparatory stage was to consider various specific problems, such as (1) Whittier's long life in feeble health; (2) the truth about his sex life in relation to his personality and achievement; (3) the exact degree of his influence in getting Sumner elected to the Senate; (4) the story of his interest in Elizabeth Lloyd.

Beginning with the health problem, I read George Milbry Gould's *Biographic Clinics* (6 vols., Philadelphia, P. Blakiston's Sons and Company, 1903-09), not only his article on Whittier, (in Volume II), but his papers on other celebrities in order to form my opinion of his opinion. I verified the professional standing of Whittier's physician, Dr. Henry Bowditch, and his reputation for good sense. I reread numerous Whittier letters referring to his health—heart palpitations, lassitude, headaches, limitation of working periods, etc., etc. And then I discussed the symptoms with two noted physician friends to whom I sell early American medical books—only to find that migraine is still a nerve and perhaps a gland puzzle imperfectly understood.

Regarding Whittier's sex life, I accepted Mordell's army of facts and tried to apply to them the common sense of a not-cloistered life, including many years in newspaper, publicity and theatrical managerial work, stuffed to the brim with personal problems far more spectacular than those of highly respectable nineteenth-century American men of letters.

The proof of Sumner's explicit obligation to Whittier I found in a letter published by Pickard (*Life and Letters*, I, 352-53), the full significance of which had not previously been recognized. The rest of Whittier's political and propagandist activities were clarified by a sort of three-column analysis: (1) my Pickard outline; (2) my anti-slavery outline; and (3) Currier's *Bibliography*. It was just another case, again and again, of the essential importance of the "When-ness."

The Elizabeth Lloyd episode solved itself when I took the

two sequences of published letters—those in *Whittier's Un-known Romance: Letters to Elizabeth Lloyd,* edited by Marie V. Denervaud (Boston, Houghton Mifflin Company, 1922) and those in Thomas Franklin Currier's *Elizabeth Lloyd and the Whittiers* (Cambridge, Harvard University Press, 1939), and rearranged them all in one sequence as originally written.

Other problems were taken up in the same spirit of analysis. In this connection I want it to be distinctly understood that I received help from many living sources. For instance, my information concerning Whittier's ancestry, refuting the vague French origin mentioned on the first page of Pickard's life, came to me, with authenticating references, from a distinguished professor, himself a member of the Whittier clan. When this incident aroused my curiosity as to how much further the good poet might unconsciously have romanticized his family, I got the facts regarding the fallacy of the supposed cousinship to Daniel Webster (both being represented as descendants from the notorious Stephen Bachiler) through the courtesy of the Librarian of the Haverhill Public Library and a local genealogist. My assumed explanation of a local Massachusetts political puzzle was confirmed through the kindness of Mr. Woodwell, of Haverhill, who is one of the ultimate Whittier authorities. All sorts of minor difficulties were cleared up by personal chats with C. A. Wilson, outstanding collector of rare Whittier publications, Rhodes Scholar, Guggenheim Counsel, Trustee of Williams College. And Mr. Currier, very much alive (though writing that book of his should have killed any two men), was always there in the background. Huneker used to say that the smart man was not the fellow who tried to remember everything but the man who knew just where to find printed information in a hurry. A better thing is to know the living and breathing encyclopaedias of your subject and to consult them freely.

INDEX

INDEX

Abolitionists, in 1830-40, 72; general attitude toward, 73
Abraham Davenport, characterized, 294-95; mentioned, 259
Adams, John Quincy, aided by Whittier in defending right of petition, 71; enters Congress after having been president, 77; introduces petitions against slavery, 77; contact of with Whittier, 101; poet writes introduction for *Letters* of, 110; and Pennsylvania Hall, 125; Gag Rule passed, 134; forces repeal of Gag Rule, 157, 180; sees Whittier and Sturge, 174; presents Haverhill petition and defeats attempt to unseat him, 179; monster petition resulting from Latimer case, 187; death of, 209
Agassiz, L. J. R., 310
Aldrich, Thomas Bailey, 21
Allen, Ephraim, editor of *Newburyport Herald,* 31
American Anti-Slavery Society, Whittier secretary of, 70-71, 113; publishes *Our Countrymen in Chains* (1834), 89; publishes *Narrative of James Williams* (1838), 132, 147-49; split in, 157-58
American Colonization Society, attacked in *Justice and Expediency,* 81-84; attacked in National Anti-Slavery Convention, 94-95
American and Foreign Anti-Slavery Reporter, 161, 176
American and Foreign Anti-Slavery Society, formed and Whittier allied with, 157-58, 165, 168; establishes *National Era,* 211, 212
American Manufacturer, prints early Whittier material, 37, 47; Whittier edits, 47, 55; a pro-Clay organ, 47; influence of on Whittier, 48; mentioned, 229

American Perceptor, characterized by Whittier, 64
Among the Hills and Other Poems, publication of, 302-3; mentioned, 310
Amy Wentworth, 277
Andrew Rykman's Prayer, quoted in part, 312-13
Anti-Slavery Declaration of Sentiments, signing of, 74; composition of, 93 ff.; summarized, 98-99; mentioned, 113
Anti-Slavery Record, 113
Anti-Slavery Society. *See* American Anti-Slavery Society
Apology to the Chivalrous Sons of the South, 91
Astræa at the Capitol, quoted in part, 269
Atlantic Monthly, The, publishes Whittier's writings, 213, 240, 260, 267-68, 269, 270, 271, 292, 300, 301
At Last, characterized, 309; quoted in full, 325-26; mentioned, 304, 306
At Sundown, 217, 301, 304, 324
Austin, Ann, Quaker, 12
Austin, James T., 119

Bachiler, Stephen, 9
Bailey, Gamaliel, Jr., editor of *National Era,* 211, 212, 236
Ballad, the, Whittier's excellence in, 64-65
Ballads and Other Poems (London, 1844), 191
Barbara Frietchie, publication of, 270; characterized, 254, 270-72; quoted in full, 272-74; mentioned, 259; set to music, 296, 311
Barefoot Boy, The, mentioned, 184, 193, 259; characterized, 248, 250-51; quoted in full, 249-50

343

Barnard, F. A. P., 56

Bay of Seven Islands and Other Poems, The, publication and description of, 300, 304; mentioned, 306, 309

Bell, John, 264

Benezet, Anthony, Quaker anti-slavery leader, 15, 121

Benton, Thomas H., 233, 239, 263

Billings, Hammatt, 208

Bird, Robert M., 159

Birney, J. G., and Whittier, 113; edits *Philanthropist* and heads Liberty party, 165; Whittier edits *Middlesex Standard* to support, 196; and Mrs. Stowe, 235

Bolivar, quoted in part, 66-67

Boston Courier, prints early Whittier poems, 43, 48

Boston Morning Chronicle, prints Whittier poem, 204, 310

Boston Notion, prints Whittier poem, 161

Boston Statesman, edited by relative of Whittier, 36; prints early Whittier poems, 37, 48

Boutwell, G. S., 231

Bowditch, Dr. Henry, diagnoses poet's illness as heart affliction, 42, 139; forbids poet to attend World Convention, 156

Brainard, John G. C., Literary Remains of, contains Whittier's biographical sketch of Brainard, 59-60

Branded Hand, The, 204

Bray, Evelina, early friendship of with poet, 44

Breckinridge, John C., 264

Brewing of Soma, The, 306, 308

Bridal of Pennacook, 214

Broadsides, of special importance: *Song of the Vermonters* (1843), 86; *Our Countrymen in Chains* (1834), 89-90; *Sabbath Scene* (1850), 225

Brooks, Erastus, 110

Brooks, Jerome, 57

Brooks, Bishop Phillips, friend of Whittier, 311, 326

Brooks, Preston S., attacks Sumner, 239

Brown, D. P., 125

Brown, John, in Kansas struggles, 238; in attack on Harpers Ferry and Whittier's opinion of, 241-42

Brown, John L., 204

Brown, Moses, interest of in *Justice and Expediency,* 80

Brown of Ossawatomie, quoted in part, 241-42, 258

Bryant, William Cullen, 3, 28, 29, 159, 233

Buchanan, James, 166, 170, 223, 239

Buffam, Arnold, 125

Burial of Barber, 240

Burleigh, C. C., 167

Burns, quoted in part, 30; mentioned, 248

Burns, Anthony, former slave arrested in Boston, 237-40

Burns, Robert, influence of on Whittier, 20, 29-30, 38, 69; influence of on American verse, 30

Burr, John P., and Underground Railway, 132

Burroughs, Rev. George, 323

Burroughs, Stephen, *Memoirs* of, 24

Butler, Mrs. Charles, 120

Byron, George Gordon, 4, 36, 69

Caldwell, Jacob, Whittier's brother-in-law, 111

Caldwell, Louis Henry, nephew of Whittier, 8

Caldwell, Mary Elizabeth, niece of Whittier, 8

Calhoun, John C., mentioned, 170, 221

Call of the Christian, The, 305

Captain's Well, The, Whittier received $1000 for, 301

Carlton, Oliver, 41

Carter & Hendee (Boston), publishes *Moll Pitcher* (1832), 59

Cartland, Joseph, favorite cousin of Whittier, 131; poet spends old age winters in Newburyport home of, 323

Cartland, Moses, substitutes for Whittier as editor of *Freeman,* 133

Carrier's Address for 1828, 41

Cass, Lewis, 166

Cassandra Southwick, characterized, 181, 188-89, 300; quoted in part, 190

Centennial Hymn, The, 303

Chalkley, Thomas, Quaker anti-slavery leader, 15, 121

Chambered Nautilus, The, Whittier's opinion of, 319

Changeling, The, 294

Channing, William Ellery, 174

Chapel of the Hermits, The, publication and description of, 246

Chapman, Maria, 125

Chase, Aaron, purchases Whittier farm, 110

Chase, Salmon P., 166, 206, 276

Child, Lydia Maria, excluded from Boston Athenaeum, 106; and Whittier, 315

Child Life, 302

Child Life in Prose, 302

Childs, George W., 290

Christian Union, The, prints Whittier poem, 310

Christmas Carmen, A, carol set to music, 310

Cincinnati American, prints Whittier's Clay campaign song, 52

Cities of the Plain, The, 305

Claflin, Mrs. Mary, and Whittier, 316-17

Clay, Henry, idol of the North, 47-48; Whittier's first famous song, *Henry Clay,* 52; Whittier's pro-Clay writings, 53; Prentice's life of, finished by Whittier, 57; president of Colonization Society, 73; Whittier attacks Clay's Colonization Society, 81-84, 94-95; rebukes Whittier for abandoning him, 174; death of, 222

Coates, E. H., and Underground Railway, 132

Cobbler Keezar's Vision, 277

Coffin, Joshua, twice Whittier's teacher, 23; gives Burns's poems to Whittier, 29; attends anti-slavery convention, 92; prototype of *To My Old Schoolmaster,* 247; mentioned in *Snow-Bound,* 286; Whittier relieves his dread of the hereafter, 320-21

Collier, Rev. William, 46, 47, 49

Collier, William R., 46, 47, 49

Colonization Society. *See* American Colonization Society

Columbian Star, prints Whittier poem, 48

Confessions of a Suicide, prose sketch by Whittier, 43

Conscript's Farewell, The, 48

Cooper, James Fenimore, 29, 159

Cotter's Saturday Night, The, comparison of with *Snow-Bound,* 279-80

Countess, The, 277

Crandall, Prudence, school of wrecked, 106

Crandall, Dr. Reuben, arrested in Washington for lending *Justice and Expediency,* 81, 106, 174

Crary, Isaac E., accompanies Whittier to New York, 56, 57

Crisis, The, 205

Crucifixion, The, 305

Currier, Thomas Franklin, author of Whittier bibliography, 36-37; on date of *Song of the Vermonters,* 38-39; on editions of *Justice and Expediency,* 80; dates broadside form of *Song of the Vermonters,* 86; includes *Declaration of Sentiments* in Whittier bibliography, 93; on *Poems Written during the Progress of the Abolition Question,* 117; editor of *Elizabeth Lloyd and the Whittiers,* 136; on Whittier's work on the *Era,* 213; *et passim*

Cushing, Caleb, Whittier opposes for election to Congress, 76; elected after giving Whittier anti-slavery pledge, 78; Whittier prevents confirmation of as secretary of the treasury, 176; opposes election of Sumner to the Senate, 231

Daniel Neall, 205

Davis, E. M., 131

Dear Lord and Father of Mankind, a part of *The Brewing of Soma,* 306; characterized and quoted in part, 308-9

Declaration of Sentiments. See Anti-Slavery Declaration of Sentiments

Deity, The, printed in *Free Press,* 32

Democracy, 184

Democratic Review, Whittier poems in, 161, 188, 191

Dickinson, Anna E., 131

Dickinson, Emily, 249
Dickinson, John, 131
Dickinson, Susan E., 131
Dinsmoor, Robert, "The Yankee Zingali," 200
Dinsmoor, Robert, Incidental Poems of, 38
Dix, Dorothea, 267
Dr. Holmes, 301
Dom Pedro, interest of in Whittier, 321
Double-Headed Snake of Newbury, 258; quoted in part, 259
Douglas, Stephen A., sponsors Kansas-Nebraska bill, 237; defeats Lecompton Constitution, 238; mentioned, 239, 263, 264
Drake, Francis Samuel, 58, 214
Dream of the Misanthrope, 43
Dred Scott case, 240

Earthquake, The, 48
Elizabeth Lloyd and the Whittiers, edited by T. F. Currier, 136
Emancipation movement in 1833, 79
Emancipator, The, Whittier poems in, 108, 113; investigates James Williams story, 147
Emerson, C. M., 56
Emerson, Ralph Waldo, mentioned, 3, 4, 29, 163, 199, 311; and Whittier, 145, 324
Emerson's Essays, 311
Endicott, John, 13
Essex Gazette, prints early Whittier poems, 36-37, 38; prints early Whittier prose, 40; temperance article, 46; Whittier poems, 48, 52, 60, 72, 91, 108; edited by Whittier, 51; prints *To William Lloyd Garrison,* 56; Whittier editor of, 108, 110-11; Whittier editorials in, 112
Essex Transcript (Village Transcript), 198
Eternal Goodness, The, characterized and quoted in part, 307-8; mentioned, 260
Eva, 226
Everett, Edward, 111, 119, 126
Execution of Louis XVI, The, 36
Exile's Departure, The, Whittier's first printed poem, 32

Expostulation, 150. See *Our Countrymen in Chains*
Extract from a New England Legend, relation of to *Moll Pitcher,* 59

Familist's Hymn, The, 305
Farewell of a Virginia Slave Mother to Her Daughters Sold into Southern Bondage, characterized, 132, 152; quoted in full, 153-54; crude fury of, 183
Farmer Poet, The, 199-200
Farrar, Archdeacon Frederick M., 290
Female Martyr, The, 90-91
Fields, Annie (Mrs. James T.), and Whittier, 316, 318
Fields, James T., first contact of Whittier with, 162; asked by Whittier to help arrange publication for *Lays of My Home,* 182-83; consulted by Whittier as to name and contents of *Lays,* 188; writes Whittier about *Barbara Frietchie,* 271; and *The Tent on the Beach,* 292
Fields, Osgood & Co., publishers of *Among the Hills and Other Poems,* 302; of *Miriam and Other Poems,* 303
Fillmore, Millard, 169, 207, 223
Fisher, Mary, Quaker, 12
Follen, Dr., 106
Forrest, Edwin, 57
For Righteousness' Sake, 240
Fort Braddock Papers (1824), historical novel by Brainard, a rarity for collectors, 60
Fountain, The, 108-9
Fox, John, 12-13
Franklin, Benjamin, *Autobiography of,* 24
Freedom's Gathering, 161
Freeman, the. See *Pennsylvania Freeman*
Free Press (Newburyport), started by Garrison, 31; Whittier's first poem printed in, 31-32; prints other early Whittier poems, 36
Frémont, John C., Whittier attracted to, 232-33; first Republican candidate, 239; Whittier loyal to, 263; influenced by Whittier, 275-76

Frémont campaign song. See *What of the Day?*

Friend, The, prints Whittier poem, 161

Fugitive Slave Law, 218, 224

Furnace Blast, The (to the tune of *Ein' Feste Burg*), sung in Union camps, characterized and quoted in part, 276, 296, 326

Gag rules, passed by Congress, fought by J. Q. Adams, 75, 157, 180

Gallows, The, 184

Garrison, William Lloyd, entrance into anti-slavery movement, 15; early life of, 31; discovers Whittier, 32-33; interviews Whittier's father, 32-33; recommends Whittier for editorial post, 46; joins Lundy, 50; founds *Liberator,* 61; imprisoned in Baltimore, 63; enlists Whittier in anti-slavery movement, 62-64; influence of on Whittier, 72; mobbed in Boston, 75; activities of at anti-slavery convention, 92-99; and the *Declaration of Sentiments,* 97-99; promotes Thompson anti-slavery lectures, 102; rescued in Boston riot, 105-6; disagrees with Whittier, 113-14; speaks at Pennsylvania Hall, 125; views of differ from Whittier's, 157, 158; fruitless conference of with Sturge and Whittier, 174; mentioned in "Round Robin" letter, 330-31

Garrison, To William Lloyd. See *To William Lloyd Garrison*

Garrison of Cape Ann, 258, 259

Gates Ajar, by E. S. Phelps, 317

Genius of Universal Emancipation (Baltimore), 50

Goldsmith, Oliver, 29

Goodsell, P. B., publishes *Literary Remains of John G. C. Brainard,* 60

Gould, Dr. George Milbry, cited on Whittier's eyesight, 141

Gove, Sarah, 323

Greeley, Horace, 233

Greene, Mr. and Mrs. Nathaniel, 30, 37, 47

Greenwood, Grace, 205

Grimké, Angelina and Sarah, 109; and Whittier, 125

Gundalow, term used in *Snow-Bound,* defined, 289

Gurney, J. J., 171

Hale, John P., 204, 228, 236

Halleck, Fitz-Greene, 57

Hanmer & Phelps, publishes *Legends of New England,* 57-58

Harriman, Edward, Whittier letter to, 50-51, 76

Harrison, William Henry, 166, 175, 207

Hartford Iris, prints Whittier poem, 60

Haskell, George, 23

Haverhill Academy, 35, 36-37

Haverhill Gazette, edited by A. W. Thayer, 33; prints early poems of Whittier, 36-37, 204. See also *Essex Gazette.*

Haverhill Iris, prints Whittier poems, 76, 107, 108

Haverhill Petition (1842), a sarcastic rejoinder to other threats of secession, 178-79; started movement for repeal of gag rules, 180

Hawthorne, Nathaniel, 3

Hazel Blossoms, publication and description of, 303, 310

Healy, Joseph, publisher of *Pennsylvania Freeman,* 130; publishes *Moll Pitcher and The Minstrel Girl,* 131; publishes *Poems* (1838), 132

Henry Clay, Whittier's famous Clay campaign song, 52

Higginson, Thomas Wentworth, 137, 238, 248

History of Haverhill, by B. L. Mirick, Whittier gathers material for, 41; published, 58

Holmes, Oliver Wendell, mentioned, 3, 4, 29, 59, 199, 301; Whittier's relations with, 314-15, 319; Whittier's last poem to, 324

Home Ballads, characterized, 246

Hooper, Lucy, meets Whittier first in Brooklyn, 114; letters to, 118; further relations with Whittier, 135; death of, 135, 161, 176

Houghton, Mifflin & Co., publishes *The King's Missive and Other Poems* (1881), and all later publications, 303-4

Houghton, Osgood & Co., publishes *Vision of Echard and Other Poems* (1878), 303

Howell, Mrs. *See* Lloyd, Elizabeth

How the Women Went from Dover, 191, 300, 304

Human Sacrifice, The, 184

Hunters of Men, The, 91

Hussey, Mercy, Whittier's aunt, position of in family and death of, 8; mentioned in *Snow-Bound*, 285

Hutchinson, Anne, 12

Hutchinson family, the, troupe of entertainers, sing *The Furnace Blast* in Union camps, 276; descendants of sing at Whittier's funeral, 326

Ichabod, characterized and quoted in full, 205, 218-19

Independent, The, 267

In the Evil Days, quoted in part, 226

Incidental Poems by Robert Dinsmoor, the Rustic Bard, contains a Whittier poem, 38

In School Days, characterized and quoted in full, 193, 260, 298-300

In War Time, 269, 270, 274, 277, 311

Irving, Washington, 29, 159

Jackson, Andrew, 47, 53

Jackson, Stonewall, and *Barbara Frietchie*, 272

Jay, William, and opening of Pennsylvania Hall, 125

Jefferson, Thomas, attitude of toward slavery, 72

J. G. W. to the Rustic Bard, 38

Johnson, the Misses, Whittier's cousins, 323

Journal of the Times (Bennington, Vt.), prints early Whittier poems, 37; established by Garrison, 46

Justice and Expediency, published, 63, 70, 74, 77, 78-79; value of as collector's item, 80; analyzed, 81-83; quoted in part, 83-84; effect of, 92; Dr. Crandall arrested for circulating, 81, 106, 174

Kansas Emigrants, The, set to music, 240, 246, 296; characterized, 242; quoted in full, 242-243; mentioned, 245, 248

Kearny, General Philip, 276

Kelly, Abby, 125

Kennedy, John Pendleton, 159

Kennedy, William S., biographer of Whittier, cited, 119

Kent, George, 103

Kent, William, 103

Kimball, J. H., 103

King, Thomas Starr, 241

King's Missive and Other Poems, The, publication and description of, 303-4

Kittredge, George Lyman, quoted, 161

Knapp, C. L., 197

Knapp, Isaac, co-founder with Garrison of *Liberator*, 61; important in anti-slavery movement, 94; publisher of *Letters from John Quincy Adams to His Constituents*, 110, 115; publisher of *Poems Written during the Progress of the Abolition Question*, 110, 116-17; mentioned, 108

Knickerbocker, The, Whittier poem in, 108, 161

Kossuth, on speaking trip in U. S., 233

Kossuth, 245, 246-47

Ladies' Magazine (Boston), prints Whittier poem, 48, 52

Lady's Pearl, The (Lowell, Mass.), prints Whittier poem, 161

Lament, A, 91

Larcom, Lucy, edits *The Lowell Offering* and meets Whittier, 200-1; life and later relations of with Whittier, 201-2; first to whom Whittier wrote of sister's death, 277; work of on Whittier anthologies, 302; as editor of *Our Young Folks*, 319

Latimer, fugitive slave, 169, 184

Laus Deo, 269-70; set to music, 296

Law, Jonathan, 54, 56, 70

Lawrences, the, of Massachusetts 238

Lays of the Emigrants, 246

Lays of My Home, 59, 156, 162, 300; publication and analysis of, 181 ff.

Leaves from Margaret Smith's Journal, published as actual colonial document, 87; 213; 215; characterized, 215-16

Leavitt, Joshua, 113, 114, 133

Legends of New England, The, 25; Whittier's first complete published volume, a valuable collector's item, 57-58, 59

Leggett, William, 57

Letter . . . , A, 204

Letters from John Quincy Adams to his Constituents, with Introduction by Whittier, 110; characterized, 115; contains two Whittier poems, 150

Lewis, Sarah, 131

Liberator, The, founded by Garrison, 61, 63, 72, 74; publishes *Our Countrymen in Chains,* 89; other poems, 91; influence of, 92; mentioned, 107, 108, 119

Liberty party, formed, 165

Life of Clay, by Prentice, completed by Whittier, 57

Light & Sterns, publishes *Mogg Megone,* 62

Lighting, The, 200

Lincoln, Abraham, Cooper Union speech by, 79; elected president, 166; attitude of Whittier toward, 232-33, 274-75; supported by Whittier after nomination, 263; authorizes singing of *The Furnace Blast,* 276-77; Whittier's comment on Marshall's engraving of, 318

Lines on the Death of S. Oliver Torrey, 108

Lines Written on the Passage of Pinckney's Resolution, etc. See *Summons, The*

Lines on the Portrait of a Certain Publisher, 205

Literary Recreations and Miscellanies, 216-17

Literary Remains of John G. C. Brainard, published with biographical sketch of Brainard by Whittier, 59-60

Livermore, Harriet, 24-25, 279, 322

Lloyd, Elizabeth, meets Whittier first in Philadelphia, 131, 135; subsequent friendship and influence of, 136-38, 161

London Literary Gazette, prints Whittier poem, 52

Longfellow, Henry Wadsworth, 3, 4, 29; publishes *Poems on Slavery,* 120; publishes *Voices of the Night,* 159; *Ballads,* compared with *Lays of My Home,* 189; contrasted with Whittier, 260, 314

Lost Occasion, The, quoted in part, 220

Lost Statesman, The (Silas Wright), 205

Lovejoy, Elijah P., murdered in Alton, 16, 75; Wendell Phillips's speech on, 118-120

Love to the World!, 171

Lowell, James Russell, prints Whittier poem in *Pioneer,* 162; compared with Whittier, 181, 184, 314; as editor of *Atlantic* buys Whittier material, 213; during Civil War replaces Whittier as leading political literary force, 267; mentioned, 3, 29, 181, 314

Lowell Offering, The, edited by Lucy Larcom, 200

Lundy, Benjamin, becomes forefront of anti-slavery movement, 15; discoverer and partner of Garrison, 15; selects Whittier to follow him, 16; meets Garrison, 47; associated with Garrison in publishing *Genius of Universal Emancipation,* 50; summons Whittier to Philadelphia, 118

Mabel Martin, publication and description of, 303, 304

McClellan, General George B., 275, 276

Macy, Thomas, Quaker, 13

Marais du Cygne, Le, 240, 242, 245, 258

Martineau, Harriet, 115-16, 110

Mary Garvin, 248

Massachusetts to Virginia, mentioned, 151, 160, 181-82; occasion of, 182-83; characterized, 184-85; quoted in part, 185-86

Mather, Cotton, description of in *Double-Headed Snake of Newbury*, 259

Maud Muller, mentioned, 184, 193, 260; characterized, 248, 253-54, 258; quoted in full, 255-58; set to music, 296

May, S. J., revises *Declaration of Sentiments* with Whittier, 93; reads the *Declaration*, 97; Haverhill lecture of stopped by rowdies, 102

Meeting, The, reveals Whittier's philosophic attachment to Quakerism, 310

Memories, relation of to *Moll Pitcher*, 39, 188; as interpreted by Mordell, 42, 45; characterized, 192-93; quoted in part, 193-94

Metacom, 58

Middlesex Standard (Lowell, Mass.), Whittier edits, 158, 196-97

Milton, John, *Prose Works of*, reviewed by Whittier, 40; influence of on Whittier, 69; and Whittier, 289-90; Whittier writes memorial quatrain to, 290

Milton Memorial Quatrain, occasion of, 290; quoted, 290

Minot, Judge, 40

Minstrel Girl, The, only issue of, 59

Miriam and Other Poems, publication and description of, 303

Mirick, B. L., 41, 59

Mogg Megone, publication of, and characterized, 62, 100, 110; quoted in part, 66

Moll Pitcher (1832), 42; *New England* incorporated in, 56, 65; first publication of, most valuable of Whittier first editions, 59

Moll Pitcher and The Minstrel Girl (1840), publication of, important and rare volume, 59, 131

Moloch in State Street, quoted in part, 226; mentioned, 232

Monster petition, 157

Mordell, Albert, interpretation of Whittier by, 35-36, 42, 54-55, 140

Mott, Lucretia, 131

Mott, Richard, 171

Music, Whittier's attitude toward, 316; songs of Whittier set to music, in sheet music form, 296-97

Mussey, B. B., publishes *Poems* (de luxe edition, 1849), 208-9

My Playmate, as interpreted by Mordell, 42, 45

My Prayer. See *Andrew Rykman's Prayer*

Mystic's Christmas, The, quoted in part, 310

My Summer with Dr. Singletery, 213, 216-17

Narrative of James Williams, An American Slave, publication of, 132; controversy concerning, 147-49

National Enquirer (Philadelphia), Lundy calls Whittier to edit, 118 ff.; renamed *Pennsylvania Freeman* in 1838, 121; Whittier edits by mail, 122, 128; Whittier's editorship of, 132 ff.; mentioned, 125, 127. See also *Pennsylvania Freeman*

National Era (Washington), Whittier co-editor of, 146; corresponding editor of, 198; account of, 205, 211-14; mentioned *passim*

National Lyrics, 269

National Philanthropist, prints early Whittier poems, 37; history of, 46; Whittier's connection with, 46-47

Neal, John, 159

Neall, Daniel, head of Pennsylvania Hall management, 126, 131

Neall, Elizabeth, 131

Newburyport Free Press. See *Free Press*

Newburyport Herald, Garrison works on, 31

New England, published, 56; used in *Moll Pitcher*, 59, 65; quoted in part, 65-66

New England Magazine, publishes Whittier poems, 60, 90-91; *Song of the Vermonters*, 86; *Mogg Megone*, 100

New England Review. See *New England Weekly Review*

New England Weekly Review (Hartford), prints early Whittier poems, 37-38, 43; Whittier retires from editorship of, 44, 54; prints poems, 48, 52, 56; edited by

George D. Prentice, 51; Whittier as substitute editor of, 51-52, 53 ff.; *New England* published in, 56; Whittier resigns from, 71; Whittier as editor of, 75; mentioned, 142, 156, *et passim*

New Wife and the Old, The, characterized, 191; quoted in part, 192; mentioned, 214

New Year, The, published, 132; characterized, 151; quoted in part, 152

New York Courier and Enquirer, 57

New York Ledger, prints poem by Whittier, 301

New York Mirror, prints poem by Whittier, 106

Nicholson, Elizabeth, writes verses on Whittier's leaving and returning to the Cause, 168-69

Noah, Mordecai, 57

North Star, The, anti-slavery gift book anthology, edited by Whittier, 132, 135, 162, 182

Oasis, The, prints *The Slave Ships*, 91

O'Connell, Daniel, Whittier article on, 107

Official Piety, 248

O Holy Father, 113

Old Oak Tree, The, 48

Old Portraits and Modern Sketches, publication and characterization of, 216-17

On a Prayer Book, 241

Opium Eater, The, prose sketch by Whittier, 43; in *New England Magazine*, 107-8

Osgood, James R., & Co., publishes *Pensylvania Pilgrim*, *Mabel Martin*, and *Hazel Blossoms*, 303

O Thou Whose Spirit [Presence] Went Before, quoted in part, 88; mentioned, 150

Our Countrymen [Fellow Countrymen] in Chains, published, 74-75, 89, 100, 183; quoted in part, 90; crude fury of, 161; facsimile of broadside of, facing p. 86

Our Young Folks, Lucy Larcom editor of, 201; Whittier poems in, 298, 319

Owen, Robert Dale, Whittier's interest in, 318

Paean, A, 205

Paine, Thomas, *Common Sense*, 79

Palestine, 305

Partisan Leader, The (1836), novel by Beverley Tucker, anticipates Civil War, 96

Panoramá, The, 184, 241, 246; publication and characterization of, 247-48

Parker Theodore, 170, 223-24, 238, 241, 311

Parker, William, fugitive slave, 224

Parrish, Dr. Joseph, lends Whittier his wig, 127

Passaconaway, in *New England Magazine*, 107-8

Pass of the Sierras, The, 241

Pastoral Letter, The, publication and characterization of, 108-9, 125; quoted in part, 109-10; mentioned, 150

Paulding, James K., 159

Peasley, Joseph, 13

Pedro, II. *See* Dom Pedro

Pennsylvania Freeman (the former *National Enquirer*), Whittier resigned from, 70; offices of burned in Pennsylvania Hall, 75; Whittier as editor of, 114, 122; mentioned, 146 *et passim. See also National Enquirer*

Pennsylvania Hall, dedication and burning of, 75, 121, 123 ff.; building of, 121, 124

Pennsylvania Hall, 124-25, 132

Pennsylvania Pilgrim, The, publication and description of, 303, 306

Pettingill, J. M., 198

Phelps, Amos A., 114; corresponding editor of *National Era* (Washington), 211, 212

Phelps, Elizabeth Stuart, 317

Philadelphia Album, prints Whittier poems, 48, 60

Philanthropist (Cincinnati), 165, 211, 235

Phillips, Wendell, speech of on Lovejoy, 16, 75, 119-20; influence of on anti-slavery cause, 97, 120, 238

Pickard, Elizabeth Whittier, the poet's niece, daughter of his younger brother Matthew, and wife of Samuel T. Pickard, 320

Pickard, Samuel T., husband of Whittier's niece Elizabeth, and author of the official *Life and Letters of... Whittier*, cited, 5, 10, 19, 22-23, 30, 94

Pierce, Franklin, 166, 206, 223, 236, 238

Pierrepont, John, *Lays of My Home* dedicated to, 183

Pike, Robert, Quaker, 13

Pine Tree, The, 230

Pipes of Lucknow, 259

Pitman, Judge, 40

Poe, Edgar Allan, 29, 159

Poems (1938), 132

Poems of Adrian, The, prospectus of, 41

Poems Written during the Progress of the Abolition Question (1837), published, 75, 110, 116-17, 132, 207

Poetical Works (1857), Blue and Gold edition, 246

Poets and Poetry, prose articles by Whittier, 40

Polk, James K., 169, 203

Prayer of Agassiz, The, 310

Prentice, George D., editor of *New England Weekly Review*, 37-38; corresponds with Whittier to arrange for Whittier's becoming substitute editor, 51; contrasted with Whittier, 53; Whittier completes Prentice's *Life of Clay*, 57; aids Garrison, 63

Prisoner for Debt, The, 101

Proem, published, 208; quoted in full, 209-10

Prose writings of Whittier, early, 40; as editor of *American Manufacturer*, 49; in *New England Weekly Review*, 56-57; biographical sketch of Brainard, 60; characterized, 147, 197, 199, 213, 217, 267

Providence Journal, prints *Justice and Expediency*, 80

Psalm of Life, A, Longfellow publishes, 159

Publishers, of essential Whittier first editions:

— American Anti-Slavery Society Office (New York), *Our Countrymen in Chains* (1834), 89; *Narrative of James Williams* (1838), 147-49

— Bishop & Tracy, Printers (Windsor, Vt.), *Song of the Vermonters* (1843), 87

— Carter & Hendee (Boston), *Moll Pitcher* (1832), 59

— Fields, Osgood & Co. (Boston), *Among the Hills and Other Poems* (1869), 302; *Miriam and Other Poems* (1871), 303

— Goodsell, P. B. (Hartford), *Literary Remains of John G. C. Brainard* (1832), 60

— Hanmer & Phelps (Hartford), Prentice's *Life of Clay* (1831), 57; *Legends of New England* (1831), 57-58

— Healy, Joseph (Philadelphia), *Poems* (1838), 132; *Moll Pitcher and The Minstrel Girl* (1840), 131

— Houghton, Mifflin & Co. (Boston), *The King's Missive and Other Poems* (1881), and all later publications, 303-4

— Houghton, Osgood & Co. (Boston), *Vision of Echard and Other Poems* (1878), 303

— Knapp, Isaac (Boston), *Letters of John Quincy Adams to His Constituents*, with introduction by Whittier (1837), 110, 115; *Poems Written during the Progress of the Abolition Question* (1837), 110, 116-17

— Light & Stearns (Boston), *Mogg Megone* (1836), 62

— Mussey, B. B. (Boston), *Poems* (de luxe edition, 1849), 208-9

— Osgood, Jas. R. & Co. (Boston), *Pennsylvania Pilgrim* (1872), 303; *Hazel Blossoms* (1875), 303; *Mabel Martin* (1876), 303

— Piercy & Reed (New York), *Views of Slavery and Emancipation* (1837), by Harriet Martineau,

Publishers (*continued*)
with preface by Whittier, 110, 116
— Thayer, A. W. (Haverhill), *Incidental Poems by Robert Dinsmoor* (1828), 38; *History of Haverhill* (1832), by B. L. Mirick, 58
— Thayer, C. P. (Haverhill), *Justice and Expediency* (1833), 80
— Ticknor, Wm. D. (Boston), *Lays of My Home* (1843), 162, 182
— Ticknor & Fields (Boston), *Literary Recreations and Miscellanies* (1854) and all later publications to and including *The Tent on the Beach* (1867), 292-97
— Ticknor, Reed & Fields (Boston), *Leaves from Margaret Smith's Journal* (1849), 215-16; *Old Portraits and Modern Sketches* (1850), 216; *Songs of Labor* (1850), 200, 246; *Chapel of the Hermits* (1853), 246
— Waite, Peirce & Co. (Boston), *The Stranger in Lowell* (1845), 199; (in association with Thos. Cavender of Philadelphia and Wm. Harned of New York), *Voices of Freedom* (1846), 207
— Wiley & Putnam (New York), *Supernaturalism of New England* (1847), 214

Quaker influence: beginnings, 12; early American persecutions, 12-13; anti-slavery activities, 15-16, 17; anti-slavery influence, 64; representation at anti-slavery convention, 94; anti-slavery leadership passes from Lundy to Whittier, 118; Whittier aided by "inner light," 163; Whittier's spiritual awakennig, 172; Whittier's interest in the supernatural, 215; Quaker persecutions pictured in *Margaret Smith's Journal* and elsewhere, 215-16; Whittier's qualms at the thought of encouraging war, 266; Whittier's Quakerism, 297, 309-16. See *To Members of the Society of Friends.*

Quakers Are Out, The, characterized and quoted in full, 265
Quantrell, Mrs., and *Barbara Frietchie,* 271

Randolph, John, frees slaves, 73-74
Randolph of Roanoke, 91, 205
Rantoul, 248
Rantoul, Robert, 101
Reformers of England, The, 184
Relic, The, 183
Religious Poems, 305 ff.
Rendition, The, 240, 242, 248
Revelation, quoted in part, 309
Riot at Concord, The, 108
Ritner, Governor, of Pennsylvania, 127-28, 133
Round Robin, important recently discovered letter by Whittier and two friends, 329 ff.
Rowson, Mrs., *Charlotte's Daughter,* by, reviewed by Whittier, 40
Russ, Cornelia, Whittier's interest in, 55

Sabbath Scene, A, published, 149-50, 205, 225; characterized and quoted in part, 227
St. Gregory's Guest and Recent Poems (1886), 304, 309
Scott, Walter, 29; Indian in plaid of (*Mogg Megone*), 62, 65, 86
Scott, Winfield, 166, 206, 236
Sedgwick, Catherine Maria, 159
Sentence of John L. Brown, The, 204
Sewall, Samuel, attacks slavery, 17
Sewall, S. E., 92, 157, 187
Seward, William H., 166, 206, 228, 233
Shakespeare, Whittier buys first copy of, 31
Shipley, Thomas, 131
Shoemakers, The, 218
Sicilian Vespers, The, 48
Sigourney, Mrs., as friend of Whittier, 56
Sims, Thomas, fugitive slave, 170
Skipper Ireson's Ride, set to music, 126; characterized and quoted in part, 259-61; dialect of a suggestion of Lowell, 261
Slavery issue, the; attitude of clergy, 17; studied by Whittier, 72;

Slavery issue (*continued*)
  growth of slavery, 72-73; chronological list of events, 73-75; slavery in Washington, 77; England
  frees slaves, 79; Whittier publishes *Justice and Expediency*,
  79-85; attack on Clay and Colonization Society, 81-82; *Our Countrymen in Chains*, 89-90; Anti-
  Slavery Convention, 92-99; attack
  on Colonization Society, 95-96;
  anti-slavery riots, 102-6; murder
  of Lovejoy, 118-19; burning of
  Pennsylvania Hall, 123-28; pro-
  slavery influence in Pennsylvania,
  124; Gag Rule passed, 134; table
  of pro-slavery and anti-slavery
  presidents (1840-1860), 166;
  schedule of outstanding slavery
  political events (1842-1860), 169-
  71; effect of Harrison's death, 175;
  Haverhill petition and attack on
  Adams, 179; Gag Rule repealed,
  180; Whittier's *Massachusetts to
  Virginia* arouses ire, 184-86; Mexican war as slavery issue, 198,
  205-6; *Ichabod* assails Webster for
  Seventh of March Speech, 218;
  deaths of Adams, Clay, Calhoun,
  Webster, 222; additional free and
  neutral states offset by fugitive
  slave laws, 224; case of Thomas
  Sims, 225; *Uncle Tom's Cabin*,
  235; election of Pierce, 236-37;
  Kansas-Nebraska bill, 237; An-
  thony Burns Boston riots, 238; vir-
  tual war in Kansas, 238; Dred
  Scott decision, 240; campaign of
  1860, 263-66; Whittier thinks of
  reviving slave purchase plan, 266;
  Laus Deo, 269
Slave Ships, The, 91, 101, 150
Smith, Gerrit, 113; and opening of
  Pennsylvania Hall, 125; and John
  Brown, 241
Smith, Mary Emerson, Whittier's
  early attachment for, 42-44; mar-
  riage of and revived friendship
  with Whittier, 44; inspiration of
  Memories, 42, 192-94
Smith, William, fugitive slave, 224
Snow-Bound, characterized, 278-80;
  financial and literary success of,

288-89, 289-90; publication history of, 280, 288-89; quoted in
  large part, 281-88
Song for the Times, A, 241
*Song Inscribed to the Frémont
  Clubs*, 241
Song of the Negro Boatmen, The, set
  to music, 296
Songs, many of Whittier's set to mu-
  sic, 296-97
Song of the Vermonters, The, date
  of, 38-39; publication of, 85-86;
  very rare in broadside form, 86;
  regarded as genuine 18th century
  poem, 86-87; quoted in part, 87
Songs of Labor, publication and
  characterization of, 200, 217-18
  246, 306
Songs of Three Centuries, 302
Southworth, Mrs. E. D. E. N., and
  Barbara Frietchie, 270, 271-72
Spirit of the North, The, quoted in
  part, 48-49
Spofford, Harriet Prescott, 301
Spofford, Jeremiah, editor of *Essex
  Gazette*, 112
Stanton, H. B., 113, 120, 133
Stanzas, 43
Stanzas. See *Our Countrymen in
  Chains*
Stanzas for the Times, in *Letters
  from J. Q. A.*, 116; quoted in part,
  150-51
Star of Bethlehem, 305
Stedman, E. C., 326
Stevens, Thaddeus, and opening of
  Pennsylvania Hall, 125
Stowe, Harriet Beecher, interest of
  in mysticism, 163; writing of
  Uncle Tom's Cabin, 235-36; Whit-
  tier says the spirits naturally pre-
  fer Mrs. Stowe, 317
Stranger in Lowell, The, publication
  and characterization of, 197, 199-
  200, 207
Sturge, Joseph, early contact of with
  Whittier, 113, 131; close association of and travel with Whittier,
  173-75; leaves fund for Whittier,
  175; Whittier finally accepts aid
  from, 268
Summons, The, included in *Letters
  from John Quincy Adams*, 115;

quoted in part, 150; mentioned, 241, 245

Sumner, Charles, Whittier sponsors, 16; meets Whittier, 50; early career of, 229; Whittier picks for Senate, 71, 230; delays and difficulties in election of, 231-33; corresponds with Whittier, 233; assailed and injured by Brooks, 239; Whittier's poem on death of, 302; Whittier at funeral of, 317-18

Supernaturalism of New England, The, 25, 192; publication of, 214

Swan Song of Parson Avery, The, characterized and quoted in part, 258, 259, 260

Sycamores, The, characterized and quoted in part, 258-59

Take Back the Bowl, 48

Taney, Chief Justice, 240

Tappan, Arthur, 63; financed large edition of *Justice and Expediency,* 80; house of sacked, 106; mentioned, 113

Tappan, Lewis, 113, 268

Taylor, Bayard, and *The Tent on the Beach,* 292-93

Taylor, Zachary, 166, 169, 206, 224

Telling the Bees, characterized and quoted in part, 258, 259, 260; Whittier's own evaluation of, 319

Tent on the Beach, The, quoted in part, 164; background and enormous success of, 292-93; discussed, 293-96

Texas, 204

Thaxter, Celia, Whittier guest of, 311, 323

Thayer, A. W., friend of Whittier, 33, 34; publishes *Incidental Poems by Robert Dinsmoor,* 38; Whittier learns editing from, 41; Mirick's *History of Haverhill,* 58; mentioned, 46; opposes Cushing, 76; in Philadelphia, 130

Thayer, C. P., publishes *Justice and Expediency,* 80

Thompson, George, New England anti-slavery lectures of, 70, 102; on trip with Whittier is in Concord "riot," 103-6

Thompson, Maurice, 159

Thoreau, Whittier's comment on, 318

Thurston, David, oldest delegate to Philadelphia Convention, 92, 97

Ticknor, William D., publishes *Lays of My Home,* 162, 182-183

Ticknor & Fields, publishes *Literary Recreations and Miscellanies* (1854) and all other publications to and including *The Tent on the Beach* (1867), 292-97

Ticknor, Reed & Fields, publishes *Leaves from Margaret Smith's Journal* (1849) 215-16; *Old Portraits and Modern Sketches* (1850), 216; *Songs of Labor* (1850), 200, 246; *Chapel of the Hermits* (1853), 246

To the Author of the Improvisatrice, published in London, 52

To Charles Sumner, quoted in part, 230, 302

To the Daughters of James Forten, 91

Todd, Dr., 56

To Delaware, 205

To Faneuil Hall, 204

To John C. Frémont, characterized and quoted in part, 274-75

To Mary, 43

To Members of the Society of Friends, a circular by Whittier on Quaker war obligations, 267

To the Memory of Charles B. Storrs, 91

To My Old Schoolmaster (Joshua Coffin), characterized and quoted in part, 247

To S. E. M., 43

To a Southern Statesman, 204

Toussaint L'Overture, 91

To William Lloyd Garrison, published, 56, 64, 150; quoted in full, 67-69

Training, The, 199-200

Trinitas, quoted in part, 306

Trumbull, Mr., 56

Tucker, Beverley, author of *The Partisan Leader,* 96

Tufts, Henry, *Memoirs of,* 24

Turner, Nat, leader of insurrection, 74

Tyler, John, 169, 207

Uncle Tom's Cabin, in *National Era,* 226, 235-36
Underground Railway, 124, 132
Underwood, F. H., 266
United States Magazine and Democratic Review, Whittier poems in, 108; *Supernaturalism of New England* published in, 214

Van Buren, Martin, 112-13, 175, 236
Vesey, Denmark, leader of insurrection, 74
Vestal, The, 43
Views of Slavery and Emancipation, by Harriet Martineau, with Preface by Whittier, 110, 116
Vision of Echard and Other Poems, The, publication and description of, 303
Voices of Freedom, 207-8

Waite, Peirce & Co., publishes *The Stranger in Lowell,* 199; in association with Thomas Cavender of Philadelphia and Wm. Harned of New York, publishes *Voices of Freedom,* 207
Walden, Whittier's comment on, 318
Walker, Captain Jonathan, 204
Wardwell, Lydia, Quaker, 13
Washington, Bushrod, first president of Colonization Society, 73
Washington, George, attitude of toward slavery, 72
Webster, Daniel, not related to Whittier, 10; opposes Clay, 53; supports Whittier for Congress, 177; attacked by Whittier, in *Ichabod,* for Seventh of March speech, 218-19; Whittier's memorial poem to (*Lost Occasion*), 220; joins Fillmore's cabinet, 228; death of, 222
Weld, Dr. Elias, 40
Weld, T. D., and Whittier, 113; husband of Angelina Grimké, 125
Wells, Martin, 56
Wendells, the (Ann, Margaret, Isaac, Evart), Whittier's Philadelphia cousins and friends, 130-31
What of the Day? (Frémont campaign song), 241; quoted in part, 243

What the Voice Said, 305-6
White Mountains, The, 58
Whitman, Walt, 29, 278; compared with Whittier as war poet, 270; Whittier contrasted with, 278
Whitney, Eli, 73
Whittier, Abigail Hussey, poet's mother, marriage, children, death of, 7-8; descent of, 10; in *Snow-Bound,* 284
Whittier, Alice Greenwood, niece of poet, 8
Whittier, Charles Franklin, nephew of poet, 8
Whittier, Elizabeth, poet's younger sister, close association of with poet, 8; escorts S. J. May, with Harriet Minot, from Haverhill anti-slavery meeting, 102; in Boston during 1835 riot, 105; poem by, 116; with poet in Philadelphia, 134; influence of on brother's work, 163; friendship of with Lucy Larcom, 201, 202; illness of, 267; death of, 277; in *Snow-Bound,* 285; poems by in *Hazel Blossoms,* 303
Whittier, Elizabeth Hussey, niece of Whittier, 8
Whittier, John (son of Joseph II), poet's father, life of, 7-8; early business experience, 24; interviews Garrison regarding poet, 32-33; attitude of toward poet's education, 32-33; in *Snow-Bound,* 284
Whittier, John Greenleaf, ancestry of, 5, 7-8; refutation of Huguenot descent of, 5-6; homestead of, 6-9; sells farm and buys Amesbury cottage, 9; no relative of Webster, 10; errors of in own genealogy, 10-11; Quaker background and habits of, 12-15; inherits Quaker anti-slavery responsibilities, 16; paraphrased by Phillips in Lovejoy spech, 16; opposes Mexican War, 17; boyhood of, 18-26; social background of, 24-25; earliest travels of, 25; writes verse, 27-28; has long productivity, 29; influenced by Burns, 29-30; first Boston visit of, 30; "discovered" by

Garrison, 31-33; earns money for term at Academy, 33-34; writes ode for opening, 34; education at Academy and adolescent affections of, 35-36; influence of Byron on, 36; published writings of (1826-28), 36-37; publisher contacts of, 37; pen names of, 37; first book publication of in *Rustic Bard*, 38; *Song of the Vermonters*, 39; early prose of, 40; received in best households, 40; assistant to Thayer, 41; *Poems of Adrian* and *History of Haverhill*, 41-42; relations of with Mary Emerson Smith, 42-43; refutation of sex repression theory as cause for illness, 42-44; relations of with Evelina Bray, 44; editor of *American Manufacturer*, 46-47; meets Lundy and supports Clay, 46-49; *Spirit of the North*, 48-49; meets Sumner, 50; called home by father's illness, 50; letter *re* pretty girls, 50-51; edits *Haverhill [Essex] Gazette*, 51; after death of father, accepts Hartford position, 51; poems of 1829 and first printing in England, 52; Henry Clay ballad, 52; visits New York, 53, 57; resigns from *New England Review* because of illness, 54; *Garrison and New England*, 56; life of in Hartford, 56-57; finishes Prentice's *Life of Clay*, 57; *Legends of New England* and Mirick's *History of Haverhill*, 57-58; *Moll Pitcher*, 59; *Literary Remains of . . . Brainard*, 60; recovers health, 60; *Mogg Megone*, 62; inspired by Garrison to anti-slavery activity, 62-64; and Milton, 69; dedicates himself to anti-slavery cause, 70-73; habits of life and work, 71; early political activities of, 75-78; *Justice and Expediency*, 77, 78, 79-84; *Song of the Vermonters*, 86-87; *O Thou Whose Spirit [Presence] Went Before*, 88; *Our Countrymen in Chains*, 89-90; delegate to Anti-Slavery Convention and relation of to *Declaration of Sentiments*, 92-99; attacks Colonization Society, 94-95; *Yankee Girl*, 101; in Massachusetts legislature, 101; on lecture trip with Thompson, in Concord "riot," 102-4; in Boston, Garrison anti-slavery riot, 105-6; goes into semi-retirement from writing (1834-37), 107-8; *Pastoral Letter*, 108-9; moves home to Amesbury, 110; edits *Essex Gazette*, 110-12; edits anti-slavery papers in New York, 113; disagrees with Garrison, 113-14; meets Lucy Hooper, 114; *Poems Written during the Progress of the Abolition Question*, 110, 116-18; writes preface to J. Q. Adams's *Letters*, 115; called by Lundy to Philadelphia, 118; "plagiarized" in Phillips's Lovejoy spech, 119; "mobbed" in Newburyport, 120; boards with Thayer in Philadelphia, 120; edits *Pennsylvania Freeman*, seeks freedom with union, 122; "ideal practical crusader," 122; inauguration and burning of Pennsylvania Hall, in which *Freeman* office is located, 123-28; writes ode, *Pennsylvania Hall*, 124-25; saves records by wearing disguise, 126-27; first Philadelphia health collapse, 128; boards with Healy, establishes circle of friends, portrait painted by Otis, 130-31; *Moll Pitcher and The Minstrel Girl*, 131; interested in "underground railway," 132; publishes *Pennsylvania Hall, Narrative of James Williams, Farewell of a Virginia Slave Mother*, and first authorized edition of *Poems*, 132; visits Governor Ritner, 133; visits J. Q. Adams, sees Gag Rule enacted, 134; second Philadelphia health collapse, 134; relations of with Lucy Hooper and her death, 135; friendship of with Elizabeth Lloyd, 135-38; invalidism of analyzed, 139-45; fails to attend London Convention, 139; in controversy concerning authenticity of *Narrative of James Williams*, 147-49; opposes Garrison, 157; poverty of, 158-59; resolves on

Whittier, John Greenleaf (*cont.*) distinct literary effort, 158-59; explains change in *The Tent on the Beach*, 164; local and national affiliations of, in 1840, 167; suspected of abandoning the Cause, 167-68; ethical ideals and spiritual awakening of, 171-72; travels with Sturge, 173-75; uses Sturge's gift for the Cause, 175; prevents Cushing's confirmation as secretary of the treasury, 176; barely escapes election to Congress, 176-77; writes letter accepting nomination of Liberty party, 177-78; relation of to Haverhill petition, 178-80; through Fields, seeks new publisher for *Lays of My Home*, 182-83; Latimer case and monster petition, 184-86; *Cassandra Southwick*, 188-90; first book published in England, 191; *New Wife and the Old*, 191-92; *Memories* and other reminiscences, 193-94; edits *Middlesex Standard*, 196-97; edits *Essex Transcript*, 198; *Stranger in Lowell*, 199-200; second group of anti-slavery poems, 203-5; *Voices of Freedom*, 207; Mussey edition of *Poems*, 208; as corresponding editor of *National Era*, 211-14; *The Supernaturalism of New England*, 214; qualities of as antiquarian, 215; *Leaves from Margaret Smith's Journal*, 215-16; *Old Portraits and Modern Sketches*, ends major prose efforts of, 216-17; *Songs of Labor*, 217-18; *Ichabod* and *The Lost Occasion*, 219-20; *Sabbath Scene*, 225, 227; *In the Evil Days*, 226; *Moloch in State Street*, 226; picks Sumner to succeed Webster in Senate, 229, 230; engages in practical politics to elect Sumner, 231-33; writes to Sumner, 233; endorses new Republican party, 237; supports Frémont, first Republican candidate, 239; celebrates events of fifties in series of poems, 240-41; *Kansas Emigrants*, 242; estimates John Brown, 241-42; writes more important literary verse, 244-46;

Chapel of the Hermits, 246; *Panorama*, 246; *Home Ballads*, 246, 258-61; *To My Old Schoolmaster*, 247; *Barefoot Boy*, 248-51; becomes Harvard Overseer and receives master's degree, 252; *Maud Muller*, 253-58; *Skipper Ireson's Ride*, 261; loyal to Frémont but supports Lincoln, 263; in election of 1860—*Quakers Are Out*, 263-65; prior to firing on Sumter, temporarily ready to dissolve Union to avoid war, 266; drafts Quaker wealth for war relief, 267; death of mother and illness of sister, 267; financial distress relieved by Sturge, 267-68; virtually retires from politics, 268; writing and sources of *Barbara Frietchie*, 270-72; dissuades Frémont from running against Lincoln in 1864, 275-76; *Furnace Blast* approved by Lincoln over heads of army chiefs, 276-77; non-militant poems of *In War Time*, 277; sister Elizabeth dies, 277; *Snow-Bound*, 278-79, 288-89; contrasted with Milton, 290; quatrain for Milton memorial window, 290; receives Harvard LL.D., 290; *The Tent on the Beach*, 293-96; *Abraham Davenport*, 295; songs set to music, 296; *In School Days*, 298-99; receives $1,000 for *Captain's Well*, 301; late life and prosperity of, 301-2; poem on death of Sumner, 302; books published after 1867, 302-4; devotional poems, 305-13; *The Eternal Goodness*, 307-8; adherence to Quakerism, 310-11; *Andrew Rykman's Prayer*, 312; character and appearance of in old age, 314-15; anecdotes concerning, told by Annie Fields, Mary Claflin, and others, 317-18; comments on Lincoln, *Walden*, and *The Chambered Nautilus*, 318-19; writes Lowell *re Telling the Bees*, 318; dialogue of with Joshua Coffin about hereafter, 320; residences at Oak Knoll, Newburyport, Centre Harbor, 322-23; last summer and death at

Hampton Falls, 324-25; *At Last*, 325-26; funeral, 326-27; remarkable "round robin," partly by Whittier and describing him in 1832, 329-331. *See also* Prose writings

Whittier, Joseph, son of Thomas, 7

Whittier, Joseph II, son of Joseph, 7

Whittier, Mary, older sister of poet, vital facts, 8; sends Whittier's first poem to Garrison, 31-32; Caldwell, husband of, buys *Gazette*, which Whittier edits unsuccessfully, 111; as portrayed in *Snow-Bound*, 285

Whittier, Mary Peasley, wife of Joseph, 7

Whittier, Matthew F., younger brother of poet, sketch of, 8; in *Snow-Bound*, 283

Whittier, Moses, uncle of poet, 8; mentioned in *Snow-Bound*, 284

Whittier, Richard, of England, ancestor of poet, 5

Whittier, Ruth Green, wife of Thomas, American founder, 5, 7

Whittier, Sarah Greenleaf, wife of Joseph II, 7

Whittier, Thomas, American founder, settles in America, 5; ancestry English, not French, 5-6; descendants of, 7; supports Quakers and involves family in that sect, 14

Whittier's Unknown Romance, 136, 137

Wiley and Putnam, publishes *Supernaturalism of New England*, 214

William, James, Negro subject of Whittier sketch, 147-49

Wilson, Carroll A., collector of New England first editions, 52

Wilson, Deborah, Quaker, 13

Winthrop, Robert C., 228, 231

Wish of Today, The, 306

Woman's rights, and the abolition movement, 169, 174

Woman suffrage, Whittier's attitude toward, 315-16

Women, in the anti-slavery movement, 93, 125, 167

Woodman, Mrs., Whittier's cousin, 323

World Convention, The, 132, 156

Woolman, John, Quaker anti-slavery leader, 15, 121

Wordsworth, William, 4, 29

Wreck of the Rivermouth, The, 294

Wright, Elizur, 113, 125

Yankee and Boston Literary Gazette, prints Whittier poem, 48

Yankee Girl, The, Whittier's first use of pure narrative ballad verse form, quoted in part, 101

Yankee Zingali, The (Robert Dinsmoor), 199-200

WITHDRAWN

JUN 2 8 2024

DAVID O. McKAY LIBRARY
BYU-IDAHO